To:
Flory

Thank you for your
wonderful
friendship

BD

JASBIR
RAI

G-D's Eye

UNIVERSAL AWAKENING

Bobby Dazzler

Vancouver BC

G-D's Eye: Universal Awakening
© Jasbir Rai, 2018

ISBN: 978-1-988368-03-0

Cover Design by Diane Feught

Created for Bobby Dazzler by Alpha Glyph Publications
Vancouver, BC, Canada

www.bobbydazzler.ca

Dedicated to humanity.

May *G-D's Eye: Universal Awakening* bring you love, and help you return to the source so you can awaken to your true nature.

That is my intention for you and the world.

Let's raise the vibration of Mother Earth together.

ACKNOWLEDGEMENTS

With the deepest gratitude, I wish to thank every person who has crossed my path in life. Some people have come and gone but that was the way it is supposed to be. They had done their work. Many amazing people are in the NOW and will be honored. I would like to acknowledge and express my gratitude to the following people for all their support and contributions in my awakening process and to the creative processes of this book.

First, foremost, I would like thank G-d who has spoken through me to reveal this knowledge, this awakening and the inspiration to write this manuscript as a way to serve humanity in an uplifting manner. Thank you G-d for giving me the power to share this writing with the world to nurture our planet.

The magnificent human beings that make up the *G-D's Eye: Universal Awakening* team:

Carol Sill, my Editor/Publisher, who has provided me with confidence, guidance and support that I never thought could be found instantly. This was a divine connection, indeed. She has truly made this manuscript magical. Carol, you are a genius and I honor your abilities, tenacity and persistence in making this project a success. I also appreciate your motivating me to continue writing and your assistance in my website design/business which will be the next chapter in my life as a spiritual innovator.

Dan Sonnenschein in his assistance in copy-editing of my book. Thank you for your kindness and help.

Diane Feught for the amazing design created for my book cover. Your ingenious creativity is inspiring, not just in my book cover but in all the other covers that you have done for other amazing authors. You are gifted!

My amazing clients and patrons who shopped at the Bobby Dazzler retail stores for 27 years. Without all your sales, there would no way that I would be able to materially support myself and arrive to this point in my life of spirituality. Thank you for shopping Bobby Dazzler and making my business such a success, your loyalty is valued. Many of you inspired me to write this after dealing with all you wonderful people.

My precious friends are too many to list, but Susan and Steve Mah have certainly helped me in so many ways in times of need and during odd times of night/day. Thank you for your computer assistance, your computer technical know how, your abilities to recover my files from USB sticks or wherever they went and helping me to get my computer unfrozen. You helped to recover my book so many times that I can't even recall, and, yes, I have now started to back up my files.

Karolina Turek for the amazing photos that were taken of me. I never thought that I could look that great. I don't know what you do but you do it well.

My siblings, Ruby and Tony Rai, for their support in my life, who put up with their awkward super-nerd sister. And my two nephews, Arjun and Ari, who bring me happiness and joy every day.

My precious parents, Nihal and Pritam, who had great strength and the balls to move to Canada from the State of Punjab, India, so their children would have a better life. Mom and Dad, this book would have never have happened had you made the choice to stay in India. I felt as I have won the parent lotto when I chose your souls to be my parents. I would not be who I am without the two of you. You make awesome children.

And finally, to my closest confidants, my children, Ya'el and Izack Kastiel. Dearest Ya'el who gave me a new meaning to real life as a mother for the first time. You are an amazing gifted artist who inspired me to leave the world of retail for the artistic world of creation. And, to Izack, who is my solid rock man and son. You are so strong, level headed, outspoken and full of life with so much love for your eccentric mother. Both of you are the jewels of life, Thank you and your souls for choosing me to be your guide in this life journey. I also thank their father for helping me to create these two amazing angels.

I also would like to acknowledge the British Library for the use of black and white images in this book which have no known copyright restrictions. They really made the book come together.

Note:

In the book, G-D refers to Creative Intelligence, Ashem, Allah, Divine Intelligence, the Divine, the Creator, Creation, Christ Consciousness, Light, Inner Voice, Universal Awareness.

Contents

Foreword
Introduction: Fives

About the Author

FOREWORD

In *G-D's Eye: Universal Awakening*, Bobby Dazzler offers an overview of aspects of modern life in the West that we take for granted. Selecting from the innumerable five-letter words in the English language, she writes short pieces on each word. She examines ideas, fads, seeming-essentials of life, concepts of religion, all from a point of view that asks the questions: Does this lead to our awakening? How can we become more aware of the Divine in our daily life?

She turns the G-D's Eye on the various topics selected here, to reveal whether or not the activity or event can help us toward awakening. From religion to Vegas and back again, Bobby Dazzler touches upon pre-conceived notions, the imprints of childhood conditioning, and the awareness of a Divine purpose. The reader is led toward the stillness of the inner life, and away from the glitz and glamour of modern striving for sensory stimulation, travel, novelty, and greed. *G-D's Eye* also looks at religions, culture and family, as these influences too often can be barriers to awakening.

Bobby Dazzler's spiritual awakening called into question much of the everyday life around her. By becoming still, nurturing the body, mind and heart, she became able to see the world, and her place in it, in a whole other light. The transformation of awakening permits greater awareness and increases life-force. As her life changed to match the new awareness, she was inspired to write these brief pieces on aspects of life, based only on five-letter words. Never having been a writer before, she created this intuitive expression of transformation. Part self-learning, part advice for all, part play with words and images, her writing soon became the book you now hold in your hands.

As you read, watch for the five-letter words, think about them and their impact. Make some of your own connections with five-letter words. Each one is a star of a specific frequency. While Bobby writes, she decodes this frequency as she sees with G-Ds eye.

Some of the words here may appear light but the message is profound, for it is connected to the perennial quest for truth that brings humanity to the awakening. Like Bobby Dazzler, who left a successful retail business after nearly three decades, you may find priorities shifting and changing to fit your new understanding of life, and of your role in it. By seeing from the point of view of the Divine you can discover for yourself what is best for your own peace, health and wisdom.

This book is for you. Take a moment to dip into this easy-to-read modern guide to becoming aware, alert and alive. Tune in to Universal Awakening.

- Carol Sill

FIVES

"The sacrifice is fivefold; The animal is fivefold; the person is fivefold; all this, whatever there is, is fivefold. Whoever knows this obtains this."
- Upanishads

In the *Upanishads* is written this description of our lives and environment: Earth, middle-air, sky, directions, intermediate directions; fire, air, sun, moon, constellations; the waters, plants, trees, space, self; so much regarding beings. Now regarding oneself; breath, diffused breath, lower breath, up-breath, central breath; eye, ear, mind, speech, skin; cuticle, flesh, sinews, bone, marrow. Dividing them up in this way, the Rishi has said, 'All this is fivefold. By the fivefold, one wins the fivefold.'

Following the advice of the Rishi, this book retells the story for modern times using five-letter words, applying the fivefold to our modern world so those in the West may easily understand the path to truth. Five is a good and important number for many different reasons. According to Indian numerology, five is the number of the intellect and is associated with destiny. Fives favor freedom and freewill. The destiny of an individual can be a five and names can have vibrations of fives.

John 1:1 *In the beginning was the Word, and the Word was with G-d, and the Word was God.*

The Word becomes words as they make up the texts or scriptures of G-d. Words is a five-letter word. So many powerful words of life are five-lettered. Five-letter words come up often and seem to be the ones we live our lives through. There is something very important about these fives. The time has come to write about them and how they relate to everyday life. The words that are five-lettered are more influential than the rest and there are more of them than one would think.

The power of five manifests so much influence and ability in our lives. (Really this is not crazy to think. Even the fact that crazy and think have five letters in them make you think already, right?!) Of course, other words that exert a profound influence may have 6, 7, 8, and even 9 or more letters in them. Yet, we seem to come up most frequently with these five-letter words on a daily basis. They appear over and over again and define much of the way we are influenced. Read them and think, learn, and realize. Embrace them as they will allow you to see the world differently than if you ignore them. They play an integral role. Look at them deeply, not just on the surface. The lives we all live depend upon and are impacted deeply by the meaning of these words.

When we look, listen, learn, and accept this, these words will reveal the profound meaning of many things we do daily, determining how well we do in this life. As some of the most often-used words in the English language, they reveal the source of our thoughts that become our actions. These are the words that make things work in this life. A careful analysis of them will allow us to become more awake, alert and aware of ourselves in the present moment.

This book will highlight a key selection of Fives to help show their importance and assist the realization of their significant impact on your life. They reveal the most important issues and hottest topics of today. This call to attention upon the words can enable a pause for a moment before you make a decision to speak or take action. The practical purpose of this is to help us live our daily lives with success. This "pause, think, and then speak" dance will better allow you to respond to the demands of life and deal with it from a higher, spiritual level.

These fives are valuable, crucial, and critical for our daily lives. Use them wisely and feel their impact while they play in and out of your world, as they have in all our lives in the past, present, and future.

Of course, it is impossible to point out all the fiveletter words but take notice here of some that are opposite of each other, which we refer to as the duals or duality. To start to grasp duality is when one does not see either of the opposites any longer. It is no longer clean nor is it dirty. It is just what it is. Examining some of the opposite duals makes this discussion interesting. Since the seeker no longer sees this or that, the opposites and duals of life diminish. It is what it is.

In these examples some five-letter words are compared:

birth vs. death	truth vs. false	awake vs. sleep
giver vs. taker	clean vs. dirty	smile vs. frown
steal vs. earns	loves vs. hates.	happy vs. sadly
north vs. south	black vs. white	daily vs. never
shark vs. softy	purge vs. forms	large vs. small
bulls vs. bears	doubt vs. knows	lease vs. owner

close vs. opens	mommy vs. daddy	sever vs. mends
newer vs. older	tight vs. loose	break vs. build
starts vs. stops	frown vs. smile	group vs. alone
upper vs. lower	night vs. light	argue vs. merge
final vs. began	relax vs. tense	loves vs. hates
fresh vs. stale	lover vs. hater	quiet vs. noisy
inner vs. outer	stink vs. scent	micro vs. macro

What a coincidence that the names of the three main books of the three main Western religions of the world have five letters in them. They are the Bible, the Koran and the Torah. Sure, religion is important as so many people of the world follow religion and live by it. It would be foolish not to mention faith as one of the significant five-letter words of the world. Many people have faith - be it in a higher power, an energy, a spirit, or some other forms that are yet to be discovered.

Some of the most famous and common Western or Eastern religions of the world rely on this five. All numbers can have significance of some sort when explaining truth. Fives became the number of choice due to the fives' prevalence in so many scriptures of the past but most importantly, it was the number used to teach during these times - NOW!

Five Levitical offerings (Leviticus 1-5.) And it also is the number Jesus used to multiply to feed 5,000 (Matthew 14-17.) The list of five's significance can be seen in many paths in the religions of the world. Buddhists have the five precepts or the five virtues or rendered in English as the Pali. The Sikhs have the five K's which are the articles of the Faith as commanded by the tenth Guru, Guru Gobind Singh. Islam has the five basic acts of Islam which are known as the five Pillars of Islam. In Judaism, the five represents the five books of the Torah. It is also the fifth letter of the Hebrew alphabet, Heh, which is one of the holy names of G-d. In the Upanishads, the animal is fivefold; the person is fivefold. The five saman in the worlds should be contemplated upon: earth, fire middle-air, the sun and the sky.

Faith of the world falls into one of each of these categories. Torah=Moses (Torah also coincidentally has five books.); Bible=Jesus; Koran=Mohammed who brought the word of Allah for Islam which in turn has five pillars or tenets.;Books (Texts)=Bodhi (Buddha); Agdas=Baha'i; Sidur=Nanak (Sikhs); Vedas=Hindu; Jians=Jinas

We belong to one of the races in this world: White, Black, Brown, Asian, Latin, Mixed, Mocha, Cocoa, Local - This is everyone else. Needless to say, we are all part of the human races of the world.

We even have five days in the week that we work in!

Four of the five senses are words with five letters in them: Touch, Smell, Taste, Hears (hearing), Sight.

The five-letter words are also present in our five elements: Metal, Earth, Water, Fires, Winds (Air, Ether.)

How about some hot spots of the world to visit? Vegas, Ibiza, Miami, Italy, India, Chile, China.

Or what about when they decided to name the award ceremonies? We have the Oscar, the Junos, the Emmy's.

Or better yet, what about some of the most spoken about crucial aspects of life are five letter words. These are all the topics that news tends to print in our local newspapers as well. The news tends to cover the headlines and each section of the newspaper consists of: Sport, Money, Homes, Birth, Death, Foods, and so on. Check it out for yourself. The major news only makes the paper for print if the article consists of: Foods, Power, Crime, Crook, Thief, Stole, Death, Gangs, Money, Stock, Bonds.

Lists of the matters of life go on and on. On a daily level, the main issues of life more often than not entail a five-letter word. Is it just a coincidence or is there some other underlying meaning to the fives that connects us to these words? Everything is always related, as many spiritual leaders in the past have shown. It wouldn't hurt to examine the effects of the fives in our lives as an attempt to better understand ourselves and attempt to find unity in humanity while awakening ourselves.

Patterns exist throughout life. They are especially understood in science and math. Patterns also exist in words, and those certain words can be used to understand awakening during modern times. The number 555 in numerology denotes major shifts and/or spiritual growth. Five has been chosen as the number of letters for each word that indicates a new chapter, as it made sense to express this divinely inspired text for everyone to understand easily. It is true that all numbers have significance of some sort when explaining truth. Fives became the number of choice for this analysis due to its prevalence in so many scriptures of the past but most importantly, the five-letter words are used to teach and express the point. They will remind the reader to pay attention and remember that word, and discover its significance.

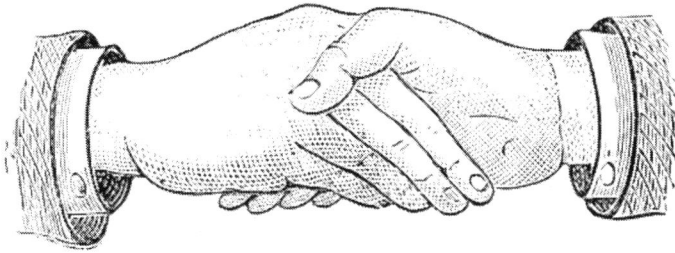

AGREE

"Agree to arrive at awareness and truth."

At the time of birth there is no choice but to agree to what our parents or caretakers give us. There is no opportunity to disagree with the cultural and societal arrangements made for us by our caretakers upon our arrival. We are, in a way, forced to agree to how things have been done in the past. A baby doesn't have a voice or a developed mind to be able to know what is true and what is false. Yet a newborn does know the truth. The many Masters agree that a child, so very pure and untouched, is closer to the truth than any adult.

We agree to take on the religious paths given at birth since we don't have a choice. We agree to all the ideas, plans, words, and thoughts that society has planted in our minds. We agree to listen, for from the time we are born until early adulthood most of us rely on others for guidance.

Parents, environment, and schooling, plus external programming and conditioning provide us with standards and truths that we take for granted.

When we take the next step to become a spiritual seeker, we discover that we can disagree with this conditioning. At that time, we agree to learn how to arrive at awareness and truth for ourselves. We agree to become awakened!

AH HAA!

"There is no going back, this is it!"

It was Oprah who made this phrase a household word. Ah haa! refers to the moment when we realize something. It could be a turning point in life or when an understanding emerges. This ah haa moment is great but it is even greater when one comes to self-realization. In self-realization, the Ah haa or aha moment is even more intense, for it builds up through years of study or processes to bring us closer to the truth. Once truth arrives there is no going back, baby! This is it! This moment is more than euphoria: it is the eureka of all life. We realize the true essence of our being: it is why we are here!

We do not have to worry any more. There is no sorrow, there are no more fears, we know we are ageless and deathless. We come to realize who we are and what defines us: bliss and nothing else! Life becomes simple. We cannot be hurt anymore after crossing the threshold of birth and death. Everything is peaceful, now. Ah haa! We have pierced the veil of life.

AHEAD

"Look beyond what is before our eyes."

Getting ahead is what it's about in the Age of Materialism. Nobody wants to be left behind. Many self-help gurus today encourage us to go for success and make our dreams come true. They say we must find our gift and excel at it to make a living for ourselves and our families. Getting ahead means to be part of "the doers." We learn to put up vision boards to reach our goals. This is correct. But once we gain that house on the vision board, the ideal or trophy partner, the cars we dreamed of, the amazing job, and the other props we put on the board, do we then re-create another board with bigger versions of everything on the original board? Or is there another way we can get ahead? Is there another ahead that we can aspire to?

There is another form of ahead we can discover. In materialism, it is easy to lose our way in the whole "getting ahead game" of gaining the stuff they say we should own. They call this stuff "props" - props to prop us up. Nobody is saying having those props is wrong. Nobody is saying that we should stop getting ahead in a material way. In the natural human cycle of life, getting ahead should also have a spiritual component, one that heals the body and mind and nourishes the soul. When we meet our material goals, then a time must come for us to get ahead in spiritual goals as the human cycle evolves.

What does ahead mean for us when speaking of self-realization or awakening? It goes back to discovering who we are at our inner core, once we finish acquiring the outer stuff. We then return to the state we were in when we first arrived here on Earth, and become awake like the day that our eyes first opened at birth. We become conscious and leave behind the delusions that other humans make-believe are important. These things that humans create to appear important are only outer stuff. Getting ahead in the spiritual world means going past the door of intellect and coming home to the house of the promised gift. This is humanity's highest aspiration.

Awakening is not attainable without taking the opportunity to advance in life and to become doers in our chosen activity. It doesn't matter what work we take on. What matters most is to do the best action possible without constant reaction to what is going on around us. Relying on others to take care of us builds up the false notion that we can self-realize by only sitting and meditating - without doing a thing.

If we are not contributing to humanity or society in some way in our daily cycle of life, it is impossible to see the best we can do. Engaging ourselves to serve others, even if it is only volunteering, is a way to become doers in society. Takers wait for others to take care of them. But going to a job or volunteer position that one can enjoy, loves, or hates is still doing something rather than nothing. You may ask why doing nothing is not going to get one ahead? It has something to do with the notion of entitlement, the idea that everything will come to you rather than you going after what you want. Nothing comes to those who wait for the "self-entitlement card".

That card has the word "title" in it. When individuals seek a title then they are no longer leading. This is a favorite saying from the writer and leadership guru, Robin Sharma. Getting ahead requires us to push ourselves to the limit. Why? Because that is what the human being is meant to be doing. We are meant to be challenged and to learn. Getting ahead is part of our internal drive to find out who we are and to discover what gifts we are blessed with. And all this is part of awakening and the coming home to truth.

Getting ahead requires us to focus, have discipline and drive, and to set very strong goals for ourselves, beyond the material objectives. It requires rolling with the punches, as Calvin Arye puts it when he describes what business is all about. A person can't be a negative or pessimistic thinker if they wish to get ahead. Pessimism can cause one to give up, and giving up is not even an option in realizing truth.

Ahead is the one who thinks bigger and larger, without any need to react in every instance of interaction with our fellow humanity. It requires us to be in possession of the unique ability to think beyond the closed box and to have a open mind; always, not just sometimes. It requires us to use our intuitive abilities. Those abilities open through an alchemy that leads us to the truth.

Some of the traits that lead to the Divine are the power to complete, persistence to always follow through, determination to go the distance, and tenacity to do very difficult tasks without giving up when all looks bleak.

Another aspect of getting ahead entails looking beyond what is immediately before our eyes. It means using intuition as a guide by developing our sixth sense. By nourishing the sixth sense, a seer begins to see things that are not just physically in front of us, but other things and activities outside of our limited vision.

These G-dly traits are seen when true greatness is sought.

ALIKE

"We are not only alike, we are one."

We are all alike. All people are the same. Often when we get to know another person, we look to identify the common ground we have with one another. We encounter many who say, "That's just like me!" or "Ho, that's like me!" Or:

"We are so much alike!"

"We think the same!"

"I am like you!"

"You are like me!"

"I'd say the identical thing!"

Human beings long and seek to be alike. We search for similar associations. Yet on top of the soul a sense of separateness piles layers and layers of conditioning. These layers have programmed each of us at birth. The layers can be cultural, religious, national, linguistic, ancestral, ethnic, social, economic, and so on.

Removing them is like peeling an onion. The outside layers represent the conditioning added onto humanity over the centuries and millennia. To find the one unique core of the onion which is the source, we must shed all the top outer layers. We discover we are not only alike but one. Humanity's search to be like another leads to the realization that we are part of that same one. Locating the inmost centre is what spiritual awakening or self-realization is about. It is the whole point in life!

ALIVE

"Everybody should strive to feel alive"

Running a retail store allowed for a lot of people-watching. It soon became apparent that many people are not looking or feeling alive. Over the years, many retail clients were observed not taking care of themselves yet making huge purchases for other people. The core is to become awake, alert, and aware in order to become alive. That can only happen when an individual cares for themselves rather than focusing on the outer world of making more and more purchases. Observation in retail showed me that people were taking care of others rather than themselves. It appears that the conditioning to please others supercedes taking care of the self. This starts to make the self less alive. The focus needs to shift to the self for self-realization to begin.

Everybody should strive to feel alive. Then the body is free of all habits, pure and full of energy. How do we become pure and full of energy? Being alive is totally embracing whatever one is doing. It you aren't alive, you are dead. Being alive is being lively, living and being then means being happy even if there are things in one's life that make one sad. Part of being alive is awareness that death will happen. Knowing this allows one to better deal with the opposites and duality of life. Where one is alive, there is inevitably death. Know that in life the opposites exist. Rather than getting upset at one end of the spectrum, it would be wise to move to a non-react mode. It seems cold yet that is required when one is moving to become more alive in life. A pragmatic approach to life allows humanity to feel alive.

Being alive is being able to appreciate; to love music and dance, to eat foods, sing, work, be good at many things, cook, work, love and be loved. Being alive is having good energy and looking at the good and the bad with indifference. Being alive is important not only for the way the world sees us but it is important for us, too, for personal growth. Nobody wants to deal with someone who is looking or behaving like they are part of the dead. In the retail world many people came and went. Some were alive while others were clinging to the dead aspects of life that made them lifeless. They seem to be living but are, in a sense, the walking dead. All it took was one bad thing to happen to them and suddenly life was in a tailspin, and spiralling into pessimism and everything was no longer alive.

Alive means self-care first. Easy modern self-care techniques that are available to feel better and allow the human vessel to nurture itself include getting a massage once or more per month. It means getting a manicure and pedicure once per month so the human body looks great and properly maintained. If we feel great, look great, and focus on self, that enables us to pursue the self-care that is absolutely necessary for self-actualization. So it might be better to splurge on the self and not worry so much about accumulating more stuff. Start to feel alive!

ALONE

"Never say you are alone, for you are not alone, your G-d and your genius are with you." - Epictetus

The Talmud states: "For this reason was man created alone, to teach thee that whoever destroys a single soul…scripture imputes [guilt] to him as though he had destroyed a complete world; and whoever preserves a single soul…,scripture ascribes (merit) to him as though he had preserved a complete world." (Sanhedrin 37a)

One cannot become one with all until one is able to spend time alone. The word "alone" holds the term "one" and the word "all". Words hold mysteries in their meanings. Once we begin to pay attention to them, soon we can decipher them. Nothing is a coincidence, even in the language of words.

Did the Masters of the past forget to point out in their books, texts, and scriptures that the most important word for self-realization and awakening was the word alone? It is the exact opposite of the word for group. Or has the word been removed through later revisions, interpretations, and rewriting that took place century after century, or yuga after yuga? If mastery required it, why was this word not included in many of the texts of the world's religious paths? Was this an oversight? Or were the various paths that were always meant for one to self-realize just kept back from humanity, so those who controlled the masses kept everyone engaged with one another and the group? Was humanity being deluded into believing the 'group' version of self-realization was the sole method to attain to truth, so awakening would be kept for a selected power elite? Did those few require everyone to always engage with the social group?

The word alone is a most important word for self-realization, seeking truth or coming to find ourselves. Western culture and society is trained and conditioned by media and society that being alone is not normal. The word alone has a negative connotation from this deep conditioning.

We may find it difficult to be alone, for we have been made to believe we are never supposed to be alone. We are bombarded with comments like: "You shouldn't be alone!" "Loneliness kills!" Says who? We have bought into this attitude so much that when we have time to be alone, then anxiety, depression, and other afflictions or diseases of the mind/brain arise. This is due to our own expectations based on the conditioning of society. But, says who?

Masters of the past spent significant time alone. Jesus spent 40 days and nights in solitude, prayer and fasting in the Judean wilderness. Moses, also, went up to Mount Sinai alone for 40 days and nights in prayer and fasting. It was he alone who received the message of G-d from the burning bush, that later came to be known as the Torah. Mohammed often went to a cave on his own. It was there that the word of G-d was revealed to him by the Angel Gabriel. He had many occasions when he was alone and not in the company of anyone else. From the age of six, he was not subject to the watchful eye of his mother since he was known to have been an orphan. He lived in the barren empty desert. In that vastness he found true solitude and contemplation. Deep contemplation can begin through the space that the Masters found only when they became alone.

Alone is a central theme of many masters, spiritual teachers, yogis and awakened beings. Like Jesus and Moses, Buddha sat beneath the Bodhi tree so the meaning of life would come to him. He, too, was alone and on his own, having left a wife and an innocent, newborn son in his home to find "truth". There doesn't seem be any other way to reach awakening unless one goes about it alone. Most organized religions are based on small and large groups that come together to pray, read, and congregate. They then segregate from the main groups that have different beliefs of their own, and smaller groups that separate from the larger groups, such as the Shiite and Sunni in Islam. But never does religion promote being alone. These groups resort to outer means of prayer. Each religion or faith then makes its congregates believe that looking at the world in their one way is the right way. Segregation starts its deep conditioning. Nowhere does it state that we must chant, pray or meditate in groups. Nor does it say we can only find G-d in a church, synagogue, mosque, temple, Gurdwara or any other specific place of worship. It can prove difficult to meditate in a group setting in any church, temple, synagogue or mosque. Places of worship are very busy due to the many distractions.

People have been made to believe that G-d, the Divine Source, is outside the human being. None of the organized religions promote being alone and seeking union with G-d, truth or awakening on our own. Instead, groups congregating in a religious institution or place of worship is the sanctioned way of prayer. A pray here and pay over there policy seems to exist in many places of religion.

Group prayers can be a dispersal of one's energy. We can read every single book for all faiths in our own home where we can become still, quiet, and can be alone. Groups are more loud, noisy, cause more 'mental noise' and distractions. Conversations, and the desire to be understood through speech occurs in groups. There is little quietness in any church, temple, synagogue or mosque, since so many congregate there. It is quiet when nobody is there, but people are everywhere causing us more and more interactions. Time to meditate, to be quiet, to be still, to contemplate, and be alone is crucial in the path to becoming awake.

Masters of the past spent plenty of time alone. Yet, the collective conditioning and programming of humanity is such that this is seen as bad or negative. This fixation on being social extends by being in touch and keeping in touch all the time. When we are engaged with the other outer people around us, how is it possible to hear the inner voice of the Divine?

The time must come that the inner voice will prevail over the much louder, outer voices of the other. It comes when we allow ourselves to be comfortable being alone and try to do things by ourselves. When we are alone, deep contemplation can begin. It is here that intuition is fostered, psychic abilities are developed and the Divine begins to reveal itself in us. Enjoying our own company is necessary even if it is so very difficult in modern times, due to the outer chatter, or as modern Master Eckhart Tolle put it, due to "mental noises".

Right from the beginning, the conditioning we receive makes us think we should be social. It is one layer that is very difficult to peel away as we learn to be alone. Some of us find it easy to be alone while others are alone by no choice of their own. Introverts or those who choose to be alone are called "loners". We are told that nobody likes to be alone, so right from the beginning our conditioning takes over the mind. The terms "you shouldn't be alone," or "nobody is supposed to be alone," or "loneliness kills" makes us feel we should keep in the company of people all the time. In this social programming the mind and brain become transformed or fixated. We think in the opposite manner from how we were originally born at Source to be. Humans are social beings but even social beings need down time. That down time is when the spiritual seeker is born and begins to be awake.

The truth is that at birth you come into this world alone. No two people are born at the exact same second, millisecond of time or place. This is also true upon our death. No two souls die at the same instant of time. Yet we are constantly being fed society's command that we should not be alone.

Becoming aware, alert, and awake requires spending time alone. It is something that one needs to make a positive habit of, instead of loathing it. Being alone makes us totally and absolutely depend on G-d for all guidance. It can be difficult to be alone when we marry, live with others, have a child, and must deal with 7+ billion people in the world - and counting - through our everyday social interactions. Techs and media control so much of this cycle on Earth that it is now impossible to be truly alone, unless we disconnect from it all or at least limit it, so those forms of keeping in touch are no longer irritants.

Being alone is one of the trademark aspects of coming to our own light. When one becomes alone, the light which is the creative force turns on and shines. We cannot become awakened when we spend no time alone in space and solitude.

Choosing to do things alone must become a habit until being alone is preferred over being social. A constant need to be social is counter-productive to awakening processes. Spending time alone is the only way we can truly get to know ourselves, to answer the big question, "Who am I?" Will the "I" realize it is self-reliant? One can listen to the inner voice when no other voices from the outer are in its way. The other voices all around us are the limitations imposed on human life, and they are the voices that prevent one from being free. These are the "mental noises". They belong to the other people we interact with daily either through physical contact in person or through cyberspace, email, phone, texts, mail, cable, media, tweet, and pages. (Note the five-lettered words.) And yes, it includes the voices of family, caretakers, co-workers, people chit-chatting in the mall, friends, siblings, aunts, uncles, mommy or daddy. Having people around tempts us to look for the answers to our own questions from the other. Being alone is not only necessary but mandatory for us to come to the point of "Who am I?" and "Why am I here?" You are the only person who can look into yourself with introspection.

Given we must be alone to answer our own questions, this is one of the hardest things to do today with so many distractions. The techs, the other, media, chatter, noise, children, work, school and everything around our lives prevents us from being alone. Even when we are alone, we are wired to the world. This makes being alone very difficult.

Often people feel the need to resort to the other for a path, an answer to their prayer or even find the right way to live. How can this someone give you the right answers when over 99% of the world does not have the answers to their own problems? Sure, asking is good for guidance but real truth is found in or through personal experience. Wisdom of this sort is referred to as experiential wisdom. Few 'others' can tell one what to do. They are the outer voices that sometimes confuse rather than give the correct answer that we seek.

If we take a closer look, nobody is alone unless they think they are. Too much of life can circle around ideas of blame such as "I am all alone, poor me - I have nobody!" Yet in reality many accomplishments in the world can attest to this often-quoted sentence: Once you listen to that inner voice within you, you are simply never alone. That voice can get lost so very easily when we seek the other for an answer. We all know the answer but need to find it ourselves. The inner voice is that of G-d or the Divine, for we are all part of G-d.

Alone can be found in two ways. Some of us are alone by choice while others just are naturally alone. Since we are creatures of habit, we can become used to being alone if we have done it for long enough. One can manage being alone if that is all they have been accustomed to. It becomes harder when you have to deal with people all the time and then are forced into being alone. Alone does not mean literally alone but having to rely on the self in all facets of life with limited or little interaction with the other. Figuring things out by ourselves enables us to better understand ourselves, and leads us to become strong, independent, and self-reliant individuals.

I learned to be alone and make the habit of being alone until it became comfortable. My childhood circumstances before the teen years show how important it was to be alone. By grade five, wearing heavy, large reading glasses, having braces and a severe acne problem made sure that not too many people wanted to hang out with me. Add to this the plain fact that I was one of the two only brown people in school, the other being my sister. Brown-colored people in an all-white school means being alone all the time with little effort. In all of these childhood experiences I did not have a choice, but had to deal with it as a part of life.

From personal experience, children can be mean, but there is not time to feel sorry for ourselves and take things personally. Children can only mimic conditioning given to them, knowing they may have only been taught hate or meaness by their upbringing or environment. Living in a lower income class with immigrant parents who could not help with homework only meant relying on the self. These dynamics meant that the teen years were spent alone more often than not. Nobody was going to ask me to a party or prom anytime soon.

It was in this alone that a total, absolute surrender to G-d started to take place, and the inner voice began to lead. A total dependence on G-d occurred without me even knowing it. The "in" crowd in school walked by as if they had never seen anyone so hideous. What was I to do? Well, the library was great place to start. It was quiet, there were many other people just like me who were alone or might like to be alone by no choice of their own, to actually study in school rather than socialize. I discovered the library is a great place to study, with plenty of books to read and learn from. Nobody bothers anybody in the library. It is the only place in the school accessible during recess or lunch, and even after school. Children conditioned by racism cannot yell remarks like "Hindu!" "Paki!" "Brown girl, who put shit on you?" and "Eew, a Punjab!" It is an open place where people are not social.

When people are social, people may get anxiety and become susceptible to depression, in part due to people making comparisons with one another via social media and techs, which tend to exacerbate this problem. The focus shifts from the self to the other. When we hear things and take them personally, it affects the mind. To keep the mind clear and clean makes sense. We must remove ourselves from that negativity that gives rise to afflictions of the mind due to what other people say or make us believe is truth.

In a quiet library, one hears none of these schoolyard words or children's evil lingo lingering in the mind after it has been said. The library puts on a mask of silence for students to engage in whatever they like to do without so many words or the need to speak unnecessarily. The schoolyard is loud. The library is quiet. It was a great place to be alone to concentrate, escape and get myself together. It was a silent place that allowed me to see how all negatives can be made into a positive.

I had to figure out fast what kind of edge can be had with what I had been given. In the library, the alone time paid off by getting focused, with utter silence for schoolwork and perfect marks in school. This allowed my self-esteem and confidence to rise. Receiving excellent marks and being number one in school was something many kids who had looks did not achieve. That was when the Ah Haa moment came to be, from all this quiet, aloneness. I was being smart, learning fast and getting amazing grades in school. Alone worked out like this for many years including high school and university. It was a matter of making this alone time work somehow. Simply planting the ass on a chair to learn is not everybody's forte. Learning requires discipline, goals and focus which can't be had if one is a social butterfly or socially engaged with others. Ah Haa, the Divine, had given me a direction and a brain but not looks. So what?! Just do what works.

As time fast-forwarded to today, it became obvious that being alone was necessary for me to find the light in awakening, for it makes me self-reliant, self-sufficient and self-confident. When you are among the alone, you find intelligence. Comfortable in your own skin, you can survive by yourself in a crowd. You have the unique ability to eat, dance, listen to music and work alone.

Since I came to be a retailer, other people were always around. Interactions with others were daily, hourly and sometimes by the minute. I learned that some connection was necessary while other communication was not. Interacting with co-workers was unnecessary after training. Retailing involves talking and hustling. That energy must be kept for the clients, not co-workers who wanted to share what they did last night. Being self-employed meant that the calendar could be made with only one person working during non-busy periods. Working alone made productivity and sales increase, with a decrease in the time spent in chatter with the co-workers. This work enabled me to spend hours alone. Dealings with clients were kept to a minimum as discussions were to do with the sale. Extra staff was not kept on during the day as it meant the engagement of extra idle talks, ideas and yadda-yadda-yadda that nobody wanted to hear. It was this way for over 27 years. Of course, during that time, quiet time was spent in meditation on the Divine/G-d, rather than engaging in useless gossip.

Being an entrepreneur in business helped me to quickly come closer to self-realization. It makes it possible to deal with people and without people. Alone, therefore, became a choice rather than something imposed. Over time a level of comfort arose. That is important for spiritual success. It allows for growth and brings us closer to knowing who we are. Being alone can be seen as a call to being me, myself, and I all in one, alone. It becomes the starting to point to self-realization.

Start by seeking to spend time in quiet solitude, so that time is made for the G-d or the inner voice in yourself. Soon, spending time alone becomes such a habit it is sought after and yearned for. It only becomes a problem when we listen to the outer voices that keep claiming we "should never" be alone! How ironic, as this is the only way one can come back to G-d and self-realize. It appears to be the exact opposite of what we are taught in schools, through media, by the large companies and all those techs who feel we should always keep in touch.

Alone can apply to being self-reliant, independent, and able to challenge ourselves to try things without help. Being alone also ensures that we mind our own business. If we focus so much on what other people are doing, then we cannot learn how to become ourselves. When the brain is involved in things that don't matter to us personally, it engages us in things that matter to the other people. And all the outer stuff doesn't matter at all.

APART

"A perpetual apart is always carved out."

People tell each other they grew apart, divorcing or disconnecting from another. Apart is not relevant for those who marry, live together, or are friends. Apart describes many circumstances in personal and professional life where a person grows apart from something, concluding that they need "space" or they prefer to be alone. Growing apart occurs for many reasons in our times. Divorce is one field where apart is more widespread. In some religions it is viewed as negative, but it is not such a bad thing to focus on the self (and a child if there were children).

Divorce is not abnormal and is common in this time when the soul endeavors to be free to find out who the self is. There is a rapidly growing number of those seeking divorce. Many are those who should seek self-realization rather than pursuing yet another other who will meet their needs and wants based on their senses. Growing apart is natural as the universe moves through a cycle or shift in the consciousness of humanity.

Humanity is now expressing love for all, not only for one person. Loving all people no matter what their sexual preference shows this spreading of love. Self-realization is often prevented by the conditioning of society towards the need to marry. External pressures, including parents, the other, cultural and religious standards, foster societal programming/conditioning. We are ingrained to think we should marry again for love. Nobody asks why so many people are divorcing or growing apart. After gaining freedom, an individual who grew apart decides to go back into a relationship again rather than to explore the real self.

We marry because either we have to (pregnancy) or we determined it was the right time, or we are in love. We think we should because that is what everyone does, the soul's continuing struggle to find the other half, we want a younger/hotter partner to please our senses, we want a change, we want something new, we don't want to be alone and the list of reasons goes on and on.

When consciousness is not in unity, a separateness is created in humanity which divides. Division shows with the establishment of nations, further separated by regions. Once regions were established, religions based on beliefs created ethnic groups, races, and groups founded on social, economic, political and material lines. Many layers of dividing humanity continue as we spiral out of control into a world where languages, religions, ethnic groups and others continue to hold their superiority over other humans. A perpetual apart is always carved out. The drama expands without even a screenplay. It is time to recognize who you are and escape this plane based on division, separateness and being apart from other humans. It is time to look at unity and share.

AWAKE

"Spiritual awakening is found when we return
to the exact same point at the time of birth."

We humans do not remember when we first became awake because that was the time we had just arrived from our mommy's womb. When we first awoke, we as babies did not eat meats, did not drink dairy from cows, did not care for views, did not engage ourselves with others through sexual relations, care for the trips, homes, cars, foods, money and everything else that humanity has made important during this "cycle" or "yuga". We came naked, empty-handed. This clean slate has been referred to as "tabula rasa." We did not arrive with anything except our desire to suckle milk from our mothers (mommy), being able to cry and then calm down when comforted.

How can humanity come to the level of awakening we experienced at birth during this time of materialism? The spiritual awakening or truth as some call it, is found when we return to the exact same point as at the time of birth. It is a most difficult process to arrive at. During modern times, humans cling to materialistic stuff as if they are losing something. Humans during materialism are so far from spirituality it is difficult to teach the awakening process. Bringing the human back to humanity seems like an impossibility when there is so much keeping us busy and desiring to come back for more on Earth. Clinging to earthly desires subjects humanity to continue the cycle of birth and death.

The second awakening is comparable to the first, yet during the second awakening one is older, wiser and more experienced, plus it is by choice. In this awakening, we remember the love we once arrived with. That love is everywhere and in everything. We return to the Source and seek the same things we once did when we first arrived as a baby. Yes, the human will forgo the desire to eat meats, eat dairy, engage in sexual relations seeking more penis or pussy, the desire to gain more stuff - homes, autos, money - and will forgo greed, power, and everything else worldly to obtain union with the

Divine Source. There is nothing as beautiful as this union. Once found it is the ultimate drug of life. It is pure bliss and ecstasy!

We awoke first at birth. From that moment on, in the words of Rumi, the 'hangover' started. Until then, we belonged to the Divine Source. The doctor, the nurse, mommy, daddy and others came and looked at our face then gave us a race, a name, a religion and more. After that came all the other things that nobody ever asked for but got. They were all predetermined due to the caretakers (mommy and daddy) we were born to. We were given many things we never asked for, ever. We were even given a religion based on our parents and society. We were given a culture by those vultures around us who wanted to shape our new life. We were made to believe there were already plans in life made for us by society and the others around us, as we were heirs of someone or an important child of a childless couple.

We awoke with a "tabula rasa" only to have our life written before we learned to speak. We were this and that, and were supposed to adhere to it because of dogma all around us. We were given our conditions that would become so very hard to escape later when we awake for ourselves again. These pains and the suffering would last until we become awake once again. This is referred to as returning to the Source. It is a return to the way we were the day we opened our eyes to humanity. To become awake is returning to the world with open eyes. The day we knew the truth and knew what true love was, before humanity gave us the 'headache' to fill our entire lifetime with anguish, stress and worry. It is one of the most difficult tasks to overcome this, and we try to escape it all our lives.

When we awoke from the sleep of illusion, there was no care for the brand, the biggest house, the most money, the shows, the desire to beat someone or many other trivial matters that humans have created. It was all nothing! Everything all around was nothing. "There is nothing down here!" some say. People walking around in the need for greed, desire for power, beast-like appetites for foods, money being their honey, the desire for the fames with their names - and the joke was on us.

Awakening brings relief. There is no more grief! People, places and things are the way they are supposed to be. Nothing is wrong but nothing is down here either. We smile at people in stress, chaos, or despair because we know that fundamentally there is none. We have awakened from the sleep that the world made us wallow in. Everything around seems fake and unreal. Life begins again, only this time you are not a baby but an adult who knows what to do and how to do it. Everything is easier for there is no more pain or suffering. We become in control of the outcome of the life we create in sync and in union with the Source. This is true liberation. It is being free.

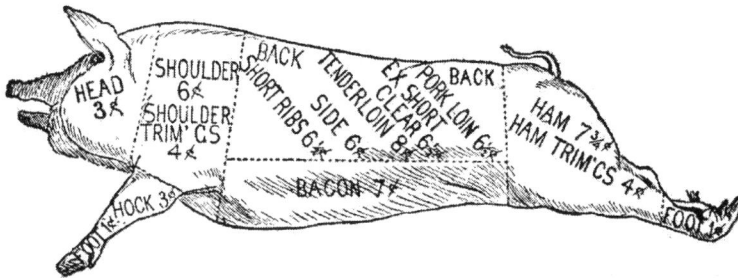

SHOULDER 6¢ · SHOULDER TRIM'GS 4¢ · HEAD 3¢ · HOCK 3¢ · BACK · SHORT RIBS 6¢ · TENDERLOIN · SIDE 6¢ · CLEAR 8¢ · SHORT · PORK LOIN 6¢ · BACK · HAM 7¾¢ · HAM TRIM'GS 4¢ · BACON 7¢ · FOOT 1¢

BACON

"The bacon infatuation was out of control."

Bacon is swine. Yes, the pig and pork. It is part of meats yet it deserves a section in this book on its own. What is so fine to dine on the swine? The West enjoys the swine even at the crack of dawn when the sun is about to shine. It is one of the dirtiest animals and humanity can't seem to get enough. It is dirty not only because science has studied the swine but also because many religions already discovered that it was not fit for consumption. Yet, almost every single "gourmet" breakfast, lunch or dinner meal that chefs consider a delicacy contains swine. Incredible! Many in the West love its unique flavor.

Looking at the health effects of eating it makes one wonder why we would eat it in the first place! What is so popular about clogging your body with additional fat from another animal? Sure, it has a unique taste that cannot be replicated and is often used by chefs as an add-on. It is the secret recipe to make things taste good. Bacon is made from the belly of the pig (the pork belly) which is the fatty meat portion of the pig's stomach. Science and Google Baba says, "A 100-gram serving of pork belly has about 520 calories. The calorie breakdown is: 92% fat (53 g), 0% (0 g) carbohydrates, and 8% (9 g) protein."

The popularity of bacon was so high that Bobby Dazzler was selling bacon toothpaste, Christmas tree ornaments shaped like bacon, bacon bandages, bacon gummy candy, bacon t-shirts, bacon-scented air freshener, bacon candy canes, gummy bacon, bacon soap, bacon body wash, bacon frosting, bacon lollipops, bacon mints, bacon gumballs, bacon candy necklace, bacon flavored jelly beans, bacon board games, bacon bendables, bacon wrapping paper, bacon gift bags, bacon candy canes, bacon chocolate, and bacon air deodorizers!

Bacon was also being used by the local cupcake store as topping over the frosting to make those mini cupcakes for "manly" boys. This was just the tip of the iceberg. The bacon infatuation was out of control. Everything was wrapped in bacon! What was next - a body wrap in the spa where humans can wrap themselves up in bacon for full on bacon body wrap?

Pork belly is put through a brine of salts, food coloring, flavor and cooking to arrive in the bacon form that stores sell. It was so popular in the West that other meats are wrapped in bacon; for example, steak in bacon - just to ensure that we have enough fat, flavor, calories and more of the meats.

Bacon is everywhere in North America and Europe. This is amazing when one examines what they are eating. Pigs eat anything and everything! Islam and Judaism consider pigs unclean and not fit for consumption. Becoming awake means that we take foods such as bacon into consideration before we decide if we should open our mouth to them.

On the road to consciousness we learn how we take care of the temporary body that the Divine has given us to carry out our duties on Earth. Being driven by our sense of taste alone means we allow diseases such as heart problems, strokes, heart attacks and clogged arteries become a major killer. Carrying on with this behavior shows that eating 92% fat is giving in to living in ignorance. Studying bacon and making in depth research into these foods allows one to conclude that it is not very healthy at all. One should abstain from bacon along with other meats.

BALLS
"Humans love balls"

We collectively spend a lot of time watching all sorts of sports, particularly ball sports. This relates to our spending time watching others rather than focusing on the self. The difference here is if we spend time playing with those balls, we become active. Once we play sports, the human body is active and this assists the body to become alive. The Divine vessel is taken care of when it is in shape and is able to come close to G-d.

Bobby Dazzler promoted itself as a "got what's hot!" retailer. Often it would take balls to carry some of the risky items we carried. Much of life requires balls when we become awake, alert, and aware. Humanity spends so much time on watching kids' ball sports that men played for millions of dollars during the age of materialism. So, to cash in on this trend, Bobby Dazzler carried novelties based on hockey, soccer, baseball, football, tennis, golf, bowling balls and any other ball sport that humanity played or watched. Carrying balls made sales.

Humans love balls. They love golf balls so much that we watch people put them in holes for hours at a time. Some watch baseballs, footballs, soccer balls, pool balls, tennis balls and even hockey pucks (flattened balls) for up to four hours to see who will win. We have not won a thing, since we haven't engaged our body in any physical activity while we watch the other. Why not just check the local paper tomorrow to see who won? Why waste this human life on all these balls which are part of the games that society has given importance to. So many of these same games associated with balls are just another avenue for groups to get together so they can drink, smoke, party, enjoy foods and spend more money on. It appears to be cool to pay huge amounts of money to go to see these events. Why not engage the Divine heavenly vessel, our body, in a sport instead?

BANKS

"A bank is a place where they lend you an umbrella in fair weather and ask for it back when it begins to rain." - Robert Frost

Bobby Dazzler could not have become a successful retailer in business without having to deal with banks. Banks provided us with an account to deposit our sales, credit cards to pay invoices, loans when we didn't do well, and coins for our clients' change back when they made purchases. There is no way any business can succeed without dealing with banks. Since there were so many banks to choose from, it is important to deal with banks that serve the needs of the retail business. It was important to look for banks that could help Bobby Dazzler grow. While we searched for the right banks, Bobby Dazzler learned much about the banking industry.

During materialism, it is all about the banks. To talk about banks in a spiritual book may seem off topic, but it is not. Banks deal with money and money seems to have become the new G-d. They also have tremendous influence on our daily lives. Banks dominate during materialism as they hold all the money for all the people. No one goes without an account, unless we choose to operate solely in digital cryptocurrency. But, even then, it is necessary to convert cryptocurrency into funds for use. Banks make us think about money all day long without ever giving us time to seek the Divine. Banks have installed screens inside their buildings, the ATM's have screens and then there are screens we use in our handheld devices to look at more of the same subliminal messages the banks put out to us. Through this influence, money becomes the focus and the new G-d for us, replacing the actual Source.

Banks have a tremendous influence in our lives. One cannot do business in this world without them. Our society does not work on cash alone so our banks store our money, use our money, and provide us with money through loans. Even those who work on a cash basis have learned that money still needs to be laundered through banks so it can be used. It is not practical to store large amounts of money at home or in a safe.

Banks are institutions we deal with daily. They are associated with debts, money, loans (mortgages), RRSP's, credit cards and credit lines. Transactions involving money are all a normal part of daily living. Banks send us many subliminal messages we don't even realize we are seeing. Banks grow and become even more profitable because we are making them rich. We buy into everything they tell us. This is fuelled by all the material "get rich quick" gurus who convince us that making more, more, and more money should be our priority.

Banks are no longer working "bankers' hours" of 9 am to 3 pm. The longer they stay open, the more money will come in to them. Today, banks are everywhere, open as late as 8 pm, some open Saturdays and Sundays so we can continually do our banking with them. They are available 24 hours a day and 7 days a week online when we can't get our car through one of their drive thrus.

Humans are hoarding money, yet creating huge amounts of debt. We are so focused on money that nobody is looking for the Source. Society is being made to believe money and banks are the main issue today. While banks are growing, people are made to worry they will never have enough when they retire. Banks brainwash humanity into believing money is the centre of the universe.

With the past meltdown of the economy, it was interesting how the mounting debts were dealt with by the banks. The stimulus package passed in the United States comprised some $787 billion dollars with money going from top to down. As simple as it may seem, wouldn't it have been better to provide each American one million dollars? Okay, give each person $2 million! Okay, divide $787 billion by the number of people and disperse it evenly? Sounds so easy and common sense, but nothing makes sense!

Not only would the average person get the benefits of the stimulus package but the costs would be far less. This other method of helping to improve the economy would cost $670-700 million. This is a considerable saving, plus a much less scary prospect regarding the financial burden for the taxpayers to carry in the long run. If only every person were given this amount to be held "in trust" as funds to be used against any outstanding loans (mortgages), debts, credit lines, or other money which may be owed to the banks, the average Joe would be better off. They would pay off the monies owed to these large banks. The banks would gain back their certainty and be in a better financial position.

Why was a top-down approach used? Because the large was enriched once again at the expense of the small. The small just got smaller, and the large got larger. The gap between the rich (haves) and poor (have nots) was just made a little larger after this so-called stimulus package and the other bail-outs were put into play. Putting this in a spiritual book is significant, for truth was revealed when the stimulus package payments were arranged. The small (i.e., almost all of us) is always playing a losing battle with the large. The only way to escape this battle is to become awake, alert, and aware by returning to the Source, rather than running the rat races that the banks and large business have installed for us to engage in. Banks just make humanity chase greed.

How could something created by humans for the exchange of goods and services be the new G-d? Money is materialism that enables us to buy more stuff. We are talking about a lot more stuff: homes, autos, brand names and just about anything purchasable. Alan Greenspan who was head of the Federal Reserve is quoted as saying the following in 2008: "It was not supposed to happen. It was the worst financial crisis in history. It had never happened before. It will not happen again for 50 years. But it will happen... I always thought people in their own rational, long-term interest would sustain the system." It is safe to surmise that even the geniuses of money know money is something that is not forever.

A final note on banks: they are as susceptible to failure as many other large and small businesses. This was seen in countries like Cyprus where the banks were closed for withdrawals and many people found out that a portion of their money was taken to pay off the debts of their major banks that had collapsed. In 2008 the American banking crisis was another instance that saw banks melt down due to the mortgage crisis, caused through the lending of bad debts and/or loans to people who could not afford them. The government had no choice but to bail out the banks. By now, even good old Canada renewed the financial sector regulations by introducing a bank recapitalization "bail in" regime. Shareholders and creditors would be on the hook for any or all losses in the unfortunate event of a large bank failure or losses due to the banks' risks. If banks can take the money to pay off their debts, is there any point to hoarding money or seeking to attach ourselves to money? We all know that when the game of Monopoly is over, everything goes back to the bank (house). Game Over!

BASIC

"Shift to the basic."

What does basic mean? It means we need to go back to the good old stuff and purge all that outer stuff. It means leaving those processed foods, being an owner of one house and one car, not multiples, and stop hoarding behavior. Materialism cannot keep going like this, for some will awake to this madness and realize the basic inner stuff is missing in ourselves and those around us. Sounds simple, right? Wrong. The outer stuff must first be shed to get to the basic inner stuff.

Once we realize that we can only live in one house at one time, the need to acquire the second, third or even the fourth is left to those consumed in greed. Shelter is possible in one house. Greed is ownership of multiple houses so the ego is satisfied and others can see how "well" you are doing. Real estate is such a hot topic around the world. We need to realize that one should not pay outlandish prices just to own in some of the most desirable cities like London, New York, Vancouver, and many more. Their real estate markets have become a gathering point for speculation based on the bulls and bears or the rises and falls of any market.

A seeker need not play into these games. A seeker knows "mortgage" means that it is a death pledge to the shelter. Becoming awake means we realize one house is enough and the rest of the resources can be used to better mankind in some way. The shift to basic can apply to anything that we only use one of. It is materialism that makes us end up with multiples. The shift to basic means we may eat foods that are not so novel. We might even grow our foods in place of the lawns we water for no reason other than to keep them green so others can see just how beautiful our multiple homes look. The shift to basic means we feed ourselves to live. Time is spent on finding the Divine within ourselves. The focus becomes the inner self. The ego melts away.

The basic is always difficult to affirm when we accumulate so many things in life. Our garages are full. Why are we collecting so many possessions? It might help to examine just how this hoarding behavior damages not only Mother Earth but us, as we attempt to figure out how we should give up on "hoard".

BLACK

"Given that the qualities of the Divine/G-d are light, brilliance, bliss, happiness, joy and energy, wearing black doesn't make sense if one wishes to awaken."

Fahima gave up her family traditions, cultural ideals and religious black clothing when she joined the world of retail sales. Fahima came to Bobby Dazzler to be the best salesperson we ever had. She had great energy, and it showed. She quickly shot to the top as Store Manager. She knew she had skills as a salesperson and quickly was called the "natural born hustler." Being able to follow her heart and show the world her real gift in life meant she could live happily without feeling repressed in garbs that no longer served her calling in the modern retail world in Canada.

Doesn't anybody wonder why the color black was chosen by religions as the color to wear when deciding to dress modestly? Is black even a color? Nowhere in any of the books, texts or scriptures does it say we shall walk around in the color of death during the human cycle. This has to be a cultural or man-made thing, adopted for no perceptible reason. Many religious people dress in black. Did Jesus, Buddha, Moses or even modern day Master Eckhart Tolle wear black all day before their awakening as an indication of being modest? Black is just a color that appears to have been adopted from a past age.

Why do so many people wear black in religion? Scientifically, black is not even a color. It will definitely keep everybody looking homogenous and obscure. Some religions thought it was necessary. Why would one walk around in a colorful life without color? Why would such an ugly, dead color be associated with G-d? It turns out that the color black appears to be the color of choice for showing humbleness and resignation, not standing out, and having an awareness of the Divine or G-d only. This was a color that may have prevailed in past times or cultures, but it is not the color for contemporary Western awakening.

Wearing black is common in all three Western religions. The Kalimakion is worn by Greek/Russian Orthodox Christians, Fundamentalist Christians, Mormons; black is worn by the Amish for worship or formal occasions, the black Hijab or Burka/niqab is worn by women who follow Islam and the Orthodox Jews of many sects (Hasidic/Haredi Judaism.) Ultra-Orthodox also choose long black jackets, pants and hats. The older forms of religion love black since it permits them to practice and worship as they did in the past. But living in the past does not mean one is living in the present. The present is living in the now.

Ironically, black is also the color of death and the color one wears traditionally to funerals or when someone passes away. It seems odd to display the color of death all the time. G-d is love, light, joy, creative, happy and full of color. The Divine is found in everything around us. Green trees have 600 shades of green, for example. The many shades that humans come in are also examples of the Divine's choice to make us different shades and not the same homogenous color. If black were the color of spirit, then everything would be black. Yet, the sky and water are in different shades of blue. We could not have been the same color, as the Divine created many shades of humanity. Humanity was not meant to be homogenous. But wearing black makes the human to appear dark.

In modern times, often one finds the Gothic (Goth), Punks, Victorians and Elizabethans moving to black as their color of choice. Many wear black on their nails, hair dyes, as make-up and as their choice in the garbs they wear. They also emit a dark force by choosing to wear black from head to toe. Almost devilish. By wearing the color black, black auras exist that some people give off, to show they may be holding onto negative emotions not positive ones, since the color is so dead. Typically, black shows an unwilling and unforgiving spirit. The color can be a sign that disease is being held in certain regions of the body (i.e., Black Plague). Many other colors have different meanings but black has one of the most regressive and negative explanations for it.

Given that the qualities of the Divine/G-d are light, brilliance, bliss, happiness, joy and energy, wearing black doesn't make sense if one wishes to awaken. Black is only one color. It least represents those words or descriptions of the Divine or G-d, so for Western awakening other garbs can be chosen. Choosing to wear black is the decision to cover up the Divine (the self) in a dark and unhappy color to live our life through. It is as if one is putting a lid on the sunshine (light) within ourselves.

One can show respect for the Divine and G-d even if they are in modest clothes like a pair of jeans, a knee-length skirt and a t-shirt. One stands out much more when one wears black from head toe in the Western world where the general population doesn't wear the types of garbs or clothes from past periods. Ironically, for those who are seeking to be obscure, black clothing achieves the opposite, for they make them stand out.

Black is least of all 'fitting' for the general crowd and very noticeable in the United States, Europe, Australia and Canada. Fitting in without being noticed today means wearing clothes similar to what everyone else is wearing. It even seems that wearing just a regular pair of pants or jeans and shirt would make one blend in better and not stand out while paying heed to the Divine. The Divine is hope, joy, light, love, and positive energy. Black is the opposite of these descriptions. Grey, navy blue, cream, white, yellow, and green are all happier colors to wear when seeking to give respect to the Divine or G-d while still being modest.

Clothes are simply outer coverings that have nothing to do with the inner self. Nor does it mean that one is more awakened if they decide black is the color they wish to wear. It should be one's own choice. If a specific color makes one more happy then that color should be worn with no force. It is symbolic and would have more to do with the signs, symbols, cultures and traditions of the past than of modern times. The color one wears has little to do with self-realization but more to do with dogma.

Self-realization, truth, and realizing our consciousness relates more to our sense(s) and inner self than the outer garbs we wear.

BOOKS

"Books generate ideas for learning and experiencing life through the eyes of those who have already lived it."

What seems so redundant about following just one path is that one is expected to read the same books over and over again and again to become awakened. Isn't there something so very boxed in about this logic? Would it not make sense to read all the books from many paths so we can become one with all and not just one specific group? To awaken and be open one gathers from all those who have awakened. It is boring and useless if one is attempting to "turn the light on" to become awake, only to turn it off by going to just one path we have been conditioned to believe is truth.

Books allow us to learn about the various paths in life and broaden the mind. Interactions with people from different paths, books such as the Kalpa Sutra, the Aqdas, the Guru Granth Sahib, the Quran, the Bible, the Torah and the Vedas open us to see life from many facets.

Has anyone come forward and said because of this one book from this one religion, humanity has been awakened in current times? Does anybody else wonder about these things? Since first being created by the original Masters of the books, who has awakened since that book was produced after the original Master had? Does anybody want to go beyond one book? We may discover the possibility of a revision, omission, or deletion that occurred over time, done by those in power who might want to control the other from having too much information. Are we to believe a scripture written thousands of years ago is in its absolute form? As time goes on nothing is absolute except Absolute Vodka, right? Is there room for error or is each book considered real truth? Good science demands progression. Awakening or spirituality is no different. It, too, should challenge past ideas and thoughts to ensure if they are indeed true or false.

Everything in life is open to some errors and omissions with the possibility of progression. Words can be changed to mean something other than what was first intended. Some Earth cycles differ from others. This is why all books of as many paths as possible should be read, not just those one has come across due to their birth parents, caretakers, culture, society, religion or those that are forced or imposed on a nation. Books from all paths are available for reading in the West. Democracy allows this freedom of religion to explore all paths. The West is best for books and thanks to our wonderful libraries plus cyberspace, we can awaken with a wealth of information.

It is always a shock when a parent states "reading too many books confuses the proper direction that you should take to become awakened." That is what the Guru also said to his Sikhs. The Guru instructed his Sikhs (disciples) to be students for the rest of their lives, with the same book over and over again. This ensures that the students or disciples stick to Sikhism's teachings and no others. This approach is contrary to what modern awakening is about. Reading as many books as possible to learn and dabble in as many concepts is a way to learn, get knowledge, and experience life, so the door to the house of the promised gift opens one day.

How sad that some have resorted to reading only one book over and over again to find awakening. Did it ever occur to them that, other than the original Master, not one from his religion of 27 million or so has stood up and said, "From reading this book over and over again, I know G-d!" What a shame, not to wonder and ponder if the books our parents, caretakers or grandparents had given were the actual path to awakening, or not! It is a little redundant when a Master asks his students to only read the same book(s) over and over again. Does anybody ever want to go beyond one book to discover if there is the possibility of a revision, omission, exclusion, reprint, reinterpretation, missed interpretation, as understood by so and so, or deletion? Aristotle recognized that scientific knowledge is progressive, subject to revision. Religion and spirituality must adopt that same view to move forward and progress humanity to a higher spiritual level. Following only one book in complete and absolute form ensures that the religion keeps the power to itself and grows.

Books are guides to awakening, not meant to be taken literally. They act as guides in life. They add to our personal, independent and private experience to help awaken us. Many have read books of one religion and gained amazing insight, but to become awakened by only one book has not occurred. Subsequent editions of any book results in errors, interpretations, omissions, and changes sometimes without even any intention. It is almost certain that everything in life is open to some errors, omissions, and interpretations. Words can be changed to mean one thing when they mean another. When they are written in so many languages they are even more subject to interpretation. This is why all paths have books. The spiritual seeker should aim to dabble in as many books of all paths, and not rely on the one they are born into.

The beauty of the West is that we have freedom of religion in our laws. This makes one wonder why those in North America, where this freedom of religion is ingrained in our constitution, are not seeking awakening as the path on their own. Why not add to the religion that was given to us at birth so we gain more insight? This gives us an opportunity to keep the path we are born into or choose to become awake. By sticking to one religion, intolerance arises that leads to an us-vs.-them scenario: our books are right and theirs are wrong. However, democracy allows all of humanity to learn. Libraries, online searches, schools, religious institutions/organizations, wellness, spiritual groups, new age groups and so much more are all available. Awakening in the West promotes self-discovery, it develops us for a private, personal and independent experience of all paths, not relying on only one book to find the Divine, G-d and awakening.

Nowhere in any of the books does it state that the books are only to be read inside a church, mosque, temple, synagogue, Gurdwara, ashram, or any other place of worship. A book is no more holy there than in one's own house. Reading each of the religious books, there is no mention of a need to create a place where many people should gather and read the books that the Masters have given. Each of us can read all books in the privacy of our own homes in a quiet setting where the potential for meditation or union with the Divine is more likely to occur than in a noisy place of worship filled with many people all around us who are interested in socializing rather than realization.

The predominant books that are being read in the West are the Bible, the Torah and the Koran. Other books are also common such as the Guru Granth Sahib (Sikhs), the Holy Vedas (Hindu), the Aqdas (Baha'i), Tipikata (Buddhism), Zoroastrianism (Yasna which part of the Avesta) and so on. Examining all books opens new ideas and concepts. (It should be noted that many of the books have titles made up of five letters, which keeps bringing up those fives.)

The literate world realizes that anybody with something to say has written it or will write about it. So, we need to know how to read and write. Yes, write books. Printed books can be passed on to others and are re-used over again in libraries. Books are where movements, ideas, and thoughts are born. A world without books would be a fearful place. Books generate ideas for learning and experiencing life through the eyes of those who have already lived it. They are teachers without having to have a physical human being talking to them. Books that are non-fiction and based on philosophy, spirituality, or on previous awakening periods are of most significance for the seeker to become awake. Reading the Bible, Torah, Koran or other such books allows the Western world to understand what shapes and conditions other peoples' thoughts and ideas. Reading all the different books from various paths enables one to experiment, conduct tests, and choose a path that works best. This is one of the most crucial pieces of information for a seeker: understand others' religions, books, ideas, thoughts, and knowledge of "truth". Books allow us to become open. Without reading other books, we are locked into one path so we cannot self-discover and self-realize. Locking into one path ensures that life is seen in one way only and not in the many ways it can be.

An excellent example of the power of books is seen by examining the Nazis of Germany. When the Nazis wanted to eliminate the Jewish people, they targeted their books by burning them. To get rid of printed books they had to be burned. The same occurred when the Taliban of Afghanistan looked for people who were educated and learned by attempting to locate the books they read, hid, or had in their possession. Many had their homes raided and vandalized. In their attempt to suppress society, the Taliban did not encourage reading or writing, especially for women. This keeps control and power in the hands of the Islamist extreme group. It is a means of keeping society in the dark through their veils of evil. The Egyptian government's attempt to suppress the rebels was clear when during the 2011 overthrow of Mubarak, Egyptian rebels were coerced, threatened and asked what books they had been reading in the days that led up to the revolution known as the Arab Spring.

During major human movements or wars, books have played a very significant role in the shaping of political ideologies. People need printed books. Not necessarily electronic books since they are just part of this cycle. Written books can be passed on as legacies of ideas, knowledge, know-how, techniques, styles, social/political/economic trends and many other topics of life. Written books keep for a long time if preserved. Electronic books have not yet proven themselves to stand the test of time. Printed books have gone through many cycles on Earth.

Books are crucial to society and future progress. Anybody who has anything to say writes books. Anybody who wants to learn reads books. We, the adults, already know a child is like a sponge when you teach them to read books. If one's intention is to raise a genius, then it would be prudent to give them as many books as possible rather than another screen to view. This includes opening a child up to the dictionary at the early ages of three, four or five, whenever they can read. The path to awakening of a child is being surrounded by books, music, and adults whose interaction is as positive as possible. Books allow us to become awake to new ideas, creative thoughts, and stories. One can introduce all books that relate to the main religious books of the world along with the books that are associated with their own faith. A child can become more aware and open to all people. They will not live in a boxed world that only deals with "their own kind", their own culture, their own people and their own religion given by our parents (caretakers). Not only do books make people more aware of how others around the world feel but people are better able to align themselves with their own belief system.

By opening the mind, one can reduce how we judge people before we have seen how they are educated. One of the most helpful books one can read is the dictionary. Giving kids this book opens their vocabulary and gives rise to whole new ways of speaking and writing. The dictionary helps them to write more interesting stories and enhances language arts skills. Other useful reads for children, teens and adults are the Charter of Rights, the Acts and Statues of any province or state, or the laws of the city you live in, Read the Income Tax Act, and eliminate worry about taxes. Helping to understand the why takes fears and worry away.

Books must be reusable, recyclable, rereadable and available to all people no matter what their economic or education level may be. Kids often collect books for school book drives, so these books are donated and shared. This means many people may enjoy the words of knowledge and intellect, not only those with money.

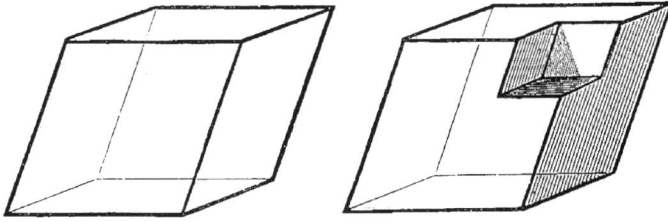

BOXED

"Getting out of the boxed up mentality means change."

Being boxed makes people want to live close to those who are like them in looks, religion, language, culture, norms, and ideals. Life is so much easier following the status quo generation after generation. This is living boxed up. And so we are subject to birth and death over and over again in a stuck pattern. Living easily and comfortably doesn't mean we are keeping knowledge and wisdom in mind. We want to live pleasing our senses rather than to look outside of the boxed up village, culture, religion, social group, or any other boxed version of us that exists. When we open the boxed up nature of the self, we become open to the new. We soon see how alike we are to those we once thought were so different from us. When we open the boxes, we come closer to truth. We can see the similarities rather than the differences. We see just how boxed we were.

This opening is possible in cosmopolitan cities in the West like New York, London, Los Angeles, Toronto, Sydney and Vancouver where many different people live. Here we can find people with competencies covering almost every market and culture of the world, without leaving the city. Living boxed up means living like the sheep who are asleep. It is tunnel vision that is manipulated by those around us who convince us life is an "us versus them" scenario. But we are all in this together. Everything, along with everyone, is connected to each other because we are from the same Source.

A group of people speaks the same language, has the same foods and looks the same. Anything different is taken as a threat to that town or city's way of life. This gives rise to a group feeling that all things that belong to their way of life are superior to any other group so different from their own. This then propels the ego's momentum. This is how boxed up ideas gain momentum, making individuals feel superior to others.

Getting out of the boxed up mentality means change. It is essential to the path to Truth. Change may even be shunned as it means that something different from the outside is brought in. Perhaps this is how whole nations become so boxed into one religion or even boxed so much that progress is hindered. This could be the problem that the Middle East is experiencing, where one faith seems to feel superior to versions of the same faith, causing wars and fighting in well over twenty conflicts in that area of the world. Western ideas, cultures, and ways seem at issue with the most radical religious individuals.

Free thought is a means of change and progress, so why would one nation read one set of books and take them as the only set of books? Why would any nation not want its people to be open-minded? Well, power and control, for one. A boxed nation cannot become free until it opens its boxes. These boxes are difficult to open as they remove power from the elite political, social, economic, and religious leaders whose main desire is to secure the people into submission. The boxed are those who are unable to be free due to autocratic religious, political, or economic leaders who instill their system into the people so control and power are always maintained. They keep the lid closed on their populations by ensuring they are moving around only within the boxes they have in place. A classic modern day example would be the conflict in Syria. "Destroy the country" seems to be the motto instead of installing democracy in the nation.

Many in the West feel free, but this is not the true scenario for the rest of the world which attempts to overthrow its corrupt leaders and overcome the boxed lives that have been created by them.

Has the West improved the situation? We still have issues with equality, gender, and race. We still have many who follow religion verbatim, and we still buy into the next "big thing", we still allow the movement of status quo (sheep) to lead us where we are supposed to be and we still love getting boxed in on Boxing Day when the same deals will be available the next day, the day after, and for the whole week. We are a boxed society, like it or not. Doing, thinking, and behaving outside of these and other boxes of society would make us more free. Why not be free?

In the West, we are lucky. We can become open-minded and freer because we are exposed to so many different people that it would difficult to stay closed-minded. Apostasy is allowed as we can convert, recant, or forsake if we wish to find our truth. Blasphemy which is violent and not peaceful is still carried out by many countries that force one to believe in just one religion. This is prevalent in many Islamic countries where one can be executed for not believing in the religion of the state - Islam.

This is not the problem of the West. Free speech enables truth and light to reveal itself. Although blasphemy is still illegal in modern Canada under the Criminal code, freedom of speech is not. Freedom of speech enables that "old" outdated law to be squashed in our search for real truth. Turning on the lights in our heart, mind, and brain is that much easier in the West which is in the best position for awakening to take place. People are ripe to turn for change. The SBNR (Spiritual but not religious) groups are rising in the West and Europe; they feel that religion is no longer the path to becoming awake, alert, and aware. The beauty that is discovered through the interaction with our fellow humans will allow the light to be bright. Reading up on different spiritual material assists in at least bringing us closer to awakening. It opens the mind to the new possibilities we can experience ourselves, not those that were experienced by a Master, a Guru or Teacher from a past cycle.

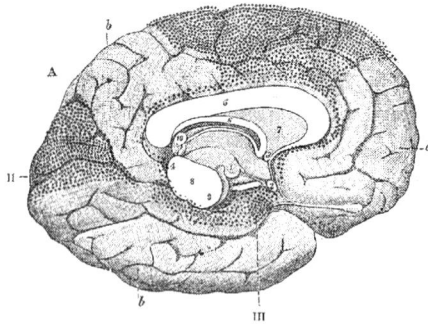

BRAIN

"The mind is like a muscle - the more you exercise it, the stronger it gets and the more it can expand." - Idowu Koyenikan

The brain holds the mind, and the mind is where all the action takes place. The mind and body are connected. Buddha stated, "To keep the body in good health is a duty, otherwise we shall not be able to keep our mind strong and clear." The brain has so much potential with its ability to generate ideas, learn and bring in all that needs to be gained in life. The brain of a baby is so free and open when it arrives. It is a tabula rasa. The brain is limitless in its ability to gain all that needs to be known, if the right conditions prevail. Those conditions are preset determinants such as genes and the environment, including the influence of the other. The brain is affected by the DNA of the two people who join together to make our physical body. Environment includes those around us upon birth. Conditioning or programming comes from the other people we interact with from the time of birth. In our constant intercommunication with the world, like it or not, the others are all around. You can avoid them and be exclusive or you can get sucked into their words. The brain will decide. Family we cannot choose, but friends, work, and the daily action of the brain will decide for you who and what.

Great thinkers became prominent because they thought and worked their brain as their talent. Choosing to pursue understanding and knowledge makes the mind stronger and provides for expansion. The brain can do whatever you seek. Seek the love of drugs, smoke and drink, and soon after the brain will also choose a path of destruction for you. Whatever wish we focus on, the brain will strengthen that desire through habit. Humans are creatures of habit. Thus, if we concentrate on bad habits then those will be strengthened and if we focus on positive habits then those will grow. What you sow is what the brain reaps.

Not everyone can "get it" right away, for the degree that consciousness is developed in each individual varies. Some of us are evolved beings who are in line with the Divine Intelligence. Others are in early stages. It may take many more lifetimes to develop that consciousness of higher states that are aligned with Divine Intelligence, the Source, or G-d. Some are still in the beginnings of their spiritual progress. Everyone is not ready to wake up from delusion at the same time. Becoming awake, alert, and aware is for those who are on the upper levels of human consciousness. That is for those souls who have already been here, and they know the laws of nature that are a fact of life on Earth.

BUY IT

"The crazier the stuff, the faster it sold."

The famous line in retail is just "buy it!" All retailers used this line often. Clients would mull over if they should get something or not. Usually, a sales pitch of just "buy it" convinces the client to go for it. Often, the salesperson is what makes the sale. The product may be something that the client doesn't even need but a salesperson pitches the item in such a way that client couldn't say no to "buy it". At Bobby Dazzler many clients just bought a product even when they don't need it or want it. "Buy it" was also something that many clients did because so many other people were doing it.

People in the Americas buy into whatever is being created, even if it is useless. Did anybody think of the ramifications of taking water, putting it into bottles, labeling it and then selling it for profit? Where were these bottles going to go when we finished drinking all that water? That is just a simple example during materialism. What about saying: I don't buy it that we need to eat three meals a day; I don't buy it that we need to eat from four food groups. Who said and why?; I don't buy it that we need to celebrate this holiday on this day; I don't buy it that the religion that my mommy and daddy gave me will be mine; I don't buy it that I must marry; I don't buy it that I must have a child.

The conditioned "buy it" mentality means "get it, got it!" Buy it means "get it now!" Being a retailer helped to understand humanity. People purchased so many items that were useless. Yes, useless! How would a retailer know this? Well, prior to the consumer choosing to buy it, the retailer bought it from the wholesaler. The wholesaler bought it from the manufacturer. The manufacturer buys it from the creator. Running a store that sold novelties and party supplies meant that I got to know what people wanted. It was unbelievable when I saw some of the stuff that people bought. Fake poop and fake dog poop! I didn't know there was a difference until I sold the fake stuff. Fart noises galore and fart smells that nobody would ever get near. Why? We sold everything from Swearing Polly the Parrots to the craziest shirts. It makes one wonder, who would buy any of this stuff? The crazier the stuff, the faster it sold. The weird stuff went quicker and the wacky stuff was never in stock because it was gone before the weird stuff. Yes, humanity was going further down the toilet when they came to ask for more weird and more wacky.

A client of mine asked who would buy a singing fishing bass fish that sold for $65.00? Yes, you read that right! A singing fish which sang the tune "Don't worry be happy!" Our shop sold so many that when the supplier ran out of them, we would purchase them from Walmart for $9.95 and sell them in our store for $49.00 (in-store) and $65.00 at YVR. It was just ludicrous to see who would buy it! The West and developed countries buy it because there is nothing else to worry about. We just buy it!

CAMPS

"These camps add to an already nervous world we live in."

With summer camps, playdates, and sleepovers a child will be engaged with people all the time, with no time for pure meditation or being in a state of unhurriedness. Humanity is going over the top crazy for more of this activity. Living in an Indian household, sleeping at other people's houses was never even a question. Why do we sleep at other peoples' houses when we have a bed of our own? Why should we pay to send our child away from us? Because we have the material means to do so? Do adults send the child to camps so they have more free time to enjoy life while someone else takes care of their child? It makes little sense to send a child to camps or to pay somebody to take them on trips, go to movies, swim, or do the things that a parent can do with the child. These camps add to an already nervous world we live in.

A child who is going to camps, or to friends' homes for playdates and sleepovers is intensifying the societal-created madness for techs. iPads, iPods, and such keep the child staring at screens for hours. Before this, the child was hooked up in cable, videos, or games. The child jumps around from screen to screen in life without interaction with real people. How can a child realize who they are when they are are always kept busy and on the go.?How can they be grounded in reality, deal with face to face social situations, or develop emotional intelligence through relational play? This has been examined by David Elkind who wrote about the unhurried child. It is time for us to stop all this hurry! And not worry so much about the play-dates or camps. Spreading ourselves so thin into so many camps is no way to develop the one special gift a child or human has. The special gift is found in meditation and in quietness at home, not in the noisy camps.

CHEFS

"Chefs allow us to relax."

During materialism, chefs have become the new celebrities. Their status rises as people not only watch how they prepare foods but also eat the foods they prepare. They cater to all people since we all have to eat. The foods are made into 'art' and become part of our daily 'entertainment'. Foods sustained human life but chefs make the foods more than just a means of sustaining our lives. We eat foods with the eyes before ever using the sense of taste to know if the foods are even edible or good for us.

The chefs allow us to relax a little more, making it easy for us to go to restaurants, food cafes, coffee shops, pubs, clubs, lounges and grills. Basically, they do all chores associated with cooking and eating, leaving us more time for drinking and socializing. Chefs train for years so they can make tasty foods that keep people coming back for more. Foods prepared for hundreds of people cannot have health in mind. Profit is the motive for a chef to go into the business of catering to people and desire for foods.

The chefs and those who prepare our foods cater to our needs. If they cannot do this they will hire a company who will cater our foods to our desires. Foods are part of our desires and our ego desires so much. Those of us who are chefs and cater our foods know this. And the foods industry is flourishing. These two groups know how to please the taste buds. They aim to please our taste buds because that is what the West is doing when they are not depressed, taking pills, complaining about the weather or even having something to do. Chefs know if they cater to our foods we will come back, for humans are creatures of habit.

Why? Because the chef's secret recipe is salts and sugar. With these two plus a spice or two added in with the lards, we have our foods. Foods are based on heavy salts and sugar which now are being considered a detriment to our health. They both elevate the risks of heart disease and diabetes.

CHILD

"The soul is healed by being with children." - Fyodor Dostoyevsky

The Bible states in Matthew (18:2-4), "Truly I tell you, unless you change and become like children, you will never enter the kingdom of heaven. So, whoever takes the lowly position of this child is the greatest in the kingdom of heaven."

We were each an infant and then a child at one time. Children are most untouched, unconditioned and pure when they are infants and they are closest to the source at the time of birth. The spiritual seeker can consider several different aspects of child and/or children when pursuing awakening. The first is that a seeker must choose to become more child-like, trusting and naive, choosing the inner self rather than the voices or noises from people and the outer world. This is difficult due to the layers and layers of false and toxic conditioning. The open mind of the child takes in all that the adult gives like a sponge. Some call it brainwashing, others refer to it as conditioning. Whatever it is, the child is no longer the same person as when they arrived with a mind of tabula rasa (blank). It may start with "you are this race and it is the superior race." "Indian people are like this or that." "Chinese people are like this or that." "Islam is this or that." In reality, it is neither this nor that. The list goes on and on, for peeling every layer of falseness that we have been given by our family, friends, caretakers, society, religions, cultures, and so on. Others around us all the time shoot constant noise into our ears even when we don't ask them to. This mental noise shapes, forms and conditions us and keeps us separated from the real truth. Certain beliefs, fears and limitations must be shed, for they have passed on to the child concepts that make some things seem impossible. A child lives from the soul more than the programmed/conditioned adult. A child is naturally able to make the adult see that we are all spiritual beings living in temporary human bodies, going through human experiences of learning, evolving and advancing towards self-realization.

A child needs care, guidance and love to realize their gift in life. Only through a human life can a soul realize, since the human has been given consciousness. Other beings like the plant and beast (animal) beings have not. Having a child is necessary for continuance of the human population, but also to ensure that souls have a chance to self-realize which is the whole point of human life. But the question remains as to how many children should we have, so our own soul may also have a chance to self-realize in this life. After having one child, there is less time for meditation due to the duties involved in caring, loving, and feeding a child to survive and thrive. Later, with the birth of additional children, the time for quietness to connect to the Divine intelligence or source is further reduced. This may be why having children is referred to as being engaged in "worldly" duties. Yet religions say we must have many children without consideration if we can or cannot care for them properly.

Religions and paths of the world have written and directed humanity to multiply and flourish the Earth. For example Genesis 1:28 states: "God blessed them and said to them, Be fruitful and increase in number; fill the Earth and subdue it. Rule over the fish in the sea and the birds in the sky and over every living creature that moves on the ground." Could this line and other lines from the various religious texts be taken out of context? Other paths such as Islam allow for multiple wives, which naturally has resulted in many children. Following some religious paths have resulted in large families with five, six, ten, twelve or more children. This has caused the world population to balloon to 7.6 billion people by 2017 and counting. Children are being born to adults in impoverished nations like Africa who are starving. How could a child and its soul self-realize if it does not even have food to survive waiting for them upon birth? Caretakers who don't have enough food, water, shelter, education, time and love or even a peaceful environment to thrive in continue to reproduce based on religious texts without consideration for their ability to provide. Many parts of the Middle East are war-torn yet humanity still brings souls to a tent with no running water, food, and no education because a religious text has commanded that the human life is a blessing. Yes, a human life is blessing if the life has food, water, shelter, love and education waiting for them. But instead a human life is put through pain and suffering when it is brought to an environment that is not conducive to a soul to self-realize. Humanity has taken words from a book literally, and brings children to the world based on what is said there. A child cannot possibly awaken in starvation, when the whole of life is spent in worry and stress in search of food. How can this possibly be a blessing? What has the West done to awaken from this?

The West and European world are hovering around two children per family on average. This gives the West a greater opportunity to come back to the self, which offers a better chance to pursue awakening. Most places where religion, poverty and authoritarian dictatorships prevail, the number of children in families remains high. The women bearing all these children face pain and suffering, giving birth multiple times. This means more mouths to feed. The West and European world are given democracy where the populations are more able to think for themselves. People can see that caring for large families is obviously difficult, time-consuming and costly. The West and Europe are collectively much more aware, awake and alert to what is manageable and workable for the life cycle. This strengthens our ability to pursue awakening sooner rather than later.

Everything is subject to cycles. When does the time come for us to come close to the Divine intellect, for those of us who have chosen to live worldly lives which include children? The time may be once we are done child-raising so they are self-sufficient into their adulthood. The faster that takes place, the faster the parent or caretaker is able to focus of themselves. This, of course, means that the child was given love, food, shelter, water, education and proper care so they are independent of the parent or caretaker. Naturally, it is easier to reach this point when there are only one or two children than when there are five or twelve or more. The time to reflect, become silent and still may seem to never arrive when we are engaged in the unending duties of taking care of little ones. This doesn't include the time required to take care of the self. That comes way down at the bottom when everybody else in the family and children are taken care of. The more children are born, the time spent on meditation on the Divine seems to diminish.

Could it be that we have come close to 8 billion people on Earth just to fulfill the promise to multiply and flourish without realizing G-d in life since the "worldly" duties of raising children take up so much of our time? Religions would not grow so large, or have so much control over people if all of humanity became awake or focused on awakening right away, or after having fewer children. There would be fewer people to control if all the religions encouraged us to meditate instead of having a large number of children. Having families that are manageable gives proper time for the parent/adult to pursue self-realization or contemplate on G-d towards the latter part of ones' Earthly life. It enables one to manage the human cycle in balance with the result of eventually awakening. With smaller families there is more time to learn, to care for the self and a chance to look after the child in a proper manner. Having a reasonable number of children would also allow some families to not worry about marrying off their girls at the tender age of nine to older men for money or a dowry just so they have one less mouth to feed at home. In the East, child brides are still a common occurrence in order to alleviate the families' financial burdens of having a mouth to feed, clothe and provide shelter for.

The next aspect of the child that should be considered by the spiritual seeker is the experience a woman goes through from the time of conception to the time of giving birth in labor. A tremendous amount of pain and suffering is involved when we bring a child into the world. Childbirth is difficult from personal experience but to be put through it multiple times only adds to the pain and suffering of the woman who brings humans to Earth, not the males. This does not include the pain and suffering after the child leaves the womb of their mother. The child must be reared, fed, given shelter, educated, and disciplined among the thousand other things that are involved in having and raising a child. These responsibilities are massive for one child. So, when we have many children, there is additional stress and worry along with the responsibilities of raising them. The main religious paths, plus books that go along with them which were all given to male Masters who don't give birth nor will ever experience the pains or sufferings of childbirth, encourage more and more children by literally writing that we are to "be fruitful and multiply". Consideration should be given to the true pain and sufferings of creating a human being from birth to death. Simply fulfilling religious commands without taking into full consideration of how a child will impact the life of the adult who brings them to life needs to be examined.

Having one child is considered being engaged in worldly matters by some Yogis, Swamis and Masters. Masters like Jesus were not known to have any children of his own. Master Bhudda had a son and wife but chose not to form an attachment to him in favor of awakening. He was known to have not even picked up his son shortly after his birth and decided that the bond that would be created would prevent him from self-realizing. The Guru Nanak of the Sikhs had two children of his own. Yet he spent 25-30 years away from his family and children in order to teach, learn and awaken. He was definitely not a hands-on father. Modern Master Echkart Tolle does not have any children either. Most of humanity does have children, so is it possible for us for awaken also while engaging in worldly duties of bringing life to Earth? Yes, it is! A child is part of the human life cycle. So humanity doesn't just stop having children. It just means that once a child reaches adulthood, the parent or caretakers who have finished their duties of raising that child should pursue awakening. This is done by "doing" what the Masters were "doing" prior to their awakening which are discussed in this text.

Another aspect of child that one should consider is that a child is a blessing. A child can help the adult in many daily aspects of life. The child can help the adult stay away from harmful distractions and habits that cause the adult to sway away from becoming awake, alert and aware. A child gives good routines, good patterns in the daily cycle so that the adult can stay focused on what is important. Taking care of a child is a big responsibility so a child can steer the adult away from negative habits such as booze, drugs, and pills (legal or illegal alike) and the desire to smoke. Having absolutely no children can sometimes cause the adult to have too much free time to engage in activities that are not conducive to awakening. The rearing of a child can keep the adult on track and even provide the adult a chance to practice love, patience, caring, sharing and teaching while learning at the same time with the child. So, yes, the possibility of awakening after living a family life in the latter part of the life is absolutely possible. We all can't stop having children. How would other humans come to self-realize?

CHORE

"A chore can be a possibility for quiet time - which is luxury time for the seeker of truth."

We all have chores to do, yet many avoid this simple time for meditation. Chores entail keeping our homes clean, and fit to live in. Part of life is doing chores. Some of us have chores at home to do while others have chores at work. Many of us loathe chores so much that we hire other people to do them, while some of us choose to live in dirty homes that are not clean. The seeker of truth will have a clean space when they are choosing to come back to G-d. We all have one chore or another, no matter who we are. Swamis, sages and yogis in the East have put those who come their ashrams to work in chores. Some students wash the floor, others clean the toilets, wash dishes, prepare meals, do seva (service) by feeding the poor, teaching the young arts/ crafts/music and the list goes on and on. The ashram always has something that needs to be done, just like we do at home. These chores bring one's ego down, brings humility to one's life. We all must do the things we are supposed to be doing for humanity, for each other. We serve each other doing chores. In America or in the West, we have a cleaning lady, nanny, and sometimes a driver to take care of our chores. We take for granted the simple chores we are supposed to do because we have been conditioned to think that chores are a waste of time and not fun. The West has different conditioning that affects daily life and living. These may even be distractions and hindrances in finding union with the Source. Delegating someone to do what each one of us is supposed to do disperses our valuable energy on others on the outside rather than reserving it for ourselves and our inner self. Chores around the house are a necessary part of secular life because we have to get those things done, and they also enable the child in the house to pick up those same habits. Habits they, too, must learn and mimic. Remember the "monkey see monkey do" line? Well, "child see and child do" means that your child will see you do your chores around the house and think that is what they are supposed to do, rather than taking the lazy, sluggish, and tardy habit up for life.

Chores are in fact meditation. Humans love routine, habit, and rituals. When the clean and dry laundry is removed from the dryer, in that quietness, stillness, and rhythmic folding, a perfect state of meditation can be achieved. It is so basic and yet many avoid this. It is so relaxing when done with right intention and right mind. The same can be said of any chore. Washing dishes quietly, cooking a meal in quiet stillness, vacuuming, making a bed, washing the floor, cleaning the toilet, washing the windows, and all the other chores of life around house can be valuable meditations. Chores are best done without talking and idle gossip. This means chores must be done without the tv on, without chitchat on the techs or phone, and without keeping in touch with others. The idea is to achieve meditation in quietness.

Just like folding the laundry, we have washing, cleaning, and vacuuming. The sound of the mop going back and forth over the floor is similar to sound of the windshield wipers going back and forth in rhythm. Simple tasks that feed our soul allow us to meditate. When chores are done alone on one's own, when the home is quiet and still, bringing attention to the simple task of the chore becomes easier.

The same system of meditation can be used for any chore that one does around the house. Gardening, weeding, and mowing the lawn can also be done this way until the habit of working quietly becomes a daily meditation. This may be the reason a swami puts the disciples to work at chores immediately in the ashrams in India. A chore can be a possibility for quiet time - which is luxury time for the seeker of truth. Chores which have to be done anyway become something we embrace, not chase away. They can be brought into life as a quiet time to be alone in one's own home. Ideally, any chore should be done alone and on one's own. The need to speak comes into play when another helps or assists in a chore. This just leads to the outer annoying voice of the other prevailing as they complain, or gossip, which takes us away from hearing the inner voice. The techs such as the phone disturb the quietness and break the slience.

CLEAN

"The seat of G-d sits within us, so it is necessary to be clean."

Bobby Dazzler was no different from any other retailer. Staff that were well-groomed and clean naturally sold the best. Staff who took good care of themselves arrived with washed and combed hair, dressed nicely, and wore make-up to make their face look great too. Being clean was essential to be successful as a salesperson at Bobby Dazzler and everywhere else. Clean was not a given. Some staff and even clients came in drunk, high or smelling as if they needed a shower. There was no choice but to turn them away. Being clean is the only way to serve in retail or to expect great service from salespeople.

The seat of G-d sits within us, so it is necessary to be clean. When "clean" refers to coming back to or when approaching G-d, it can refer to personal hygiene, the foods we eat, and also to a clean mind/brain.

In personal hygiene and care of the body, there are several ways this can be done during modern times. Clean today is not just bathing or showering in the morning. Clean today can mean cutting our nails on our toes and fingers so they are clean. Modern times enable us to take advantage of a pedicure and manicure professionally at reasonable prices so the feet and hands are clean. It is possible to indulge in a spa from time to time to have a massage or body wrap so the body can relax fully. This is especially important if the body is always in stationary or sedentary position when it is at work. The body needs to unwind and taking care of the body includes not only washing it but pampering it too. Brushing teeth and seeing the dentist are also essential so the mouth is kept clean and healthy. Modern times enable us to keep our teeth in tip-top shape. Hair must not just be washed but it also must be cut so proper care of it makes the body feel clean. It must be kept where it is not bothering one while taking care of our daily duties and can be styled to one's own liking without the need to use funky unnatural colored dyes. Dyes cause damage to the hairs and even can lead to hair loss due to the strength of the chemicals.

To be clean in your personal hygiene is not the only thing that needs to be clean in your life. Personal hygiene is at the top when describing clean. Clean on the outside also refers to order and cleanliness in the home that we make for ourselves and others. Operating daily in chaotic, messy, and unclean surroundings does not offer very much progress. Finding things, organizing items, and living a life where things run smoothly is part of living well. This does not require one to be a neat freak per se, but when all around us is clean we function smoothly and find things easily. The mind is less stressful when running our life. Clean surroundings are good for health. Living in a dusty, messy or bug-infested environment cannot be good for one's health. That also means one should not hoard.

Clean from the outside then needs to brought into the inside. Thoughts that are clean, positive, happy, and loving, plus joy, excitement, and beauty are also essential when seeking the Divine. Many Masters claim it is all in our head. This is true. The brain needs to become so clean it can seem to be mindless, without junk blocking it. Mindless is a brain that just sees what it sees, purely. A mind that is a happy observer only. A brain that does not judge, does not find answers to what is in front of them, a brain that does not question or react. A brain that is an observer of the real life dramas that unfold before us. Not one attached to the techs. The brain that is systematically ready to be strong and deal with life with no interference is a clean brain. This mode of clean makes the mind and/or brain ready to receive. Your mind does not even want to deal with things that bother it so it goes astray. The plan for the clean mind is for it to seek to be mindless, which means less conditioned or not conditioned. The mind seeks to be clean by avoiding habits that cause it to cloud. To be clean is not wanting to deal with any habit that is in excess or will cause the body to be unclean. Check it out for yourself, you will feel clean when your brain is free of all toxins and feelings that make it cloud up. Let go of all the feelings that cause anger or meanness. Think of this as a shift in focus to the self. The brain will make the shift on its own to your clean train of thought. Just love with humility and forgo any needless wasteful gossip. Just give, expecting nothing in return. Just be a clean person with no hidden agenda or plot. Just think clean thoughts that create positive feelings and let go of the negative thoughts. The mind will automatically clean itself of any toxic ideas, plans or plots.

Another form of clean refers to foods that are fit for consumption. This again means taking care of the inside of ourselves. Foods must be fresh and not processed, as those are fakes. The body needs nourishment that keeps it functioning at an optimum. This begins with examining foods, meats and dairy.

Not everything that is available is okay for consumption. Why? One cannot become awake if the foods consumed clog the body, brain, heart, soul, mind, or arteries, vessels, organ and any part of the body that disables it from performing its functions. Foods are a necessity, but pleasing our senses is not! Clean foods for eating are necessary for those who walk the path of self-realization. For example, if one eats foods that might be harmful but taste great, then one is choosing to live in ignorance.

Humanity must take responsibility to become well-informed about consuming unclean foods. With the techs, cyberspace and other tools, the time to be better informed about what we put in our mouths is now. It is too bad that humanity has not learned from the saying, "You are what you eat!" This is one of the hardest sells during the Age of Materialism as humanity has somehow made the foods that were given to us to survive upon, thrive on or live into art, entertainment and even decoration.

Since the seat of G-d sits within every single individual, then it is necessary to be clean and to eat clean foods. Judaism is one path that points this out by using the term kosher for foods are acceptable for consumption. The secular society can see that natural, organic and fresh foods are clean so they are acceptable for consumption. Determining this on our own is important as not all foods a religious person claims to be clean are suitable for the self to consume. If the physical body nourishes itself with foods that make us feel lazy or make us ill, then those are not fit for consumption. In the modern world, not everything is okay for us to eat. Clean is necessary to those who wish to self-realize. If one chooses to consume the bottom feeders of the ocean like octopus, clams, oysters, shrimps, lobster and many other shellfish that are covered up with butter, garlic and sauces without taking a look at what they consume in a scientific manner, then this is ignorance! A quick Google search reveals that the bottom feeders/shellfish eat junk and ingest microplastics and microfibres that are littered in our oceans. By covering the shellfish up with butter, garlic or other sauces just to enjoy the flavor for taste and please one's senses, is ignoring the negative aspects of this particular food. Thus in order to indulge in the bulge because everybody else is means one is not living awakened or being on alert to the possibility of introducing disease to our Divine vessel (body). It is just unclean.

COVER

"For Western awakening, it is unnecessary to cover our head."

Some cultures, traditions, and religions cover the head. Some wear the turbans, some wear a Kippah, hats, abaya, hijab, niqab, Sheila, chador, dog guan, burqa, a veil, a bonnet, a loose cap, and others wear a duppatta/chunni. Covering of the head was thought to allow for modesty, respect and humility not just to G-d/Divine but also around others who are not immediate family members. In the West, traditions of covering the head don't exist, unless one is following imported traditions of other cultures or religions. For Western awakening, it is unnecessary to cover our head. Nor was it found that other Masters such as Jesus, Moses or Buddha covered their head.

The body has many chakras but in the awakening processes final ascension takes place at the top of the head, the crown chakra. In my personal experience, there was a unique sensation that took place there daily. A slight tingling sensation increased to a constant tingle and then to a pulling of the head, at the centre known as the head chakra. It was an unbelievable experience. One who awakens in this way starts to fully appreciate the requirement, desire, and need to cover the head. That Divine Source was up there above my head. I had to experience it to realize the depth of this pull. It was unbelievable! It lasted for about seven years on an ongoing basis and was most evident upon a massage or after an energy-releasing workout in hot room doing Hatha hot yoga. At no time was the head covered, but it often felt that if the head had been covered then the energy from above would have been blocked. It didn't feel as if a cover would help, but could instead hinder the tingling sensation. When this happened, it was hard to understand why anybody would need to cover the head if they wanted to allow this connection to Divine Source to occur.

Through personal experience during prayer, meditation, in the entire awakening process and on all the occasions of the tingling sensations that took place, no head covering was ever used or needed. A head cover is unnecessary for awakening, but if one feels that it is comfortable, brings humility and there is no hindering of it in any way while carrying out daily activities then it can be used. Otherwise, it does not appear to have any bearing on whether a person will receive awakening or not. From a Western perspective, covering the head actually blocks the Divine from above reaching the center of the head chakra. When a covering is not on the head, the head is open to receiving the Divine energy, light, power, and love of G-d. It is not hindered by anything blocking an individual from receiving Divine love. This makes it easier for all in the West to engage in deep quiet meditation in our homes without worry of disrespecting the Divine source.

Each of us has a gift. Bobby Dazzler's gift was that of being a retailer in the West. The business would not be have been as successful had the traditional cover that Sikh women wear over their head (duppatta/chunni) been worn. With a head covering, the retailer which advertised itself as having "got what's hot!" would appear to be still living with family, cultural and Indian traditions that would have hindered the business. It would also make Bobby Dazzler not "fit in" which is necessary when one wants to live obscurely in the West. Western garbs were adopted so the gift in retailing could be realized.

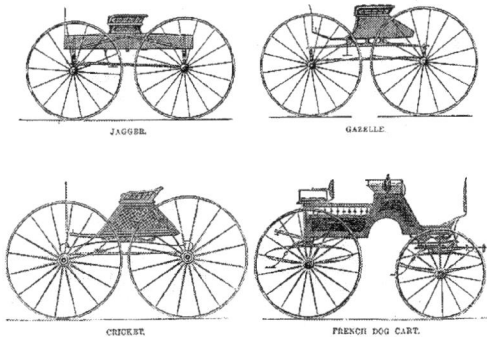

JAGGER. GAZELLE.

CRICKET. FRENCH DOG CART.

CYCLE

"Humanity is the child of cyclic Destiny, and not one of its units can escape its unconscious mission, or get rid of the burden of its co-operative work with Nature." - The Secret Doctrine 2:446

The retail world is subject to cycles like other cycles in life. Bobby Dazzler starts the year with a bang right after the busiest selling season in the entire year, Christmas. After Christmas, there is New Year's then Valentine's Day gifts. Once that is done, St. Patrick's comes up with Easter shortly thereafter. Then comes the beloved Mother's and Father's Day in May and June, respectively. This is followed by Canada Day celebrations, which would lead into the fall Back to School time for kids. With October came the busy Halloween season and then it was back to Christmas for November and December. Year after year the predictable retail cycle would not change.

Everything in world is subject to a cycle. Life is based on the birth then death cycle. A person comes into this world with nothing then gains great wealth and then dies by the desire to cling to all that is here on Earth. The person then returns to the earthly plane due to attraction to wealth on the other side of the playing field. This human then comes to see how it is to be a poor human only because in the last cycle of life this human was a person of wealth. And on goes the drama/show/cycle of life and death until the person can come to the realization that there is nothing down here if all eyes are on self-realization, truth, or G-d.

The human life should break this cycle of birth and death. Perhaps Jesus, too, knew it would be futile to wish for wealth and luxury when it was written "Those who are last now will be first then, and those who are first will be last" (Matthew 20:16) and "When someone has been given much, much will be required in return" (Luke 12:48), and "These things dominate the thoughts of unbelievers, but your Heavenly Father already knows all your needs." (Matthew 6:32).

Life is full of cycles. Woman has her menstrual cycle, the flower and plant goes through a growth cycle, the weather changes based on the season cycle, a child is born based on gestational cycle, the moon follows the lunar cycle, the sun is on a solar cycle, the earth rotates which gives us night/daylight cycle, the solar system rotates around the center of the universe, the days turn into a month which then move on to the yearly cycle to have the calendar, the body has a natural sleep/awake cycle called the circadian rhythm, and on and on the cycles of the earthly world move. The universe is on a cycle and those cycles are known in Indian tradition as the Yugas.

The current cycle we are in is known as Kali Yuga. It is the cycle that puts humanity furthest away from the Divine or central creative force. When we are furthest from the Divine, a time comes when we need to come closer to the Divine force since during the Kali Yuga, materialism prevails and spirituality is at its low point. Humanity then starts to rise, to become awake again in this cycle. The world moves in cycles and so does humanity. All aspects of life are subject to change, a cycle, or shift. This awakening, too, is subject to cycles and is no different.

DAIRY

*"Cow's milk is for calves. Mouse milk is for mice.
Human milk is for humans."*

Farmers are required to buy and hold quota for "production units", each of which gives them permission to own and milk one cow. It is like a communist business model. The Board and the Canadian Dairy Commission decide how much will be paid for his product, based on a survey of production costs, consumer prices and demand projections. Even costs like shipping to processors are pooled among all the farmers, so that milk from one part of Canada costs the same to move to market as milk from a farm across the street from a processing plant. What is the catch? Why are so many subsidies going into dairy? The government is an organization based on power so what would be the real financial benefit for investing so much money into dairy? These are the questions that one must ask in the West when a seeker desires to seek truth. So much of the West and Europe are already moving away from pure dairy by choosing alternatives to cow's milk. Choosing to forgo dairy altogether is a necessary examination into self-realization. Modern farming methods have made cow's milk contain so many toxins such as bacteria, pesticides, antibiotics and hormones that its nutritional value has become less, and it may be worthless to drink. Innovative substitutes to dairy are now available, such as lactose free milk, almond milk, goat's milk, soy milk, coconut milk, and the many other types of milks that are not dairy based. But even these dairy substitutes have ingredients in them that are "unknown", never heard of or just a mystery since we cannot pronounce most of their names. The alternatives to both dairy and the meats are processed foods which are not natural. Take a look at the alternatives before deciding to ingest them. One cup of coconut milk for example may contain carrageen, insulin, guar gum, gellan gum, zinc gluconate, xanthan gum and palmitate plus up to 25%

trans fat. So, one must surmise why we even bother with dairy alternatives that might even be just as unhealthy as cow's dairy milk. Is it necessary to continue with dairy?

Growing up in an Indian Sikh household meant there was plenty of dairy milk being purchased, served, and consumed. It was a staple of the home. If there was no dairy milk from the cow, then this was not a home. It was common to use multiple 4-liter jugs of milk every single week. It wasn't the kids' favorite beverage but we had to drink it because mommy and daddy told us to. Kids didn't have a choice back in the day. It was supposedly good for you because parents said so. Their own parents grew up on farms, with no education. Parental influences made it so that drinking milk was healthy, good and part of life. It didn't help that ads encouraged us to drink plenty of dairy. Jugs and jugs of it and G-d knows why? Drinking a glass of Homo milk which is 3.6% fat meant that a thick, mucus-like drink was going down the throat. It was disgusting. No wonder baby cows stopped drinking their own mother's milk by 6-8 months. Why did humans take up this ridiculous habit of drinking it all their lives? It was just one of those beverages that parents kept pushing on kids because they drank it. The milk today that the West drinks goes through a process of pasteurization and homogenization. It may have GMO's in it, which include pesticides when feeding those hungry cows. Production of milk is kept at the highest levels today to serve the human who is told to drink it because it is good for you.

But in modern times don't people probe into what we are drinking before buying? Who said we should drink milk, anyway? Milk that is raw rarely tastes good, and that is partly why it must be put through the pasteurization process. We had more cows in the 1950's than we do now but we produce more milk from our cows due to drugs, artificial products, and growth hormones. A quick Google search shows that the EU (European Union) government provides over $1 billion in subsidies to its dairy farmers each year. Really?!? The United States provides more than $4 billion dollars in dairy subsidies to its dairy farmers. Hey, what's the catch? What interest does the government have in making sure that the dairy farmers are subsidized so that the populations continue to receive ample supply of dairy products without interruption? If something costs so much for the government (taxpayers) then what benefit would there be to make sure that they keep subsidizing it? Are we so naïve as a public not to wonder why large organizations such as governments would spend such obscene amounts of money to make sure that we receive dairy products on our table. We must live boxed lives if these questions have not come up. Continuing to eat foods that our parents (caretakers) made us eat means that we are still living boxed up in our shell or bubble.

Given all the debate surrounding the question, should we drink milk? It almost seems like a no-brainer that cow's milk is for cows. Dairy deserved a talk of its own. This consumption of dairy and milk products continues despite the rise of heart attacks, diabetes, and other diseases common in many populations, but particularly in the South Asian communities that were linked to some of the dietary laws kept from India while in Canada. When given the opportunity to decide, should one drink milk or not? Drinking cow's milk should be left to the cows. Human milk is good for humans and cow's milk is better for cows. Simple! Their own calves don't drink it past 6-8 months so why do we guzzle the stuff down like no tomorrow?

Today we debate about the benefits that come along with raw milk but there are risks such as e-coli, salmonella, and other bacteria that may be ingested that are harmful to humans. Pasteurized milk today has so many hormones and other ingredients that it no longer is natural or healthy for humans. The best for one who wishes to become awakened is to abstain from dairy and leave it for the baby calves to drink. With the exception of yogurt, which does have good bacteriea that the gut is able to use to clean it from time to time. And, perhaps a little bit of cheese on a veggie pizza for flavor!

The body needs Vitamin D and calcium, and we can receive them from a variety of sources including vegetables, fish, soy, supplements, and orange juice with Vitamin D/Calcium added to it. There are many other alternatives to dairy or ice cream for our Vitamin D/Calcium needs to be met.

DATES

"Everybody is on dates!"

It was strange to see so many kids that came to the Bobby Dazzler store during lunch or who skipped school, just to hang out with their girlfriends or boyfriends. It looked silly to see kids as young as 10 or 11 thinking they were old enough to date or go on dates with others already. Where had the notion that children are old enough to engage in dates come from?

Dates, play dates, going out dates, date nights, online dates, blind dates, adventure dates, cupid dates, hook-up dates, one-night-stand dates and sleepover dates plus all the other dates that society today loves to put a date in their phones for! We send our kids out on play dates because that is what people do these days. That gives us more to time arrange other types of dates like those quick latte dates with the girls or maybe even wine dates instead of the latte dates. It is all about the dates these days! How do we know if we are going on so many dates in life? Large sales of online dating sites, for example, like Plenty of Fish that sold for US $575 million. That is a lot of cash based on a whole lot of people involved in online dates that lead to physical dates.

If we are not out on dates, then we are planning for the next one. This has been made so easy by the techs. Techs allow humanity to keep in touch more easily. Make dates, change dates, cancel dates and even go on two dates at one time by going on a date and talking with another date while on dates! This is a crazy time for dates and techs have added to the craze so hook-ups are faster and easier.

In hook-ups, two people who don't know each other get together to do stuff. Sometimes it's about the chats and talks but other times it gets a little more intimate, like getting some hot pussy or a large penis for dessert! Yes, dates are connected to the lusts that result after the dates, in full gear. Lusts are part of the penis, pussy, porno, boobs and butts. (Weird that they are all part of the fives that are blunt.) Dates add to societal restlessness and cause the mind to wander into imbalance. We wonder about other people, other bodies and other future dates, where all of the above will take place. This all adds to humanity's desire to go out more, see more people just for novel purposes, and it enables those who are married to partake in it secretly, too. Some websites like Ashley Madison encourage those who are married to have an affair discreetly by using their dating sites for hook-ups. Such sites cater to infidelity in marriage and make money from those who wish to stray. They facilitate people getting together so they do 'stuff'…lots of stuff that might not be moral or conducive to their own wellbeing nor to the marriage. All of this dating keeps humanity engaged in oversocializing. It has nothing to do with the self-realization process.

The West trains our children right from the start to go and socialize. It is all about those play dates. The more our children go out, the less time they have to be quiet, still, and meditate to discover what they are good at or what they want to do. In stillness, intelligence is born. So, in socializing and in over-socializing, ignorance is rampant. These play dates are counterproductive to a child being able to find that special gift they bring to this life. It is a dispersal of energy that doesn't lead to personal creativity. People go on dates to play with each others' kids while the wives engage in chats over latte or wines about what is hot and what is not. Sounds sad but life seems to circle around other people all day long. Again, techs and the need to keep in touch have made it that much easier to arrange, so people are always engaged with the other and not with themselves. Even while on dates, people rudely engage with others on the phone through texts and emails so nobody is giving the fullest attention to anything. Not even themselves when they are so engaged with so many people at once. No one has time to be alone because that is not in style. Not even when we do our yoga classes. We need to keep in touch even when we are changing out of our workout gear. People are just infatuated with what other people are doing all time. Sadly, none of these dates adds a single thing to becoming awake. They take us as far as can be from realizing who we truly are.

After receiving an email from the local community center about getting boys and girls aged 6-13 together to do a sleepover camp at the community centre, one has to wonder about the title of the email: "Who sleeps at night anyways?" It is a sleepover camp that starts at 8 pm and ends at 9 am. Something is not right when we willingly pay a community centre to take our child from us at 8 pm for the child to swim, dance, sing and watch movies with other like-minded children. Their parents must think it is a great idea so they don't have to pay a babysitter to watch the kids while they go out or party all night long. Mommy and daddy can have a date night while kids go crazy at the centre all night long without sleep. When children get together for sleepover dates they don't sleep on time and sometimes not at all. We end up with children who feel sick or not well the next day. What is the point of the entire family not engaging in a night of no sleep? The modern world has made it so that sleep is not in style. People on dates at night partake in the party habit, which is associated with the need to drink, smoke and do drugs. These are not conducive to the wellbeing of the body, soul, and spirit, which needs proper rest to come into union with the Divine.

The child gets to party with his friends all night without proper sleep so that mommy, daddy, or the caretaker can do the same. This is what the dates had done to us during materialism. Everybody is on dates! The seeker will choose to date themselves!

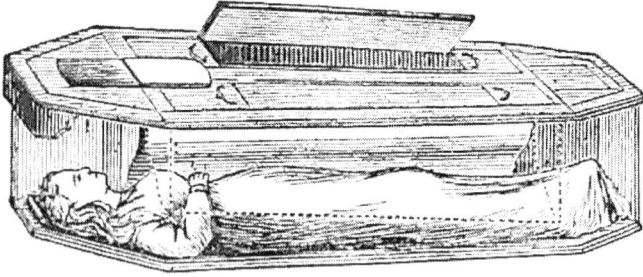

DEATH

"Death can be overcome
if we come to realize that there is nothing down here."

It has been said that only two things are certain, death and taxes. Taxes keep our social services in order but death can be overcome if we come to realize that there is nothing down here. Death to the Earthly world comes when we become nothing. That nothing is really something when it comes to realization. Death of the ego, death of the need to cling to anything down here including our heirs, money, house, cars, jewels, business or all the other stuff that is on Earth. All eyes must be kept on the final goal, which is the real death. It is the death to this world of material things.

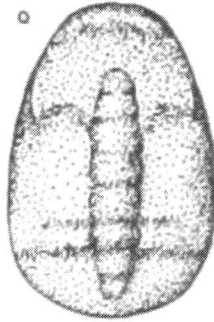

DILDO

"A form of touch that allowed our clients to use their imagination."

What does the Dildo have to do with spirituality? Well, it is part of our need for touch and sometimes we can't find that right partner to be intimate with, and a sexual need must be satisfied somehow. We all have needs! These needs are natural and shouldn't be denied. After selling gifts, gadgets, and gizmos for years, the store added the dildo as a gizmo in the batchelorette party section, which was later turned into the sex section of the store. We carried it due to many requests on Christmas during the late 90's. The demand for this item only grew as the years went on. It was something many women came into the store looking for. Some didn't have partners, so the dildo was a great way to take care of the self.

Keeping in mind that self-realization does require us to take care of the self without bringing harm to self. If there is still longing for something, or the self is still clinging to something or someone, then the self is not satisfied. The dildo took care of many, many clients' needs without them having to locate a partner to have meaningless sex with. It was a form of touch that allowed our clients to use their imagination. It was the best kept secret in our sex section in the back of the store, and many would come to purchase. From a spiritual point of the view, the desire to keep in touch is necessary for many us. Suppressing that desire for sexual gratification can lead to one obtaining it from people who are not clean, or are married. There is nothing at all wrong with masturbation or using a dildo. Ironically, the religion that forbids masturbation has had the most issues with priests who faced charges of molestation of both males and females. The need to take care of self cannot be suppressed, it is necessary. Hence, the dildo is a must-have device for modern times. It has been created and should be used. It vibrates, makes you feel great, comes in many assorted colors, is reliable, comes in numerous speeds, ensures that you come, never talks and doesn't need to be made breakfast in the morning. It makes hookups easier, safer and less stressful due to the uncertainty of having sexual intercourse with a partner whose history is not for certain. It is safe as it doesn't give you STD's, doesn't result in unwanted pregnancy, allows one to get a good night sleep without having to cuddle with it but you can if you want to. Bobby Dazzler felt that this was one of the greatest inventions. The dildo was a hot item and hit because it fit into the massage and sex section discreetly. People love to touch so it was time to get in touch with the self. This was one way to begin the journey to discovering the needs of the self, through self-touch or masturbation.

DOGMA

"Spirituality challenges dogma as it requires one to take steps to determine truth for oneself."

Sometimes clients would walk into Bobby Dazzler and decide that this store is "bad" according to their religion. Too many things in the store had to do with partying, sex, drugs and rock'n'roll. It was far too much fun and happy for them to come inside to look in according to the patterns of conditioning that their religion had provided. Bobby Dazzler was sacrilegious!

Dogma is not just part of religion but it is also a set of beliefs that a political, philosophical or moral group maintains as a core set of beliefs which they maintain as true. Dogma comprises particular belief systems that are created by an authority (be it church, a government or any other organization that has power of the masses) as being absolute truth. Spirituality challenges dogma as it requires one to take steps to determine truth for oneself. It attempts to find truth from a personal experience point of view that makes finding truth a private, personal, and independent journey different from those who pursue it by following a religion as a guide. Dogma is stringent, strict, and very hard to melt away once it has been instilled in a human as being the truth.

The desire to become awake, learn, be aware and alert requires one to seek spirituality rather than take everything that religion has taught as being the "real" truth.

DOING

"What the Buddha was doing is as important and even more important than the teachings that came after his awakening."

Not enough time is spent on examining what the great Masters were doing prior to their awakening. Humanity is fixated on the books, texts, teachings and writings that came after their awakening. While all the teachings are of great guidance when one decides to self-realize, it should be pointed out that some consistent things that the Masters were doing prior to their awakening must be examined.

Taking the example of Buddha, we could find out that the Master was sitting underneath a Bodhi Tree and in various other places in meditation. He sat alone. He resolved to remain still in meditation until his own insight had shown him the true nature of things. Some say he ate so little that he was close to death. Thus, foods and the need to socialize with the other or keep in touch with other people was not a priority. Over time, he took one meagre meal per day. Thus, he was not pleasing his taste buds with novel foods. Eating just to survive. While taking his meals, it was not stated that he ate meats or dairy. Foods were kept simple and basic. In his stillness, he spoke little nor engaged in idle talks. He did not engage in any sexual/marital relations with anybody, despite being married while sitting underneath the tree. While in his austerities, he did not engage in pleasing his senses in any way so they become distractions from reaching his goal. He was not bothered nor lost his focus by anybody who might have attempted to cause him to fail at achieving his goal. As one can see, much of what the Buddha was physically doing is not emphasized in his own teachings. What the Buddha was doing is as important and even more important than the teachings that came after his awakening. This shift in our focus needs to be understood when one becomes a seeker of truth. Observing what the Masters were doing such as the actions of Buddha prior to their awakening enables humanity to better understand the "how to" of awakening than reading all the texts, books, teachings and scriptures by themselves. It should also be pointed out that some things the Buddha was doing are also the same things humanity can aspire to do when attempting to become awake.

Another example used to explain what Masters are doing is seen by examining Guru Nanak, the founder of the Sikhs. The Sikhs are told that one should strive to live an active, creative, practical and secular life in his teachings. Secular life involves marriage and worldly duties such as the rearing of children. The Guru Nanak married and had two children but it should be pointed out that during his marriage he took five major voyages that occupied 25-30 years away from his wife and children to teach and spread the word of G-d. It is ironic that someone who wants others to live a practical and secular life did not lead such a life himself. Hence, he did not practice what he preached. His life appears to resemble someone who is closer to renunciation rather than one who was engaged in a normal, practical, and secular life.

Clearly, it is of great use to the seeker to investigate what the great Masters were doing prior to their awakening. It would be wise to search for our own awakening in a similar manner.

EARTH

"Earth provides enough to satisfy every man's need but not every man's greed." - Mahatma Gandhi

The best thing about retailing for Bobby Dazzler was that the whole world came to the store. Serving people from different cultures, traditions, religions, races, social and economic backgrounds meant the world was served. Every day, the world appeared to walk into the store This was a connection to all people of the world who made up Mother Earth, every being and every thing was connected. All people of Mother Earth were considered equally no matter what they looked like, what they believed in or how much each spent. The more customers who came into the store from varying backgrounds, the more awareness grew. It become apparent that the more people we deal with the more all people can be seen as the same.

The more time spent selling material goods to humanity, the more the mind started to awaken to the uselessness of this process to Earth. Essentially, the retail world opened the eyes up to the spiritual world through observation. The connection to selling so many possessions, novelties and "stuff" in the store just makes one wonder if this is all necessary and how it impacts Mother Earth. Looking past the parameters set by our families, relatives, society, culture, religions, races, countries, those in power and anybody else who has attempted to modify our belief system, allows for an awakening. The soul is only able to reconnect to the whole world once it establishes that there is a oneness. Oneness is unable to be accessed if the ego is still present while engaging ourselves in the collection of worldly possessions. The ego is a hard thing to smash for many, but the ego does melt when we examine the ongoing pain and suffering of humanity.

As we look at the world from a scientific point of view we are able to see that the human is made up of trillions of cells and everything the body does, the cells do, too. If we look at the connectivity and the synchronicity from that viewpoint, all things are connected. Earth has so many similarities to the human anatomy. Both are primarily made up of water. Mother Earth has its own electromagnetic field just like the human body. Animals have used the Earth's magneto reception or sense Earth's magnetic field to navigate using the subconscious sixth sense. This is something the human should start to focus on and develop. The more we make connections to the people and the Earth around us, the more we are able to feel a oneness with all. The separation that arises is due to limitations that language, culture, race, religions, programming and conditioning impose on our minds. Pure consciousness, which is the creative force or G-d, is only able to rise when this connectedness to all things prevails. This leads the seeker to ask the question if it is possible during this age of materialism to become awakened.

The answer is most definitely, yes! Earth provides enough for all our needs. And some of us have more than what we will ever need. Yet living a worldly life with money, houses, multiple cars and so many possessions makes this one of the ripest times to realize that there are others in the world who are not as blessed as the self. The self is a soul that is closer to the Divine, so that must mean it is able to be a giver rather than a taker of the creative juice of life. This realization enables the materially wealthy rich person to become spiritually rich at the same time. The exact time when the playing field in life can be better balanced by some who have more than they will ever need occurs when a letting go happens to repair the world and serve the world. The materially rich person can feed others, take care of others and provide for others who do not have. In this way the worldly individual has an even greater chance to be close to G-d by acting and behaving in a G-dly manner, by extending their material wealth to achieve spiritual wealth for those in need, in poverty and those who require education. The worldly person has infinite possibilities of helping and achieving an awakening. After all, we can't take anything with us. What the soul chooses to realize is the awakening. So why bother choosing to hoard or cling to the wealth that has been created for the whole world to enjoy.

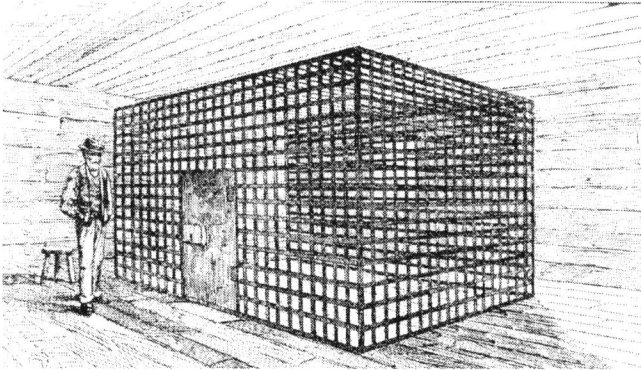

EMPTY

"To be empty, completely empty, is not a fearsome thing;
it is essential for the mind to be empty, unformed,
for then only can it move into depths." - Jiddu Krishnamutri

When we are sent down to Earth we are empty. The mind has no ideas or thoughts planted into it. So, know that we arrive empty. Learning truth means leaving this world just the way we came empty, with no need to grasp or cling to anything or anybody. Empty applies to the material things along with the thoughts, ideas, experiences, programming and conditioning that is given by those all around us and by our experiences. We arrive in the world empty just like the tabula rasa (blank slate) and that is what one aspires to achieve when seeking self-realization. At the time of our death, we are to be empty as we cannot take anything with us. Djavad Mowafaghian, a self-made millionaire who was born and raised in Tehran said he wants to leave his pockets empty when he dies. He put it simply and correctly after undergoing a stroke and found out he, too, wished to give it all away. He donated millions to many organizations including hospitals, educational institutions, charities, and facilities. This is how a man can do G-d's work here on Earth during materialism by sharing the wealth that the Divine has blessed him with. He is one example of a human who realizes that we should leave this life the same way we came into it - empty.

We are only here for the tests to see how we get along with the rest. The rest being humanity in unity. If we look at the word humanity, we will find the word unity inside it. When we realize we must leave empty and the only thing that matters is if we did what we were supposed to do and did it with success. However, one learns that we must leave without the need to cling to anything. Not a thing, including our family. Why? The world is made in duality.

Once we leave with the desire to cling to a thing or those lovely, beautiful material things, then we arrive on the other side of the material world so we can repeat that whole lesson of life once more. Just to see if we can be happy to leave empty.

Many great movers, shakers, and outstanding individuals who have made amazing contributions to this earthly cycle have already realized that they must donate whatever material wealth they have amassed to leave the world in a better place than it was when they arrived here empty. Those blessed with their gift realized this whole 'empty' concept. They have already declared that they are going away empty. Giving more to one's heirs could make them lose their drive. Each wise man or woman who has realized that is how the world works, giving to others who suffer poverty, and disease. This is true loving kindness!

Without naming every single great person who has made significant contributions to the world since that list would be a entire manuscript of its own, the following is a just a sample list and plants the seeds of leaving empty to all of us. Djavad Mowafashian speaks absolute truth when he states that he wants to leave with empty pockets.

1. Bill and Melinda Gates Foundation with The "Giving Pledge" and the multiple millionaires and billionaires who have already pledged to give their wealth back to humankind, since it is other humans who made them. The West and the developed world make them wealthy so they can give back to the rest of the world, i.e. Africa, India, Middle East and so many other impoverished nations.

2. Scott Cousens of Fortius Sport and Health donates $23 million towards the completion of a $61 million sports medicine complex in Burnaby which stood still until the donation came about. Donations to make the world a better place can be large or small. It doesn't matter!

Leaders who arrive at this point in life are overcoming their desire to cling to greed. They are pursuing spiritual goals related to karma. The actions they take now towards others will be those that they take with them. Overcoming desires for more material wealth is the gateway to the spiritual world. They choose humanity over the material world. It is a choice if one wishes to arrive empty to the Divine or if one chooses to 'cling' to this world.

Governments such as those running many of the world's nations pursue worldly material wealth instead of providing for their own people. Without naming every single nation guilty of corruption, the following is only one example of what humanity today is facing regarding the desires of materialism. The son of an African dictator in Equatorial Guinea spent $100 million of his impoverished country's wealth on luxuries such as private jets, a trove of 24 cars valued at $10 million, mansions and memorabilia of Michael Jackson, while his tiny nation of 680,000 lives below the poverty line with no access to electricity, education, or clean water.

Many wise men claim we live in a time of immense energy. Unfortunately, the energy is being exhausted on many things that are not important. Similar situations existed for Tunisia until the dictator of that nation was ousted. It just takes one individual to make the change.

We came here with nothing at birth and leave with nothing at death. Why cling to anything as we come back in the cycle of birth and death clinging to the same thing that we left in our last life? The poor in this life can arrive rich in the next. When the rich in this life will arrive poor in the next, until the soul self-realizes it is not this nor that. It is nothing and wants nothing. The Divine Source fully knows that he who clings to the material world is attracted or attached to the material world. So, the human is sent back for some lessons until we "get it". To complete this cycle properly requires one to let go. Until that time arrives, we continue these cycles over and over again until we arrive at self-realization.

EQUAL

"That revolution consists of those who are blessed to be better able to see the pain and suffering of the masses."

Bobby Dazzler was the operator of a retail store where people from all walks of life came in to browse, shop and sometimes purchase. There was no chance to treat one person better than another. All people were seen through the same eyes and treated equally as potential sales no matter what value they spent, how they dressed, what they looked like, what their race was or what they needed. The retail world of Bobby Dazzler could not be a success if some clients were treated better than others. All clients are people with the right to be treated nicely, fairly, and equally.

Equilibrium is defined as a state of calmness, maintaining a balance of the body, the forces, emotional state, and situations. Doing things in moderation is balance. This will inevitably give one peace and wholeness by giving rise to inner calmness of mind and spirit. Deep balance results in our achieving harmony and well-being. That is found when one can look beyond the outer and look towards the inner. We begin to realize ways the human body we have been given is taken care of. By choosing not to put our bodies through the rises and falls we create balance. A simple example is seen by pumping the body in the morning with an upper, caffeine stimulant - coffee, and then looking for a depressant to lower it in the evening to relax the body through booze, pills, drugs and smoke. The daily routine goes through rises and falls just like the waves in the ocean. The body gets its highs in the morning and then experiences lows in the evening. To avoid this, the highs can be removed through decaffeinated tea or another substitute, and abstaining from booze, drugs and pills. Instead the body can be given a sport to relax in the evening such as yoga, walking or any other activity that unwinds the body. From a business perspective and from a spiritual perspective, tea is the next big thing. Tea without dairy is even better as the natural taste of the flavor may flow through into the water. It can also be an ideal evening beverage due to the calming, relaxing effects it gives the body just before sleeping. Tea can be used as a beverage in the morning and in the evening to bring equilibrium to the body - especially, the green teas which are known as antioxidants, to help heal our bodies.

True balance of the mind must be continued by taking part in some sport or physical exercise of the body. In sport one can exert the body so that it heals itself of all the toxins, allowing it to detox itself of all the harmful "junk" that it has been given over the years. Namely, booze, smoke, drugs, pills and foods that are no longer nourishing to the body temple. All forms of yoga, Tae kwon do, Karate, Jiu-Jitsu, martial arts and ball sports are ideal for getting the body in gear for equilibrium. Physical exertion of the body also provides for great sleep, which is discussed separately.

Taking the word "equal" to the next step involves applying the word to the outer world as well. Looking at the world from the perspective of equality, it is easy to figure out that the world is not equal. Some are blessed with more while others are blessed with less. This can be examined by the following quote:

In the U.S., the richest 400 people have as much as 185 million people, over 60 percent of the population. As absurd as that is, on a global scale, the richest 85 people have as much as 3.5 billion people, half of humanity! Clearly, an imbalance exists, structured so a few can control the masses. These masses are those living in poverty with the rest. If the test was to determine how we treated the rest then the current system has failed miserably. That system is ripe for change, and a spiritual revolution. That revolution consists of those who are blessed to be better able to see the pain and suffering of the masses. To see all of humanity through a single eye reveals the abundance that is meant to be shared to bring some goodness and equality into the world. This is not a sudden change but a gradual shift of consciousness that requires us to collectively look at the word "share" more carefully. It is a realization that there is no way someone would be given so much unless the Divine were certain that person could share the wealth, money, knowledge, and blessings for all of us to enjoy. It requires those 400 Americans who earn as much as the 185 million to see much more clearly, to learn, to open their mind and share to make humanity progress forward. It requires the ego to let go of need for greed and the desire to hoard. The growing trend towards a share society is making significant inroads. Larger scale charitable work or philanthropy is taking off like wildfire with the help of many foundations that are helping people all around the world. This is part of realization for many that wealth is meant to be equally shared and enjoyed for the betterment of mankind. This is the awakening!

FAITH

"Faith is taking the first step even when you don't see the whole staircase." - Martin Luther King, Jr.

There are two meanings to the word 'Faith' in the context that is being looked at. Most of us are aware that Faith is a term used to describe a faith that we follow. Usually people ask what Faith do you belong to? This usually refers to a strong belief in G-d and in the doctrines of religion, based on spiritual apprehension rather than on proof. Faith is essentially another word used for religion. As a youngster, some of us are given our faith with no choice, while others are reared without any one belief system. Faith in the West is dominated by Christianity, Judaism and Islam. However, many cities in North America, Europe and Australia have immigrants who are adherents to Eastern philosophy or faiths such Buddhism, Hinduism, Sikhism and so many other faiths that come together to live. This coming together of many faiths provides us with an opportunity to learn from others. For the seeker, there is no way one can start to awaken if the focus remains just on one faith alone. Why? Well, it is looking at the world in just one way. It is choosing to see it through the eyes of just one book or belief. Awakening means opening up to different points of view and possibilities. Awakening is seeing one in all, and in the West this is much easier than in countries where religious freedom does not prevail. The chance for inter-faith studies is one of the greatest gifts that our society can give to its people. This fosters love for all. It becomes the most fundamental basis for starting out in the desire to find truth. With so many inter-faith groups, not only is dialogue, learning and awakening possible but it is the first step towards awakening. Choosing to stick to one faith in life is choosing not think outside of the boxes.

Religions are great for people who don't want to think about the possibilities of other truths or to think something else could be possible which is why it is considered brainwashing to a spiritual thinker/seeker. In the past, religion has given most of us a stable force to base our lives on. It does provide direction in many positive aspects. It has provided a peace of mind to so many and has been a powerful force. This can be discovered by reading all the main books from the world religions or teachings that give this profound feeling. However, the seeker would want to read all the books by looking into the Bible, the Torah and the Koran along with books from many of the Eastern faiths, in order to get a full understanding of faiths outside of their own. This should be done when attempting to determine what is truth and what is false. Ideally, books from many different faiths should be read in a quiet and calm setting so that one can fully grasp what is being said. Prior to any search for the Divine, it is necessary to open up to all by looking to the books that fellow neighbors read or are conditioned to believe to be true. Tremendous humility, knowledge and growth is at our fingertips if we look into all the faiths around us first, and allow ourselves to not be so boxed up into one faith. These books can all be obtained from our libraries and read in quiet meditation in our own private space, home. The spiritual seeker will be able to examine all books for self-discovery which leads us to find aspects of faith that unfold naturally. This also allows us to see what is truth and what is false rather than relying on hearsay from our society, parents or caretakers.

The second aspect of faith refers to a complete trust or confidence in someone or something. This is the faith that a spiritual seeker should be desiring; the confidence in that someone is the self. Faith in our own ability to self-discover, experience and find truth by ourselves is the faith that the spiritual seeker is aiming for. Since our search requires us to look for truth then would it not be obvious to start with ourselves first then work on all the outside stuff? Since all humans are energy, then light and faith in ourselves is necessary when overcoming the duals of life. Shifting our focus on faith in our inner selves rather to find it in a faith/religion outside of ourselves is the first step that a spiritual seeker needs to take. That is the moment we decide that this is something "I am going to figure out by myself and on my own." When we start to look for faith inside ourselves, it becomes much easier to understand than to have our parents/caretakers push a faith given to us from the outside. When anything is forced, the desire to follow it becomes harder. Children don't have a choice when they are in the care of their parents/caretakers but as an adult the spiritual seeker has a choice. Does this mean that a spiritual seeker becomes an apostate? Somewhat! A seeker does not have to believe everything that their own faith has taught but can add to what was given to enrich themselves with more choices. The spiritual seeker would look for faith in themselves rather than in religion. This is the major difference when it comes to the word faith for the spiritual seeker vs. the

Faith that has been dominated by dogma of organized religions for far too long.

Looking back though, most of the ideology that has been planted in our minds has been given to us by our parents/caretakers. The "other" around us has a profound influence in our lives from the day we were first born or awoke. We are shaped to believe in just one faith, the one that belongs to our parents or caregivers. We are not taught what other faiths do nor encouraged to search others to determine which fits our personal belief systems. But, when the seed to look for truth is planted, we search the Church, find fog in the synagogue and one feels lost in the mosque. Interfaith learning studies are not part of learning from the beginning. This is something the seeker would start to take up on their own. The seeker begins to look towards Faith in their own ways, ideas, goals, visions, plans and life aspirations rather than relying on the faith that was given to them to guide them in life. In the West, we have so many people from so many races, cultures, religions, nations, and ethnic groups living side by side that the discovery is much easier. This is why the West is the best.

Sikhism was the faith that was practiced at home. It was the path the parents were given and it was passed on from generation to generation. It was not followed in an Orthodox manner at all. But the faith was followed with very heavy influence of culture, male domination and suppression of women's rights. There will be some who read this and think that is not what Sikhs are like. That is true! However, this was from personal experience and the case was such that cultural traditions seemed to overpower the Sikh tenets at home. After going with the given faith until the age of 18 or 19, many aspects of that faith did not align with the personal belief system as what is truth. By 1990, after attending university, many different discoveries were made by reading books on theology. It was time to find a new faith that aligned with the self. A faith must align to one's own value system; a system that makes one happy, prosperous, smile, love and grow as a human being. When we become adults, a faith must be chosen by the adult on their own not by their parents or caretakers who have followed a system due to their society imposing it upon them for years and so on without ever questioning it. With so many resources available to students, courses on the study of religions, paths and other cultures allowed for a great interest into the path for truth. Judaism was one path that seemed to provide the greatest amount of interest. When a Jewish man came upon graduation in 1996, an electrical moment of truth that led to marriage plus conversion into Judaism took place. It was meant to be, or the calling had been answered for now. Oprah would call this an Aa-hah moment! Time to change the faith. It is allowed in democratic free Canada so that is what this seeker chose to do. This faith worked for many years following conversion. However, things changed by 2004. This is when intense issues in life caused a tremendous amount of pain and suffering. In 2004, the hubby walked out, leaving two toddlers to be raised by a single parent and then bitter divorce proceedings that lasted 3 years till 2007. In 2007, the most profitable business location of Bobby Dazzler was not given a renewal so finances plunged and debts mounted as a lawsuit was initiated from the landlord's actions. These intense feelings of despair and sorrow were a catalyst for some sort of inner awakening. Feelings of not wishing to go on due to tremendous difficulties that just wouldn't stop, resulted in inner transformation. It was kickstarted with a chance meeting in 2008 with a Master visiting from Malaysia. After a three-day retreat, a feeling that there has to be more than this in life arose. Even Judaism could not give this due to the fact that being complacent and not being able to think was not enough anymore. And so another great Ah Haa moment arrived when the desire to find the "real truth" awakened. It was more like "what I am doing here?" and "why are we all experiencing these struggles.?" Clients in the retail world experienced and complained about this same pain and suffering over and over again. It was around 2008 that a commitment was made to shed everything and start all over again. This was a moment that faith in the inner self would be pursued. A challenge needed to be taken and overcome so that a return to this same old drama would happen. It is in our adulthood that a spiritual seeker normally chooses to pursue awakening and this was the case by the age of 37.

Just by looking around, every generation that seeks to be spiritual knows that there is something higher, bigger or larger in life than us. Yet, we are a part of this big thing. We have this gut feeling that there is a G-d, a creative force or Divine intelligence but when push comes to shove, we seem to differ in how we come to realize the Divine. Awakening is something that requires complete and utter faith in the self. It is considered to be some sort of outside job that is unreachable for the general population. However, that is untrue. The decision to seek awakening can made by the self when we decide to put our faith in ourselves instead of relying on outside forces to bring faith to us. This can happen during the modern times by giving the power back to ourselves rather than choosing to follow outdated thoughts and ideas that have not brought the light to humanity but actually turned it off by pitting one group against another. Our idea of faith needs to evolve from being outer force to an inner force.

FAKES

"It's nice to just embrace the natural beauty with you."
- Victoria Justice

Fakes are called knockoffs at the retail level. Bobby Dazzler tried to stay away from the fakes. Nobody liked to deal with a client who complained that the item that was purchased recently is junk. Knockoff products were cheaper but fell apart fast and were not novel for long. There was nothing like ordering the real, name-branded authentic items. They were the natural first choice. Clients love to own items that were originals rather than fakes which had no warranty. The original/authentic product didn't even need a warranty as they stood the test of time and lasted forever. There was always a genuine feel to the product, it was real.

In the 21st century, humanity had materialized the simplest of tasks of life. Nannies were being hired to raise the children. The same could be said about the chore of house cleaning. It, too, had been passed along to the cleaning lady so there was more time for other stuff. The nanny was great if mommy was doing what her destiny was meant to be. But it appeared that the nanny was wonderful for the mommies who just wanted more spare time to do other things like hit the malls, gabbing, shops, clubs and grab more foods. There was no time left for meditation.

Being sexualized, the human body was used for purely sexual purposes. Even the beautiful most natural breasts that were meant to feed our babies were made into fakes with artificial implants. Humans had become convinced by others that bigger is better. Let's supersize the boob and penis with pills along with the fries! (Perhaps this is where the whole "supersize me" came into play). More to handle and much more fun to watch shake during sexual intercourse or while one walks. This also meant that humans had created baby formula to replace the mother's natural breast milk so that breasts could be used for other purposes rather than what they were truly meant to be used for. Pills enabled the simple human penis to be enlarged and even made to stand (stay hard) for longer periods of time than the natural erection would. It was all about more unnatural pills, drugs, supplements, patches, ointments and radical surgeries to alter the beautiful, perfect human natural body into the fakes. That was the trend during the Age of Materialism. Nobody wanted to be natural anymore, only the fakes were in.

People were spraying themselves silly or going to tanning beds if they weren't laying in some hot spot doing nothing to look like they had just been to an exotic place, when in reality they had just been spraying themselves brown. Humans going to tanning beds exposed themselves to harmful rays of fake sunlight to be in style or on trend no matter what the price would be later! Soon skin cancer was upon them and they wondered in awe, how did that happen?! This would be called fake and bake!

The flesh of the human being was being injected with Botox (Bottulinum toxin), bacteria, hormones and other funky junk so the human would stay young forever, along with having that large, rock hard penis or very large, breasts for the penis to enjoy. Pills were also being created for the woman to prolong her sex life to limit or avoid menopause (natural time in a woman's life when the menstrual cycle ends and childbearing also ends). Normal human function meant that onset of menopause which meant to tell the woman to pause with the man and the man to pause with the woman. (This can be read as "pause oh men" when we read menopause backwards.) Keeping in mind that the word is G-d and G-d is the word, it will not be an accident that certain words were meant to be understood as they are said, where they are written, read or spoken. Since males did not have to carry the new generation or bear the burden of childbirth nor were they the main caregivers of children, then it would be natural for men in their later age to make a shift in their thoughts to focus on the Divine Source once they had been fruitful and multiplied or had the opportunity to enjoy their sexual senses in earlier years. Yet, society, media and the large materialist world had embedded in them the need to continue reproducing, carrying on with dates, Viagra overkill, have more pleasures through the desire to go out, and anything else to increase their sexual appetites for lusts. It has additionally brought children to adults in the ripe old ages of 70 and sometimes even 80.

Foods were being processed to a degree that there was no way to determine if it is fit for consumption. Margarine, which some say is one molecule away from being plastic, had replaced good old butter. Our pure water was being put into plastic water bottles and being pawned off as being superior to the regular tap water in "Beautiful BC".

The human cycle was far from behaving naturally, which is one of the essential elements of coming home to the Divine. Normal human cycles meant that women and men who cease or reduce sexual activity due to menopause, were now being encouraged to prolong sexual activities through the creation of some artificial pharmaceutical pills and drugs. The emphasis was on using our bodies long past their expiration date because that is what humanity was made to believe is the new normal. Yet, there was nothing normal about attempting to defy the natural reproductive cycle of the human. The focus had become on lusts. What had taken place was a movement towards the body having to perform due to the human emphasis on sexual activity. This all prevented one to come to any meditation of the human body. There was only time for more sex, more penis and more pussy. This is sensory overload. We are far too in touch with others and not in touch with ourselves.

The conditioning or influence of media on society was such that nobody is supposed to be alone, ever. The large organized groups that control the whole of humanity dictate what is the next big thing and we are all collectively made to believe that we should buy it! We are all supposed to be in touch and in constant touch, one way or another, with no time for G-d or to find the Divine anymore. We were far away from the source, indeed.

Everything about the fakes was in. We had forgotten about G-d or ourselves. Humanity was being conditioned into believing they must continue with dates, drugs, pills, always stay in touch even if it meant being with the wrong person for the their whole life just as long as they were not alone. The right person was actually themselves on their own and alone! Especially in the latter part of life when a seeker is actually beginning to seek the Divine. But this was of no avail since the damage of media influence, large business, conditioning and the money-driven society almost forces humans to feel that fakes were not just a trend but the norm. Over-socialization was taking a toll on the whole. Society has forgotten how to think clearly and realize that the human body is created in a creative, complex manner that really should be left to come back to its natural state if one is pursuing self-actualization. The human body is created in cycles just like the rest of the world or anything else that has ever existed. It is a complex set of cells, organ(s), water, bones and nerve(s). It was a perfectly created system that was not meant to be used to such extreme abuse. It quite frankly disconnects from the source when it relies on the fakes and forgoes the natural. The fakes disrupt the perfect system so that disharmony or dis(ease) may occur.

What is next up for the fakes? Well, thanks to social media, relationships are so superficial that you can be a friend with someone in the morning and be unfriended by the afternoon via Facebook. Relationships are no longer face-to-face but are screen to screen or fake to fake. Socializing has taken on a whole new dimension which of course affects one being able to have meaningful, real relationships that last. Cyberspace has even created websites that encourage adultery and cheating with the motto, "life is too short to not have an affair". This was the case with the Ashley Madison website that was designed for those who wanted to step outside of their committed relationships or marriages to have affairs, yes affairs! This encourages adultery, lusts and cheating, so that the relationships and marriages can also be fake.

Fake news has only added to this dilemma. Nobody is sure any of the news that is coming our screens is real or not. This is further intensified by large companies developing AI to determine exactly what our likes and dislikes are so only what we want to see is shown on the screens. Millions and billions of dollars, time and energy are being spent on perfecting AI (Artificial Intelligence). That is read correctly, artificial not the free, natural DI (Divine Intelligence) which is found within every human being. Humanity is artificially being made to believe we need to find out if there is water on Mars. Why is it so crucial to find water on Mars when there are no humans? When we already have 7+ billion humans who are all in need of fresh clean water to drink here on Earth, now! Other fakes that are growing include digital cryptocurrency, which is not hard currency but virtual (fake).One day it is there and the next day swoosh, it is gone. Why? Well, it is digital and fake. It is not hard paper currency. It appears fake stuff and fakes are in. This leads humanity astray and away from what is important in order to create distractions from living a peaceful, progressive and positive life on Mother Earth.

The word artificial means just that: made by humans and something that is not occurring naturally. It appears the divisions between the material and spiritual world only seem to get bigger until one just steps outside of this box and looks at growing unnatural aspects of life.

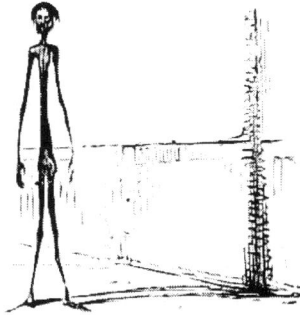

FASTS

"It is time for fasts now. Fasts were seen as a way to reach G-d."

Rumi writes:

If you take fasting to heart
You'll hear the sound
I am at your service
I am at your service
Every time you call out
My God

If fasts bring one closer to G-d, Allah, Ishvara, Jesus, Guru Nanak or to the central creative force, then foods bring the world further through excess and gluttony. Fasts need not be reserved for just the special holidays of Yom Kippur and Ramadan. Fasts should be part of our yearly, monthly, weekly and daily life. Fasts have long been an integral part of the major religions and spiritual traditions have long adhered to the benefits of fasting.

For Islam, fasting is the fourth of the Five Pillars. For Buddhists it is common not to eat each day after the noon meal. It is not considered a fast, but a disciplined regimen in the aid of meditation and good health. Judaism takes part in the fasting process during Yom Kippur. In Hinduism, fasting is an integral part of the religion on many occasions. Christianity discusses acceptable fasts in the Book of Isaiah, 58: v. 6-7. Benefits of fasts were also discussed in the Book of Daniel v. 8-16 where it describes partial fasts and their health benefits. Many accounts exist of fasts in the Bible. Eastern Orthodoxy and Greek Catholicism adhere to fasting as it is an important spiritual discipline that is tied to the principle in Orthodox theology of synergy between body and soul. The Baha'i Faith also considers fasting along with prayer as one of the great obligations of its faith.

It was only Sikhism that did not condone fasting as it felt there was no spiritual benefit to it. This was the religion during childhood, and that given by the caretakers. Knowing one must experience in life everything and then decide if it is true or false, it became necessary to try fasting. It proved to be one of the greatest and easiest things to do.

Detoxification is the foremost argument presented by many advocates of fasting. This process involves eliminating or neutralizing toxins in the colon, liver, kidneys, lungs, lymph glands, and skin. When food no longer enters the body, fasting enables the fat reserves to turn into energy. Some of the major benefits of reducing caloric intake or restricting it includes reduced risks of cancer, cardiovascular diseases, and diabetes which are all the major diseases of the developed world. Increasing one's maximum life span is one of the final results of fasting.

Fasts give so many benefits to the body. The body rids itself of the toxins that have built up in our fat storage throughout the years. The body can heal itself from the inside from all the damage over the years of eating, indulging and splurging on the foods.

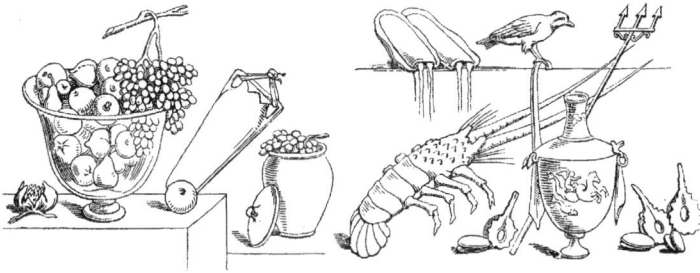

FOODS

"The mind is being made to believe we should think about foods all the time."

No book on spirituality is complete without a discussion of foods. For the seeker, foods are just a means of nutrition, a means for us to survive and thrive. Foods, and some more foods is all that the modern world is focused on. Foods are related to our sense of taste, which is one of our senses that is most "beast" like. Once we get going on foods then our sense of taste has no limit. It is not known when or how but we now see foods as forms of entertainment and art, through conditioning by large business that we must be social. Foods are a means of our being able to survive and thrive. We are now decorating them, putting bows on foods, taking pictures of food - calling it food porn. The human body has become so greedy and needy, seeking ever-more novel foods.

Foods for those seeking spiritual freedom are contrary to those novel foods. Foods known to be clean, pure and edible are termed as Satvic (pure/balanced) by Yogis and Kosher (clean and fit for consumption) by the Jewish people. Foods that are calming and harmonizing, and those that promote wakefulness are the correct foods for consumption by those seeking to bring the body into balance. Some foods that assist in mental clarity are vegetables (especially greens such as broccoli, cucumbers, tomatoes, avocados, grains, all fruits, nuts, and beans. Look for foods that nourish the brain rather than make it feel dull.

Foods are part of our cravings and desires. So much so that humanity engages in gluttony. Craving causes all suffering according to the Buddha. So why do we always crave foods all the time? It is the "in" thing to do, as we seek chefs who cater to more foods that are novel. Foods are not just a trend because some of us are even given the term "foodie" since we love foods so much. Could it be because everywhere we go, we see pictures of foods (food porn), chefs preparing foods, restaurants with more delicious foods, entire channels on cable dedicated to foods and their preparation, celebrity chef cook-offs? Or is it because we have nothing else to do but think about foods? Who said we need to eat three meals a day to stay healthy? Shouldn't we eat when we are hungry? Why do we continue to fit into some made up out-of-date model or guide to when we "should" eat and "what" we should eat along with "how much" we should eat? Are we so gullible as to believe we need three meals a day of meats like sausages, bacon and a lot of pork on that fork? Come on this is the developed world, right? Are we going from the cave and back to the caves?

Those that might need to hear this might not read it because they are too busy at the next restaurant chowing down on some sushi, pizza or steak. Foods give us energy to sustain ourselves but too much slows us down. The current diets in the West cause some diseases in humans to soar past normal readings. Cancers of the stomach, throat, and breast are out of control. Diabetes, strokes and heart attacks are harming humans, mainly due to foods and the lack of exercise that goes along with eating those foods. Living a disciplined life regarding the foods we eat is best, for discipline is based on focus or living in yoga. Mind, body, and soul cannot connect if all three are being drained by foods all day long. The mind is being made to believe we should think about foods all the time.

Foods are part of cravings and these are part of our habits or hindrances of life. Come on everyone, we have to eat to live. Why do so many of us live to eat? We need to make sure that the foods we eat are tasty and healthy. One can't just eat healthy and hate the tastes of food that we eat every day. We need to make sure we eat with taste in mind. Eating well means healthy eating. Just programming yourself into the habit of eating vegetables and fruits means that other foods will not taste that great anymore.

As a child, fast food was a treat. Today it is everyday food for all people, because we are too busy and live fast-paced lifestyles that prevent us from making healthy foods at home. People come from many places all over the world with so many delicious foods from their countries only to enjoy fast foods more. Foods from the old country are still made by many of our parents and they are tasty, plus healthy.

A very big part of self-realizing today is being knowledgeable about what we put in our mouth. It is up to us to realize whether the foods we were brought up with are good for us or not. Too much dairy, curry, meats, garlic, onion, and other foods can make the mind foggy and groggy. We can awake to what is good for us and what is not. Knowing the South Asian community is suffering from a high heart attack rate could mean that when there are so many fried foods involved, the foods are not that healthy. It is always difficult to tell ones' parents that the foods they are eating aren't good for them and they should abstain from food that is part of their cultural heritage. Foods that have been made for thousands of years in India may be hard to let go of. Foods from India are just one example. A careful examination of all foods from any country is necessary when one becomes aware, alert and awake.

Healthy eating doesn't appear to be a problem for the wealthy since they never complain about a thing as they belong to the top 5% of the population. So when you hear of one saying, "…we had a very difficult background, it was rough, we had nothing, we grew up poor, we grew up in the hood, my parents gave me nothing, my parents never supported a thing I did, it was tough.." Welcome to the club, this is 95% of the world. Having fewer foods is being closer to the Divine than one who is over-consuming them. It used to be that a rich man had the rich man's gut. Yet more and more of humanity is feeling the effects of foods, as the number of people who are obese is growing. Being obese is suffering. It decreases one's lifespan and increases the chances of many diseases. Foods today have become a habit rather than something required to just sustain our human body. Foods are being sensationalized and overemphasized. The industry makes their preparation novel through chefs who cater to the wealthy.

An industry from foods has been carved based on habit. Just like drinking, smoking, pills, and drugs, foods have become a nasty habit. The industry relies on our need to nourish but it encourages fast, easy and cheap foods. It is a bad habit that leads to health issues from obesity to anorexia. The foods we eat are a true reflection of who we are. Bobby Dazzler's store was in a mall. The food court was jam-packed with line-ups galore. It appeared to be the only place that made money. It was unbelievable to see the amount of food being consumed beyond a normal amount required for that meal in the day. The foods were not proportional to what was required for the amount of activity, age or health of the person. Watching the food court scene makes one feel not so hungry. With line-ups 10-15 minutes long, wasting a 30-minute lunch break standing and waiting for service was the norm. Why would anybody be willing to spend so much time in lineups when a lunch could be brought from home? A brown bag lunch allows for mindful eating in a meditational manner. There is a sense of peace when one opens their lunch to actually enjoy a relaxing and quiet break.

Why not bring our own foods and enjoy our break without the stares and the crowd? The fast-food industry lives off of the fact that the world is lazy. We need to drive up to a window or cashier to order a meal that costs

$2-$3. It is a wonder how a fast-food joint can make cash from a meal they retail for such little money. Well, it does not require an MBA in foods for one to figure out that through this money, the fast-food place will pay its employees, rent, cost of goods and still make a profit. Where's the food? Is there any food in the meal? There is none, we are paying for nothing. Fast food is just that, fast with no substance. You could buy a bun, yogurt and vegetables at the supermarket for much less. This is not only a healthy option but also gives tremendous amounts of great energy. The effects of the switch will amaze the body and soul after a 21-day cleanse of foods is undertaken. No kidding! You can feel better and healthier by getting into a habit of eating foods that are tasty. Even if you are addicted to the habit of foods (that is eating,) then why not be an addict to healthy foods?

We need to eat every day to sustain ourselves so it is important to be with someone who enjoys the same foods as you or who cooks. Growing up with Indian cuisine meant there was a lot of curry and spice. When the teens arrived, it was a blessing to enjoy raw, uncooked or steamed vegetables or fruit. Opening to different foods also meant not being so boxed up in everything we are given by our parents. This also allows us to select foods that make the body feel great because only the self knows how they feel. Parents will always give us what they were given because that is good for them so why wouldn't it be good for their child? Perhaps the best thing to do is go through a trial and error with foods to see which give us energy and which take energy away.

Foods can be healthy when they are simple, raw and easy to prepare. We are not talking about being a gourmet chef or something like that but it is well worth ones' while to learn some of the ins and outs of cooking. One cannot think going out and eating at restaurants is the way to live every single day. This is what we are doing. Nor can we can we believe we should eat TV dinners for the rest of your lives. This is not practical or economical. Our bodies are important to our livelihoods but we seem to disrespect the body. Part of knowing the self means we need to get rid of the excess fats, fast food, MSG's, dairy, meats, and bacon. The world is full of terrible habits that have been made into life. The time has come to stop and think about every single food you are about to put in your mouth. It is not just a saying. "you are what you eat," or "eat only those things we can pronounce."

It was once said that eating is such an intimate act that it should be done with those who are like-minded. Sitting to enjoy foods with those who love the same foods gives value to our lives and makes us happy. What happens when you see a vegan eating with a carnivore? Opposition can occur when we are in the company of someone who has bad manners, eats unhealthy foods or does not respect the life of animals the same way the seeker does. A seeker would not be afraid to eat alone as it allows for meditation to take place. Eating becomes mindful.

FREER

*"Dictatorship naturally arises out of democracy,
and the most aggravated form of tyranny and slavery
out of the most extreme liberty."* - Plato

All Masters of the world would say that to be free is at the top of their list in what they value the most while living a human life. So, when we have freedom of religion in the West, Canada, United States, EU, Australia and the New Zealand then why wouldn't progressive, intellectual and educated humans take advantage of it and become awake from the darkness. Moving to the West provides for freer thinking, open-mindedness, and the ability to add to the current faith or religion we are born into. Freedom of religion is found in the laws of many, if not all, Western countries. This makes the West the best.

A rebel dies, a group will suffer to ensure democracy prevails in a nation. To be a free, a man or woman may divorce when a couple grows apart. Getting out of jail or prison, leaving a negative job, taking part in a civil war to be free from an autocratic leader all happen for freedom. A person is freer following whichever faith/religious path they choose, or a person will sever their ties with a family, a teen will drop out of school to seek freedom and the list goes on and one of those who wish to be freer.

One is not freer when under the control of any individual or group, be it a religious group, a controlling marriage/relationship, a job or any other situation that dictates how one should live or believe. This includes our own parents or caretakers. One of the requirement of living towards becoming awake is freedom. Be a prisoner to nobody. Be free from all those who are soaked in the desire for money, power, wealth, multiple homes, or anything in life when somebody else other than yourself is in charge of your survival and your well being.

However, even in freer Canada, a nation that is voted as one of the greatest places in the world to live in the world, one can see that even it is not as free as we once thought. One cannot ignore the obvious that is taking place right now as we attempt to live in a freer country. Five very large businesses control the foods we eat daily through supermarkets and foods. It would be hard to believe food's prices are not in the hands of a select few who have full control over the foods and the prices we pay. Are food prices increasing or are they being inflated to enrich the pockets of these five large corporations in Canada? Well, there had already been a bread price-fixing issue that has been brought to the attention of the competition bureau by the end of 2017. What other foods are affected by similar price inflating?

Looking a little deeper into our Canadian banking system, one can discover that our five major banks control over 80% of the Canadian peoples' money. These five banks have control over so much more of our lives than we may be led to believe.

These banks control loans (mortgages), business and auto loans which means they control our shelter (house), our businesses/jobs plus our means of transportation/cars. These same banks control the cards - credit/debit cards, RRSP's, RREP's, saving/checking accounts and safety deposit boxes. When so few have control over so many then being free and freer is compromised.

It becomes even more surprising when we examine the enormous power that media has over our lives. When one takes a look at the media in the democratic United States thirty years ago, 50 companies controlled 90% of the media. Today, only six large companies control media in the US. Those in media are fully aware of the enormous power that media has on the people so this makes it all the more puzzling! If Americans rightfully despise totalitarian nations then why have they bowed down to "state" controlled media that is in the hands of the few? What does it mean when the so few hold undue influence over the state and the media? Well, they control your cable, radio, papers (newspapers), books (magazines) and all those lovely annoying ads (advertisements) that are everywhere - billboards, books, cable, online, papers and radio. The viewpoint become skewed.

The large keep getting larger and larger as the Age of Materialism picks up more momentum. In recent times, big dental is swallowing up practices with lined pockets of cash. Operations like DCC (Dental Corporation of Canada) and the Ontario Teacher's Pension Plan have made investments as large as $1.3 billion to purchase controlling interests in a U. S. firm called Heartland Dental. A firm that operates 375 clinics! The large have been scooping up hundreds of practices in the United States and Australia so centralized clinic management soon resembles Walmart in the dentistry world. This is not news for areas like Pharmacy and Optometry which have gone down this path years ago. One wonders just how free and democratic we are if the Ontario Pension Plan alone is controlling the oral care of so many people. Are they interested in your teeth or health or is this just another move to increase profit or to consolidate power?

The world wants to be freer but there are so many nations and their people who are not freer. Putin, along with the state of Russia, recently sent three singers from "Pussy Riot" to prison for going against him and the Catholic church for blasphemy. He also wants to fine people for being homosexual. China still does not have a rule of law. These nations along with their people are forced into dictatorships. One is not free if they are forced to follow a political, social, economic or religious movement that presents people from being who they are and doing what they are supposed to be doing. Once we escape the clutches of the autocratic dictators of the world, the democratic world finds itself caught in the web of a different prison. The West becomes freer until it succumbs to media and large business. The ideas of freer society come with maximum freedom-distractions that interfere with our being able to become still, quiet and aware.

The whole point of becoming freer is not to set up another political group/organization that fights for freedom/peace but to become freer through self-realization. The rules of power always prevail when a large group gets together to fight for peace/freedom. The only way to be free is to practice awakening, self-realization and awareness as the end goal - to not have to come back to the reborn and face the music again with life here on Earth where those in power prevent actual, full freedom. Joining the Divine is the only freer way to true bliss.

FRESH

"Eating fresh foods with fresh taste allows us to perform at our best."

In the retail world, the food court was a handy place to grab a bite to eat from time to time. The only problem was when arriving in the wee hours of the morning, those hot dogs from last night were still on the grill. Once the lights turned on, the grill turned, and suddenly the hot dogs were "hot" again. There were many instances of fast foods being served to clients that were not fresh but old, stale, and reprocessed.

It is all about fresh these days. Eating fresh foods with fresh taste allows us to perform at our best. It was funny how people who ate fresh foods looked fresh and those that ate the processed (fakes) started to look like the foods they ate. How can anything be fresh if the cans or jars sitting on our grocery store shelves read "best before June 2019" when the current date is January 2016? Are we so naïve or gullible that foods packed years ago would be fresh enough for us to consume a year or more later? What preservative is put inside to give us the great look of foods to make them look like they are when they were packed so long ago?

Going fresh is going organic, garden-grown, locally-grown without any pesticides or growth hormones to alter the actual foods from being fresh. Fresh will not be necessary for freshly caught shellfish or freshly cut meats since both should be abstained from when one wishes to become a seeker of spiritual independence and become awake.

As a child growing up with Punjabi or Sikh foods, it was always a curious thing to see how all foods would be cooked in high heat. All foods, fresh vegetables, beans or dhal would be put through a masala mix of onion, garlic and the same spices. These would then be cooked so that all the good stuff would be lost to heat and be served with roti, chapatti or rice. That was what the cuisine was based on. It was not tasty at all for a child interested in fresh, wholesome, nutritious energy foods. Foods should give the human body and the soul the best chance at working at its optimum level. So paying attention helps when one wants to become awake. Why did the people look like the foods they ate? They didn't look fresh nor did they look like they were happy. Was it true when people say you are what you eat? Eat fresh if you want to look fresh!

GANJA

"Weed had become mainstream, normal and acceptable."

Ganga is another word for pot, maryjane, marijuana, weed or skunk. By 2017, almost every other client smelled like skunk (ganja) when they came into the store. That is how mainstream, normal and acceptable weed had become. It was hard not take advantage of the growing weed industry in Canada due to Health Canada regulating its sale. People needed smoking accessories to smoke it from so that is where Bobby Dazzler came into the picture. We had grinders, bongs, pipes, hookahs, scales, screens, flavored rolling papers, and everything else underneath the moon for ganja. Ganja socks, underwear, sweatshirts, t-shirts, ashtrays, vaporizers and more. Humanity was thinking of weed as being mainstream. In Canada, drug stores like Shoppers Drug Mart had applications to Health Canada to be able to sell it along with other items like milk, cheese and eggs.

Everybody is smoking ganja or trying mushrooms to get that extreme high that awakening gives one. It is being encouraged by some leaders, some doctors promote its use for medicinal purposes while others just use it recreationally since it is becoming so mainstream. People use it and abuse it for medicinal and recreational use. The point of it is that it is not a natural way of relieving pain, stress, anxiety or depression. It is putting something into the human body to numb it from certain pains it is feeling. These days it can be the average Joe growing a couple of plants, the gangs, the government who want to control it and collect taxes on it, your neighbor, our friends, our teens, family - young and old all want to be part of the action known as relaxation. Everybody wants to be part of this going green movement. Going green regarding ganja doesn't mean that people want to recycle everything. It means that people want to smoke more ganja than ever before. Some States in the US have already made it legal, so it is no longer a big deal to grow it and make a business out of it. It is all natural and the Divine would not have created something that wasn't supposed to be used. It was just up to us to determine if it was good or not.

If it is used during the developmental years of life, cannabis on a casual basis damages the brain. In those developmental years, the tweens and teens may use it for experimental purposes, to get high or just to escape the hardships of these tremulous years of change. Changes occur in the brain but they also include changes in emotion and motivation, as the brain alters the way it perceives reward and pleasure. The brain seems to change itself in such a way it makes ordinary experiences seem less fulfilling compared to those when using drugs or ganja. These changes are not natural and cannot bring us closer to the Divine in any way. Since the brain is the key to awakening, one cannot be coming near to the Divine source when the brain is altered in this manner.

The poor in many parts of the world don't have enough to eat, drink, or live by, while the developed world not only devours foods but also seems to be going into a downward spiral, attempting to determine if we should roll ganja in a rolling paper, smoke it through a pipe, bong, or vaporizer, or bake it into cookies. These are pressing issues of the developed modern world which has so much stuff that we want to alter our brains to feel even better. When one alters any part of their body through drugs then it is not part of becoming awake. In fact, it is as far from becoming awake as one can be. The Canadian Psychological Association's task force on the legalization of cannabis says regular cannabis use among teens "is related to poorer education outcomes, lower incomes, suicidality, greater welfare dependence and unemployment", and among the populations at large increased risk of motor vehicle collisions. It further goes on to say that "cannabis use can disrupt normal adolescent brain development." affecting verbal learning, memory and attention. These same detrimental effects may also be extended to adults. Sadly, the industry is expected to grow financially to billions in the next several years. This is all due to legalization of ganja which makes it appear okay and mainstream for all to use and abuse.

GARBS

"When we wear what everybody else is wearing around us, then we can live in humility."

It is important to look great when one is in retail sales. Bobby Dazzler was no different. People from all paths of life came and shopped in the store. It was important to appeal to the general public. It would be impossible to be a successful retailer if garbs of only a certain religion or culture were worn. Having Indian parents doesn't mean that a retailer needs to wear the traditional garbs from India when attempting to sell items that are "hot". Sometimes the item was not that hot, but it was important that the salespersons' garbs were similar to the clients that Bobby Dazzler was selling to. It was good to blend in with society and be more like the clients. The sharp-dressed salesperson was always the best salesperson, as they were a true Bobby Dazzler.

Garbs is just another word for our clothes. They are worn to cover our bodies to protect us against the cold. They provide the person wearing them with a certain look which is part of the trend or fashion. When any religion and culture puts more emphasis and attention onto what is worn, it is difficult for the West to grasp the idea that garbs have anything to do with awakening. Well, they don't! The garbs have nothing to do with the human being as it is an outer covering! There are monks or swamis who wear robes of many colors similar those worn in India and the Far East. While others still think going head to toe in black is the path to awakening. These garbs may have been worn in past cycles, but clinging to past cycle fashions doesn't bring us closer to awakening. It confirms that one is attached to past ways.

One can come to have respect for the Divine and G-d even if they are in modest clothes like a pair of jeans, a knee-length skirt and a t-shirt in the

West as modern garbs. This is the modern awakening, so fitting in without being noticed today means wearing garbs similar to what everyone else is wearing. It even seems that wearing just a regular pair of pants/jeans and shirt would make one blend in better so they would not stand out while paying heed to the Divine. It should also be noted that wearing black or any other color - even orange or white - is just an outer covering of the body. An outer covering that is modest has nothing to do with the inner self. Nor does it mean that one is more awakened if they decide to wear a specific color worn by their culture or their tradition for centuries. It should be one's own choice. If a specific color makes one happier then that color should be worn with no force. It is symbolic and would have more to do with the signs, symbols, cultures, and traditions of the past not modern times. The color one wears has little/nothing to do with self-realization but more to do with dogma. Let's give orange a chance when we wear our pants, jeans, shirt or dress. The color resembles the sun which is light, energy and power.

The dress code of the West is part of our normal everyday wear for those of us who are engaged with secular society in our creative ways of service to the world. Since this is book is on modern awakening for the West, the garbs in the western world include pants (dress, casual, sweat and yoga), skirt, shirt (dress or tee), sweat stuff and the comfy shorts. Those are the clothes that make us assimilate ourselves without standing out. We can live in obscurity by choosing garbs that everybody else around us wears. Obscurity is necessary as it means that one chooses not be noticed.

Dressing modestly means we live in obscurity without drawing unnecessary attention to ourselves. Being modest means wearing garbs that cover our privates. It is unnecessary to reveal all the genitals to the world, even though in parts of India some awakened yogis choose to wear nothing. Garbs today exaggerate fashion and sometimes reveal the privates right through the clothes. This is not being modest, nor it is humbling or showing humility. Sexy wear that is see-through is distracting and causes attention to fall on the person wearing the clothes. Some of this is promoted by the celeb, advanced by the fashion world, the trend, and in the stores in the malls.

Dressing to impress draws attention and dressing according to a certain religious/cultural manner from the past also draws attention since that is not attire that the majority wears. From a personal perspective, being a retailer meant appealing to the masses by being more alike for success in sales. The gift that Bobby Dazzler had was being a successful retailer, and not many people would have made purchases from the store if traditional garbs from India such as a Sulwar Chameez were worn daily. Bobby Dazzler would not have lasted 27 years with garbs that were too traditional for a retailer that went by the motto, "got what's hot!"

Western enlightenment is the present modern awakening. When we wear what everybody else is wearing around us, then we can live in humility, be humble, and still be respectful to ourselves, the other and the Divine inside us. It is unnecessary to reveal too many body parts to others, so we can forgo the short skirt and low-cut shirts. They prevent one from living in obscurity which is the opposite of living like a celeb. Most paths agree on modesty, humility and living in obscurity when we all blend in. Western garbs suffice as we evolve and learn to assimilate, so we live drawing no attention to ourselves here.

GIVER VS. TAKER

"By giving away we feel rich; by hoarding we feel poor."
- Debasish Mridha

There are two kinds of people in the world - the giver and the taker. Let's face it! From a self-realization perspective, being a giver is the path to the limitless world of finding light and what we should aspire to be. The giver is definitely much more spiritually developed than the taker. The giver lines up their attributes with those that are associated with Divine intelligence or G-d. The giver tends to reserve personal or business resources in order to be able to meet the needs of others. They are able to give their time, energy and money toward goals that are for the betterment of humanity at large. They continually ask the question, "How can I help?" and feel there is plenty more where that came from. They take care of others in the same manner that the Divine is able to take care of them. They listen more and talk less. Givers see they are in alignment with the Divine in the manner that they were blessed with so much to share. Part of this share is to care for the pain and suffering of those around them. Limitless love, compassion and empathy towards others is the base of the giver. They tend to live consciously aware of the world around them. They can see that they are able to help and repair the world around them. Givers are able to see the bigger picture when it comes to peace, loving kindness, generosity and being a light to others. This is what makes those who wish to become more in tune with G-d, a giver. The giver is essentially able to measure spirituality in terms of resources, accountability and dependability. The giver truly wants to make a difference whereas its counterpart, the taker, tries to see what is in it for them. Givers see the Divine in all others around them while the takers simply seek attention.

The time for the giver to rise is now. The Age of Materialism has allowed so many of us in the West to amass great fortunes that cannot be used in this one lifetime. A perfect example is The Giving Pledge. This is a foundation committed to by the world's wealthiest and families who dedicate a majority of their wealth to giving back to philanthropic causes. Why? Because they have received more than they will ever be able to use, so they feel they must give to the people. Organizations such as these are the beginning of understanding that sharing makes repairing the world that much easier. They are aware that they must have been given much so they can be healers of the world around them and can undertake the work that is their soul's purpose to rise up. They are just one example of the way society is able to give back. It doesn't even have to be wealth. One is able to give time and assistance by volunteering themselves. Service to others is still possible if one doesn't have wealth to give away. All that matters is that continued service is the end goal - to be a giver to humanity. The best way to achieve spiritual satisfaction is to behave in that light by giving away to those who are less fortunate or in need.

On the other end of the spectrum, we have the taker. This is the opposite of the giver. The taker is often consumed with fears of not having enough, jealousy, envy, scarcity and thinking there is a limit to what is available in the world for all to enjoy. Takers are energy vampires that drain others. They often don't give 100% of themselves as they whine about their time, energy, agenda and schedules. Takers are not happy people and this is always easy to see in interactions with them. Their agenda is usually based on themselves and they tend to use the words, "I can do that for you!" just so you are aware that they doing you a favor. The givers' language in daily communication is different. Some takers have no choice due to corrupt regimes, autocratic, authoritative governments, war, disease or poverty. The taker has no choice in those instances but to rely on the givers such as those who contribute to The Giving Pledge to eradicate disease, provide shelter, water or other basic necessities of life. The taker in the West is consumed with hoarding, clinging and grasping onto "stuff" daily. The everyday taker fears there is just not enough to go around or clings to things having been conditioned that *you never know when you will need it* even though it has never been used in the past. The world is full of more takers than givers, unfortunately. There is a state of chaos in so many countries that are not able to see that everybody wins if we choose to become a giver rather than a taker.

GUIDE

"Do your own work. Those who have reached the goal will only show the way." - Buddha

There are many types of guides in world. There is the food and nutrition guide, the driving guide, the shopping guide, the financial planning guide, the retirement guide, the travel guide and more. But for awakening, the outer guides no longer serve the goal quite as well as the inner, intuitive guide that the self must master. The guide that our parents or other relatives have given us is known as religion. This is a guide that most of us have been given from our parents, society, country, culture or those people around us who we grew up with. Normally, that guide comes with a scripture such as the Bible, the Torah, the Koran or the Vedas, but that guide is adhered to without access to other guides/books. Whatever the guide may be, it is a guide only. What has happened, though, is that each of these guides seem to have been taken literally by a group of people who strongly believe that the guide is correct in its entirety and current form without questioning if it is even relevant to modern times, this earthly cycle, to our personal life and our world today. The guide that is being used by many paths applies to past times, not modern times. That is where self-realization and awakening comes into play. The path for the seeker requires reading all the books meant to be guides to awakening. This enables the seeker to decide what is true and what is false. It is through this trial-and-error method of life experience that one decides what to allow and what to reject.

The best guide in reality for approaching awakening is to experience life for ourselves and not take anybody's word as absolute truth. One person's truth will obviously differ from another's. By examining just how different the Moses guide (Torah) differs from Jesus (the Bible) and then once again the guide Mohammed created (Qur'an) is different from the earlier two guides. Hence the best guide for Western awakening would be to seek a personal experience of life in our search for truth. Buddha explains there are three kinds of wisdom: received, intellectual, and experiential. The literal meaning of received wisdom is "heard wisdom" - wisdom learned from others by listening to sermons or lectures, or reading books. This is another person's wisdom that one adopts as one's own. But acceptance may be out of ignorance since it is much easier to follow without questioning. People who have grown up with a certain ideology or system of beliefs may accept without questioning the dogma of that community. Acceptance can also be due to craving. Leaders may declare that accepting the beliefs will guarantee a wonderful future; perhaps even claim all believers will attain bliss of heaven upon death or receive some other present. Or the leaders will instill fear in the people of punishment or even proclaiming that unbelievers will go to hell after death. People are sometimes forced into beliefs through such intimidation. Blasphemy or apostasy laws make the crowd obey. This gives people no choice but to swallow doubts and adopt the beliefs. Received wisdom is wisdom that can be accepted due to blind faith, out of craving or out of fear. It is not one's own wisdom, not something experienced for oneself. It is borrowed wisdom. This is what most major faiths of the world are. Received wisdom becomes a bondage or barrier to attaining other forms of wisdom. One is not able to move to experiential understanding.

The next wisdom is intellectual wisdom. After reading and hearing teachings one examines whether they are rational, beneficial and practical. If one is satisfied at the intellectual level, one accepts it as true. It is still not considered one's own insight but an intellectualization of the wisdom one has heard. When one converts from one religion to another, one takes a faith that feels closer to their own belief system and drops a faith that does not align with them.

The third type of wisdom arises out of one's own experience, out of personal realization of Truth. This is where the seeker can find real truth. It is a true guide for finding truth. It is wisdom that one lives, real wisdom that will bring about change in one's life by changing the nature of the mind through direct experience. It is only through this Truth that one can liberate the mind. Buddha further points out that no one's truth will liberate us. Even Buddha's awakening could only liberate one person, Siddhartha Gautama. The guide, his books and teachings are meant to be an inspiration for others and guidelines for them to follow but Buddha said:

Do your own work;

Those who have reached the goal will only show the way.

Examine, experiment and live life through your own experiences. Use many guides to decide what is truth and what is false and do not take the truth of another as absolute truth for yourself. Books may have been subject to errors, omissions, and interpretations by different people with different ideas. Reading books to find knowledge offers the windows and doors that open our birth boxes that have kept us boxed in.

HABIT: DRINK, SMOKE, AND DRUGS

"It destroys the physical body so that the mind cannot attach itself to the Source."

Humans are all creatures of habit. It is important to know this and apply it to the way one lives in life. Habits are easy to acquire but most difficult to break, particularly the bad ones. One either succumbs to it, overcomes it or overlooks it all together. We easily fall into the traps that carry a heavy price when we fall into a habit. Books from the past cycles don't mention or emphasize the dangers of habits like drinking in excess, smoking cigarettes or doing drugs. The most common modern habits are booze (beers/wines/spirits), smoke (cigarette/tobacco/marijuana) and drugs including pills both illegal and legal. In 1990 when Bobby Dazzler first opened, we did not carry even one item related to any of the habits. By 2017, 85% of all the items related to drinking, smoking, and drugs. A quarter of a century later, times had changed. The habits of humanity are everywhere. Habits cause the physical body damage, so the soul ends up living in a body that is not clean. And when one is not clean then one cannot awake.

Everybody has stress and worry. That is part of this life cycle since duality is part of living. We all express the upper and lower levels of life. Once a traumatic event happens, the first thing that one reaches for is a drink. The adult is not the only one reaching for booze but our teens and youth also experiment with their friends. The habit of drink starts at a young age. Booze can rule one's life, turning to liquor every single day so the mind can relax, settle itself, and unwind. Unknown to the brain is that the habit becomes worse and worse as time goes on until more is needed to satisfy craving in the body.

Many teens and adults say it was just one puff, and they found themselves addicted to smoking. Many people never can overcome this habit until it is too late or harms the body. When one smokes, the smoke can also lead to many other drugs to get a higher high than just nicotine or tobacco. To smoke the following drugs is very common today and dangerous to the mind, body and soul: Marijuana, Opium, Crack, DMT, Heroin, Meth, PCP. But one cannot awaken when the habit to smoke lives in the body. It destroys the physical body so that the mind cannot attach itself to the source.

The last category is drugs. Drugs for this discussion will include both illegal and legal. Drugs of this sort are not new, but during materialism there is so much money and more free time, drugs become a habit just because people have the time to relax and enjoy themselves. Drugs are bad for the physical body and prevent the human from becoming awake. Drugs harm the body that the soul lives in. It is impossible to be in a habit to do drugs and expect to become awake.

Stresses of life cause people to resort to escape or to get over some stress or worry. People read, jog, go for walks, knit, sail, cycle, build, write, or work too much. When you find the right balance, you have found the secret to life. Living with excesses in our life can also lead us to try these bad habits. The human body is a creature of habit and will stick to the habit once it is introduced. Perhaps taking up a sport, deciding to write, focus on working or our children might be a better outlet to relax, rather than to take up a habit that will be very difficult to get rid of once in place. The modern world tends to being running on empty in the sole search for money, power, and fame. Some have let it all go so they can satisfy their habit all day long. This is a terrible waste of the human life. Bobby Dazzler saw so many people who felt it was much easier and better to deal with the world when they are high, drunk or stoned. The legal, social, physical, mental and financial considerations of habits all take a toll on society. Our teens, youth and children slide along the paths that the adult is creating.

Once your body is free from all of them, it can truly think, make plans and reach the highest goals. The body will only then be able to function at full speed and with all the right intentions. Being in constant check of the habit to drink, smoke, or take drugs will help your whole inner self to be who you want to be. These habits may seem obvious, but it is important to mention them because part of the awakening in the past did not include such habits. Drugs, pills, and smoke were rare during past times of awakening. But now they are available, created, used and abused by so many, poor and rich alike. These habits were not bound to any social or economic classes. The time had come to detox and hit rehab for many of us.

HAIRS

"Anything that is forced never makes sense."

Hairs seem to get a lot of attention when looking at spiritual seekers who shave their heads, others grow their hair long, some cover their heads altogether, and some only cover a small part. What does hair have to do with awakening? From a modern Western point of view, nothing!

Hairs seem to very important in the different religious paths. Sikhs are told not to cut their hair but to grow it and put it under a turban. Muslim women cover their hair and only show it to their husband or immediate male family members. Some Jewish Orthodox women shave their heads only to put a wig on that is sometimes nicer than their own hair so it defeats the purpose of drawing less attention to oneself. Monks shave their hair off and wear simple garbs that don't draw too much attention to them, except in the West where they stand out. But in Western awakening there is no need to shave hair, grow it or cover it. Just maintaining it and keeping it clean seems like the logical approach.

Wearing our hair in a way that is most comfortable to us is the most important part of feeling good. One who feels good will do good. Anything that is forced never makes sense. An individual may become unhappy if they feel uncomfortable with the way they appear since it is not something they themselves want to do but was imposed on them from the outside.

Hairs don't necessary need to be colored those bright colors that modern times has made the new trend. Bright pink, blue, purple, neon red, or green draw attention to the self and fails to allow one to live in obscurity. Wearing one's hair in a nice, tidy manner acceptable to the self is best. Using dyes, color, straighteners or curl enhancers can cause the hair to become thinner over time, since unnatural dyes no matter how "natural" they claim to be, still harm the hair, scalp, and roots of the hair shaft. Hair should be clean, washed, groomed, and kept in a manner that is appealing. Hair that smells clean and feels good to touch seems to matter the most. Maybe we should focus less on the hair which is the outer stuff and focus more on the inner self when searching to arrive at truth.

HAPPY

"Who doesn't want to be happy?"

The best clients to serve were those that were happy. It wasn't difficult to find in a store like Bobby Dazzler. There were always occasions to make a purchase. There was no shortage of birthday parties and the many holidays that went through yearly cycles like Christmas, Valentine's Day, Halloween and the many others. Bobby Dazzler made people laugh. Happy were the ones who came in for no reason but left with something that they thought was great. After retailing for so many years, there were many happy return customers.

It is hard to be happy all the time. For a seeker who has been handed lemons, happiness is still one of the secret ingredients when pursuing awakening. It is absolutely necessary to be as happy as one can possibly be. It means putting our best foot forward and staying positive. Smiling is free and causes fewer wrinkles than a frown. An uplifted state is also where the mind needs to be when we are attempting to reach a state of consciousness that is G-d-like. If someone makes you unhappy, let go and walk away. It is that simple.

Who doesn't want to be happy? To be happy is an inside job, some say. Well, whoever said that was right, since happy is all about the inner self and the outer self. Too much time is spent on finding happy outside of the self. We focus on the next trip we take to travel like the modern nomad, we try to fight aging with the next best cream or serum and we look to the other who will be our soul mate forever until we grow apart. The list to find a real happy goes on and on. Once we look for true bliss then happy is found. There will never be a need to look outside of where you are. You can find this happiness. This is what discovering the true self does.

HOARD

"We immortals aren't misers - we don't hoard! Such things are pointless." - Margaret Atwood

It became apparent that the retail world of Bobby Dazzler only contributed to humanity's need to hoard stuff. Clients came in making purchases just because they could or were bored. It is no wonder that hoarding has become a disease. Repeat clients would come and iron out their Visa to the tune of $500 a month on novelties to amuse themselves. As the awakening process started, all retail sales added to this nonsense of hoarding stuff. There was no limit to how many gifts, gadgets, and novelties clients could buy. It was always a wonder where they were keeping all this stuff!

Even those who claim to be minimalists cannot hide that the world loves to hoard. A minimalist may not collect so much stuff, but they can still hoard money in the banks that can't be seen by all. It is time to let some of that dough loose for the other half of humanity that lives without food, light (electricity), water, or house (shelter). In the West, you see people who are homeless yet still try to collect more stuff. Self-realization is not the collection of more stuff, junk, art, autos(cars), houses, spouses, people, girl/boy friends. You see garage after garage full of clutter, junk and stuff. If only we could ship a container to Africa, to another household that has nothing. That alone would bring us to a more even playing field. To hoard shows the new fear-mongering created by those dreaded banks and large forces in society that gain when people cling.

No wonder the population of the world keeps on getting bigger and bigger. Hoard is related to cling. When humanity clings to stuff like a house, money, jewels, autos, props, or just about anything else that is worldly, they then find themselves locked in the cycle of birth and death. Sarah Noffke says, "The belongings people accumulate throughout their lives always own them. People seem to think if they had more they'd be happier or freer, but their possessions only chain them to the Earth." We cling to things that we hoard, due to the new conditioning in the West or in some parts of the East that one must gather more and more stuff. Living in the Now as Eckhart Tolle put forth means we don't cling to those things or stuff. We simply release them so we are not attached to anything at the time of death except to G-d, the Divine Source, Allah, Hashem, Creation, or whatever we want to call the creative force. Our eyes have lost focus due to the conditioning that we must hoard, acquire, have more gains and cling to things.

HOUSE

"Humanity seeks the outer house of prayer due to conditioning as that is where we have been taught that G-d lives."

During the Age of Materialism many feel that they have "made it" or completed a cycle in life when they purchase their house and become an owner. It has been instilled in us that the American dream is to be the owner of our house. But at what price? During Materialism, the only things so many us of own are the debts or loans (mortgages) on our shelters. A house, no matter what type of house it is, is just shelter! Shelter is to protect ourselves from the outside elements, or keep us from living on the street. Who made it important that we should be the owner of the house? What a clever and ingenious idea! Condition humanity to feel as if they should always be owner of the shelter, an investor of other multiple shelters and owner of vacation properties so they "cling" to the material world on Earth. A programmed clinging to our house keeps the soul coming back for more births on Earth.

Mortgages were derived from the "Law French" term that English lawyers used in the Middle Ages. It means death pledge, and the pledge only ends with the obligation of debt being paid or when the property is taken through foreclosure. Banks and large businesses have fuelled madness in real estate to maximize profits, keeping us engaged in being the owner of our shelters. The bigger, more expensive and larger the loan, then the better for the banks who reap all the profits through those excessive mortgage payments. Taking out large mortgage loans means we continue to pay for these houses until the day we die. What does it matter if one is an owner or if one rents their shelter when we are true spiritual seekers? We can't take the house with us. We can only live in one house at one time. Anything beyond that is greed. The whole point of life is to do what we have to do by discovery of our gift to humanity. We are able pursue self-realization in our shelter. The modern world mandates that we add another house to our collection of many houses. Real estate agents or home owners who do renos to flip houses to make money will say their gift in life is to buy and sell houses. Others will say they are developers so they must make many houses to sell to humanity. When does a limit come? When do we realize that we have accumulated enough capital but can't even use it all in one lifetime? Having multiple properties also means more stress and worry associated with tenants, rentals, insurance, upkeep, theft, vandalism, and many other issues that come along with being the owner of multiple properties. A seeker would be satisfied with one house or place of shelter for themselves. This can be a suite, condo, room or anywhere else where we feel safe. We have pursued worldly wealth for long enough, and now the time has come to pursue the goal of awakening.

Sure, there are benefits to being an owner of our house. When we make the house we live in the house of prayer then we can invite both women and men into our place of worship - in our house. Self-realization is for both men and women in our own house. There are no restrictions where the men and women may sit. So the house we live in is a great starting point. When places of worship only allow men in to pray then it means women are not meant to be awakened. Children, too, can benefit from one's own house of prayer when it is a nice, quiet, and relaxing place to come home to. The entire family can engage in quiet prayer (meditation).

Humanity seeks the outer house of prayer due to conditioning as that is where we have been taught that G-d lives. Why haven't our beautiful homes that we live in in the West become our "house of prayer" as Rumi as put it? There is a constant desire to search for G-d from outer sources as we relinquish the inner sources of reaching G-d. The outer would be organized religion, churches, yoga retreats, ashrams, mosques, temples, gurdwaras and so on. In one's own house, there is time to become still, quiet, and calm. In the outer houses of prayer, there is noise, chatter, gossip, groups, distractions, over-socializing, talks, chats, need for money to keep organized religion in place, upkeep of the house of prayer, and there is no time to become alone with so many people around. Great teachers of enlightenment did not sit in any of these "outer" houses of prayer. They turned toward the "inner" houses of prayer to become awakened or self-actualized. None of the houses of prayer that organized religions cater to have been credited as the place where self-realization occurred. It is time to turn inward to our own houses of prayer in our search for G-d, or self realization, since so many of us are the owner or renter of a place of worship: our house.

IDOLS

"Guard yourself from idols." John 5:21

An obscene amount of money and time was spent at Bobby Dazzler on collecting Elvis, Marilyn Monroe, Star Wars, Betty Boop, Superman, Batman paraphernalia and any other idols' products that clients could purchase so they could have a piece of the past. Why is humanity obsessed with idols of the past in the present? This obsession has nothing to do with living in the present. The living idols of the present day are also obsessed over in the same manner. In the retail world there is a general worship of idols (celebs), which only leads to hoarding. Collecting statues of Buddha or any other religious or spiritual figures doesn't make us more spiritual. It just adds more worldly "stuff" to cling to. It is the inner actions that we do daily which count. We, as adults, can start to set better examples for our children; we can collect less,

The world loves idols and even loves to idol-worship the dead. It is unbelievable how much money is spent on worshipping those in music, movies or dance. We even have a ton of tv shows that focus on idols. This is getting out of hand, especially if we want our children to realize their own gifts and not focus their entire attention on other people and their gifts. Great, listen to music of the idols while you go about your life doing what you are supposed to be doing. The likes of Cobain, Prince, George Michael and Michael Jackson have made more money after they were dead than they ever made when they were alive. People love to worship idols. It is an odd topic. All the time spent on collecting memorabilia, pictures, movies, artifacts or other items that remind one of the famous could be spent on oneself. Is there a oneself under all that collecting? Why is it we feel the need to have so many memories of the dead or even those famous who are alive, now? Even young children start to idol worship at a young age when they watch cartoons and move on to music stars. These are just people doing what they are supposed to be doing but our children are being taught to collect, mimic and even behave like those who are caught up in the fames. This is not important nor is it beneficial to a seeker of truth. We can collect less.

INNER

"The great solution to all human problems is individual inner transformation." - Vernon Howard

The inner stuff is what it is all about and it is the juice of life. People often speak about our inner and our outer self. What is more important - our inner self or our outer self? What does the inner self mean anyways? The inner self is in your heart, your soul, your spirit, your mind and the real you. It has nothing to do with the outer stuff at all. What's the outer stuff? It might have to do with the choice of being an introvert or extrovert.

The outer is the exact opposite of the inner. It duals with the inner and this is where we are today in humanity. Our outer world has everything to do with the material world and nothing to do with the inner world concerned with spirituality. Materialism concerns itself with making all things natural into something other, outer and showy. We have materialized breast milk by making baby formula. We have made the most basic staple of life, water, into a material object by bottling, labeling it, giving it a funky name and selling it for money. We have made foods that are a necessity to life into art and entertainment by taking pictures and gastropics. We have created nonsense out of the most basic, simple things in life, leading humanity to many human-created conditions such as the desire to hoard, buy it, get more stuff and seek things that please our senses. We are as far away as possible from the Divine Source, or the spiritual eye, as can be. The outer makes it appear as if the Divine is somewhere outside, so we take part in offerings, expressions, pujas, pilgrimages, and animal sacrifices to please G-d. None of which have anything to do with the inner Divine in ourselves. Western Awakening brings the shift to the inner rather than focusing on all things that are outer.

The inner stuff is what it is all about and it is what makes you run. It has nothing to do with the outer stuff. The outer stuff is fueled by the other people, what other people think about you and those that end up taking control of you until you become lost in the mess of all the outer. When inner stuff gets forgotten and lost, we lose faith in ourselves. The inner stuff is private, secret and even protective. It never shows itself until we can get to know ourselves. That is the true awakening of the person. Some beautiful spiritually awakened souls come to us already awake and ready to heal while others come to it through their processes. How does one unlock the secrets of the inner self? Just as Buddha sat underneath a tree to find the truth, one must constantly search for it, but it can only be done when one is alone, on their own, and in inner silence. The inner voice of G-d can then be heard, as we, too, are part of that Divine Spirit. The light within. Jesus said "Light of the world! " meaning we are all light. But it is the test, we must carry out the rest to discover this light.

It was written in Corinthians, "Don't you know you yourselves are God's temple and God's spirit dwells in your midst?"

G-d's spirit is in the inner of us, it is our duty to find that spirit from within and listen to what it has to say. The inner is where the truth hides, along with love. It is the absolute and unconditional belief in that truth and love which is known as G-d. The inner stuff is what we were ALL born with and it is within every single one of us to find. It is the real stuff that is the source of you and so very pure! This is the base of why we are here. We are to realize the inner so we may lose all care for the outer stuff. Humans are pure on the inside. But the outer world which is known as our environment sets us up to face the struggles, strife, fights, suffering, and chaos which the outer world brings. Peace comes once one can find the inner spirit that is a part of G-d. That inner in them will not only give them the peace, bliss and the ecstasy they are looking for in this life on earth but the final freedom which is known as Moksha in Indian traditions. Moksha, the final liberation, is to be free from the struggle on this Earthly plane. Life is full of problems but we can be free and awake. This doesn't happen often, and it takes many struggles, grief, pains, and much love to find final freedom. A human being can come to the Source of all life, which is G-d or the Divine spirit.

JUDGE

"It is a struggle for every black man. You know how it is, only God can judge us." - Tupac Shakur

Sometimes it is hard not to judge, but daily we must move to a point of non-judgment of anybody, anything or any situation. It is one of the hardest things to do, due to conditioning from the moment we are born. Some of the judgments are taught by all the others around us: parents, guardians, teachers, society, media and anything else that has influence over our mind. But we can see with our eyes in a pure manner, just as Matthew states in the King James Bible in Verse 6:22: "The light of the body is the eye. If therefore the eye be single, the whole body shall be light." This requires us to see everything in an equal manner. It requires us to look into the universe and see only love, kindness, oneness, goodness, health and prosperity, in a world without dichotomy, no good or bad and no masculine or feminine. We no longer judge what we see. We only see what we see. There is no longer imperfection in another of G-d's creations when we cease to judge others. The seeker focuses on perfecting the self, and their own world and not trying to fix other people around them who are not like them. Choosing to judge another of G-d's beings only makes us live from darkness rather than light, and focus on what is wrong rather than what is right. Yet when it comes to spirituality, everything is right.

Judging others is a habit that we must forgo. It is a taught habit. To judge, by definition, is to form an opinion or conclusion based on past experiences, ideas or what we have learned ourselves or through others. But what is this opinion and conclusion based on? Just because someone said so doesn't necessarily mean that we must accept it. When we are young, we can't always see if something is right or wrong, for we believe that our superiors know everything and would not lie to us so it must be truth. Superiors could be our caretakers, parents, guardians, teachers, society, media, religious teachers, government and anybody else we hold with high esteem. We accept it and run with it, until we discover that it might not be true. This occurs when we decide to seek the real truth and begin our path to awakening.

We deal with many other people daily and encounter many who judge. They take one look, think that they have figured out this person, and proceed by opening their mouth based on all the facts, data and knowledge acquired over years from all those around them. They look just on the surface and fail to take the time to understand the whole of this human being who is standing right in front of them. Try staying quiet to talk to another person before you spit out the words that often are based on a judgement. Judgemental words will never get anybody far. They will cause damage in the long run for certain. It is always good to know the whole story before we start to give out our opinions. A friend once said, "Don't ever spit something out of your mouth that you will regret. It is almost as if you have thrown up vomit!" Disgusting things once thrown out of the mouth, once said, can never be taken back. Using a court case as an example during a dispute, the judge in certain circumstances indicates "please strike what has just been said" to the jury. However, once it has been said, it is really not possible to strike it from our brain. If we are what we say then we must speak in kindness, in loving kindness, with compassion and passion before we utter those words that judge others.

There is room for mistakes and errors when we judge. One of the daily rituals in life that we must work on collectively is to get over old and archaic judgments that have been planted in our brains. It is better to look at both sides and see the whole picture before deciding to judge. This is where the idea of looking at everything with equal eyes comes into play. You can never know who is on the other side of the coin. Take everyone at face value and proceed from there. Everyone is good until proven otherwise.

A classic example of a client judging at Bobby Dazzler was experienced over and over again. In retail, nobody is ever to judge - otherwise a retailer would never survive the cutthroat world of sales. Every day in the retail world, we are required to service many people from many paths. We must be nice, kind and helpful to all no matter what. It never ceased to amaze how new staff would immediately judge the poorly-dressed client and favor the well-dressed client. Sometimes the staff would not be kind to the ones that were not dressed nicely. Yet after going over to the client to ask if they needed any assistance, we discovered they were usually the biggest spenders. People don't have to dress up or dress nice when they are shopping. They go shopping when they are relaxed and want great service without anybody deciding to judge them based on what they are wearing. On the other hand, the well-dressed clients would treat the staff rudely and often were just popping in to look but not buy. The staff were always perplexed with how the outcome was so opposite to what they expected or judged may happen.

The other classic example from retail that allows us to understand that we should not judge is when a client required a refund or exchange. We were a novelty store and the novelty of an item wears off pretty quickly. We couldn't offer refunds but we did offer exchanges. This didn't happen often, but when it did, the scenario would be similar. Once they were told that they were speaking to the Manager who was a female Indo-Canadian, they would want to speak to the Owner. Once they told that they were speaking to the Owner (Bobby Dazzler) then the common thing to say was "You are lying! I want to speak to your husband or father or whoever is running this place." The answer to them is that he or they have nothing to do with this business. This business belongs to the female standing in front of them. The conversation escalates along with the nerves to the level that the husband should be put on the phone immediately. Wait a minute, he does not have anything to do with this place at all. Sadly, clients sometimes were unable to get over the fact that a man was not running the show here. They are certain that the man must be the superior of this woman in front of them. They sometimes refused to leave and threatened staff so we just had to call security. Well, that would be great since they will clear up this client's insistence on speaking to the manager/owner/husband/father. At this point, it would be difficult to help this client who has taken the whole situation out of context and decided to judge the Manager based on gender. Of course, we must not judge the client but assist them by going over the refund policy, telling them over and over again what we can do. After a few more moments of harping on the same issue, security comes in and escorts them out plus confirms that they were indeed dealing with the person in charge. The irate client turns around tell us that they won't be shopping here anymore. Do retailers really want clients like that to return for repeat business? Why bother with those who judge?

The best thing about deciding not to judge is that we move one step closer to becoming one with all. We lose duality and see everyone with single vision.

KILLS

"Choosing not to kill also aligns us with the desire to abstain from meats."

No matter which way it is put, kill, kills and killing another being brings harm, pain and suffering to another being. When one path or religion says let's kill it this way or that way, it still kills the animal (beast) being or the human being. Some paths say killing it Kosher or Halal style will bring the least amount of pain. What does it matter, the manner that the being is killed? Pain and suffering are still present when one kills no matter which way it is put. A child who loses their adult mother or father is in pain, so why would such pain not exist for the beast when a human kills for it food. There is something barbaric and dark about killing another being just to consume it. This is heinous when we look at humanity choosing to breed other beings in large animal or seafood farms just to consume them.

Humanity kills other beings for foods, revenge, hunting, fun (trophy heads in the living room), power, out of anger and sometimes due to religious books that condone killing of other beings for sacrifices to the gods or due to G-d's so-called command of killing non-believers. When a human kills, it is wrong unless one's own life is at risk (self-defense). Simple as that!

The best part of self-realization is that it doesn't matter if one is a believer in G-d or not. Self-realization brings the focus on to ourselves rather than looking for faults in all the others around us. Another person's beliefs have nothing at all to do with self, so there is no need to kill. When a human kills another being, be it a beast or human, it is wrong. It is that simple! Killing a beast-being for food out of necessity is fine to save a human life. But when one kills the beast-being just for novelty of foods then the kills are not for a good enough reason.

Much attention has been paid to the pains and suffering of other beings for foods. Halal and Kosher style of killing attempts to bring the least amount of pains and suffering to the beast (animal) being before killing it in a certain manner that is prescribed by the religions of Islam and Judaism. It still brings pain and suffering at the hands of the human. The spiritual seeker would abstain from causing additional pain and suffering to any being. Since there is already so much pain and suffering in the world, it is unnecessary to bring more by humanity's desire for novel meats or foods. How about nobody kills anything? No need to sacrifice any human or beast beings for G-d. It doesn't appear that G-d wants us to sacrifice any of his beings. Only an ego that desires novel foods, revenge, fun through hunting or desire to vent/anger kills. An ego fuelled by power kills as in the modern day case in Syria where the President has killed people who rebel against him. A book that condones killing of other beings is not for the true seekers nor the true nature of man. It would be unlikely that the creative force and Divine intelligence would want humans to kill anything other than out of necessity for their own human life or the life of another human being. When one kills another, it is a barbaric and evil act that seems to be part of this dark, ugly ego we commonly associate with the devil, satan or lucifer.

Choosing to not kill also aligns us with the desire to abstain from meats. In modern times, the vegan movement has gained significant traction because of this desire to not bring pain or suffering to other beings. The seeker kills their desire to kill or bring harm to anything, or any one of the Divine's creations.

LARGE

"Who gets the risks? The risks are given to the consumer, the unsuspecting consumer and the poor work force. The benefits are only for the corporations, for the money makers." - Cesar Chavez

The large become large when one group of small realizes that they can come together to control the masses, and others who are small, especially if money is the target of this control. It is the large that control cable, cyber space, email, tweet, phone, calls, texts, pages, the berry, the iPods, the iPads, the e-book and the list will go and on. To make sure that humans travel and marvel like the new Western nomad, they control airlines, and travel agencies, and then display on our screens how it is so cool to travel like the nomad. Humans are kept aimlessly desiring more - delicious foods, wines, booze, smoke, and go here or there looking to please their senses.

Book just once with an airline, and the company will ensure a constant flow of calls, emails and/or texts for further travels takes place, making one more and more engaged with the travel like a nomad. The large has made humanity so engaged with each other that it is impossible to become still in this nervous world. Nobody can become still as being still is the opposite of being conditioned to go out.

The large own the malls, shops, brands, banks and everything else in between. Sure, it sounds crazy to tell us to cut the cable, limit texts, phone, calls and so on because it is unrealistic, but there must be a limit put on oneself in order for the power to arrive to the individual who wishes to become awake in their search for truth. Being able to put a limit on what the large feeds us is where we must begin. The large was already in place before we got here, so we need not fight the large but we can limit how the large will affect us today. This is what it takes to become awake today and turn the light on. The large attempts to weaken the small by keeping them trapped in their ways, patterns, and conditioning until it becomes such a habit it is hard to break. So much so that people think that is the way humanity should operate for millennia until an individual comes to crack open truth through empowerment. The seeker would stay away from crowds, large organizations, institutions or other places where large groups of sheeple gather. The seeker is perfectly in alignment even being their small self on their own.

LET GO

"Some of us think holding on makes us strong. But sometimes it is letting go." - Herman Hesse

As a retailer of novelties, party products and seasonal items, Bobby Dazzler got used to the different holidays or occasions when people would spend obscene amounts of money. The material world had created a superficial nature to many of the celebrations such as Christmas. From a retail standpoint going into spirituality, the need to let go of all the different holidays, celebrations, societal standards and party occasions was apparent. The importance of these celebrations simply fell away. Certain things, people and places that were made important by people were just let go of as their significance appeared futile in relation to becoming awake. It was easy to let go of them. They all appeared so fake and made up that they did not serve the self in any way.

If we look at the words let go, the word ego hides inside these two words. Ego is what keeps us stuck. It actually keeps on hanging on. Eckhart Tolle says, "Sometimes letting things go is an act of far greater power than defending or hanging on." When we move to let go then we move to a non-react position. When we don't let go, we react and this where the snowball effect takes off. It becomes a back and forth game. Let go means that anything that does not work for you, probably should not be around. You need to let go! When you let go of those things around you that no longer serve you, then the letting go actually feels really great. Joy will not occur if you hang on to the job, the other, a spouse, a partner, the enemy or a loss that you drag around you like a very heavy backpack. Forget about it! It was not meant to be. It is dead weight, literally. Just leave it. Let it go! If they are going, it just means that they are wanted elsewhere but NOT with you. Give it up. Recycled old stuff never gets any better. Change and new experiences result when we allow ourselves to let go. A perfect example is the partner or spouse who has not emotionally been there, has no job, has bad habits and doesn't pull his/her weight around the house. Why are we hanging on to this person? Because it looks good to others around us or it is due to what society thinks is right? Or is it just because we are afraid to be alone? The seeker can realize that this person is not assisting the awakening process in any manner and needs to be let go of. For good!

A seeker needs to let go many, many different aspects of life in order to move towards growth and rapid expansion. A shift needs to take place where the seeker will let go of old thought patterns associated with ideas that were given to them by their caretakers. Let go of religious ideas, cultural traditions, society's demands, family rituals, ethnic viewpoints, racial constraints imposed by society, and all other conditioning that keeps the mind hanging on to old, past ideas that are not experienced by the self. The seeker simply lets go of old ways of doing things. This could include relatives, caretakers, parents or even a spouse who no longer is able to serve the spiritual seeker's true desire to awaken. Letting go of all these different aspects of life is hard, especially since they have been ingrained in us for so long. We let go to find the truth for ourselves.

It is hard to break up a family, lose a spouse, lose money, a job or career. But by not acting, you lose your mind, brain, soul or heart - a loss of yourself. Get a grip on yourself and get yourself together! This is when we truly live in the now. It is said that a player rolls with the punches! You need to just take them as they come. That is life! Each punch is just another way for one to learn to deal with letting go.

Let go means moving forward and not to look back at what has occurred. It is the most present manner an individual can live. Easier said than done, though. It is very difficult to move forward when major events happen in life. Never mind when a seeker purposely lets go of things in order to learn for themselves. The best you can do is just cut your losses and move ahead with the least amount of damage or further loss to your pocket book. Dwelling on it only could cause you to acquire a nasty habit to calm the mind down from all the mental noises that flare up from problems of our daily lives. Without letting go, we simply recycle the past events over and over through in the mind. It becomes impossible to make your next move if you take two steps back and one step forward. The world moves faster than we think. There is just no time to sit and think about what has happened in the past nor is there any time to sit recycling thoughts of the old world. Moving forward is far better. See it as just another test in life with the rest. You have the confidence to let go of the past and look only toward the future. Know there is a higher purpose waiting for us.

LIGHT

"We can easily forgive a child who is afraid of the dark; the real tragedy of life is when men are afraid of the light"- Plato

We were all created with light and energy. This makes us light, but it hasn't been able to shine through easily due to the layers of "stuff" that have made us think that we are this or that. Some of us even wear physical layers of clothing to cover that up. Some of us have so many layers, and layers and even more layers of life hiding that light that we might wonder if we will ever get underneath to the source of this light. Coming back to the light requires us to become fully alert, awake and aware. This is awakening. Awakening requires us to challenge the self, whereas religion (faith) keeps us engaging with other people in a cat and mouse fight that calls for peace.

To turn the light on means we choose to seek that potential, that possibility and that nectar called light - a word found right inside of enlightenment. When we turn the light on, we heighten our intuition, expand our awareness and develop deep insight. We evolve our clairvoyance and may even be able to perceive the end in the beginning. Choosing to awaken also means we move beyond the boxes that religions have created.

Light, part of awakening, has nothing to do with all the regions or any of the religions. It has nothing to do with the outside as it is based on the inside. The light can turn on in all of us when we have reached awakening. But this light can only turn on when we have a desire to awaken. Many Masters in the past have come and gone. Many have come to teach but are unable to reach humanity as it is very difficult to bring the human back to humanity. The human feels this need to be unique, different and something better, more and even a little more special than one another. The human fails to see just how much familiarity and similarity we have with all of humanity. Like vultures we look to study each of the varying cultures yet never realize that no one has won. We are all just one! We strive for the label and then even decide to fudge and judge just to be right and forget about the light. Awakening is upon us and it is for us to realize it with or without a fight.

That light is within all of us. It isn't a matter of just turning on the lights that have been turned off accidentally. Light is part of each human being and it's brightest at the time of our birth. It is shining at the moment of birth as that is the time that we first become awake. Some of us get the lights dimmed as conditioning of some sort starts to set in almost immediately by the environment or the caretakers, mommy or daddy, or whoever they may be. Others are lucky as their light remains bright until they get to school. Still others are able to keep their flame stronger by becoming resilient and not buying into or believing anything that is said to them. Some people get their conditioning later in life as adults while others remain true to their belief in the search for truth. A seeker of awakening cannot come upon enlightenment, for it is said that it just comes to those who weren't really looking. However, a certain set of circumstances can help bring about awakening.

For a child the conditioning is given by parents. But to really want to experience truth, one must not always believe everything that even our parents or caretakers say. Why? The truth that they give is truth that belongs to some book they were given by their parents, grandparents, great-grandparents or distant relatives from ages ago. It is not wisdom that is experienced by the self. It is wisdom experienced by the teacher, master, guru or awakened teacher from a cycle that has nothing to do with the modern era that we live in today. And it is a truth that belongs to that master specifically. So, one cannot obey, disobey or even agree with this as being truth since it is not one's own truth which is subject to one's own experience.

Of course, caretakers want the best for us. This concept is very, very hard to point out to them, since they are the ones who have the most profound influence in our life right from the time of birth. Coming from a very poor family of Sikhs, all that many really had was their religion at their place of worship. Parents clung to things that were from their childhood in India as it was easier for them to be around those most like them, rather than find new paths with others from different backgrounds like Italian, Portuguese and Asians who lived right next door in the West. They indicated that Sikhs must go to the Gurdwara, a place of prayer for Sikh, and pray. After going, many people were observed not being so happy but sad. They were sitting on the floor, with the men and women separated. This couldn't be the place of G-d as observed from childhood memories. This is still the personal feeling that arises today when an event occurs. This revelation didn't go over very well with the parents and was considered to be a rejection of a part of their past. After asking if an English version of the book was available to read by the age of 8/9, it become apparent this was not the book on truth from Divine memories. Of course, the caretakers take this as blasphemy as we should just be following what everybody else is doing. Right?!? Wrong! After refusing to bow down to this book, the old man, and put money in the box, there was no way that I would want to come here. Refusing to attend services and thinking that this is not truth caused problems in the family. However, going to school and doing personal research on religion helped to better understand it. The library was very helpful in my fully understanding what the Sikh religion was all about plus I used to read up on all the other religions, history of people and where all the different cultures came from. After reading the English version of the Sidur which is the Sikh bible, a better decision could be made as to whether this book was truly the book of truth. It wasn't necessary to go back to the Gurdwara since they didn't do the prayers in English. It was much quieter at home to read it and to understand it without the distractions. There was no need to worry about the separation of women from men. It just seemed pointless to go to the Gurdwara, put money in the box, bow down and pray to the book when it is right here in my hand at home. It seemed more logical to read it on my own time. In the meantime, other peoples' religions were more interesting, so the good old library provided all the information that was needed on each of the religions. I requested to my parents that I be allowed to pick my own religion not the one that they picked for me at the time of birth. This was not allowed either. This according to them this was apostasy. You must be the religion that we have and follow it because we said so and you live in our house so you must follow it. Going along with it just because I was a child was fine. But, in the heart, it was not it! This religion didn't turn the light on. After reading up on the religion, I saw that the leaders and people who were at the Gurdwara were actually not the ones who were following it the way it is supposed to be. The Sikhs were making certain things up based on cultural norms and gender-biased studies that were clearly out of context of the actual religion in its true version. Modifications of it were done so that it better 'fit' into the way the leaders and the people wanted the religion to be. This is not the path to the light of G-d as I understood it. In this way, a rejection of the current system of doing things was the start to seeking the real truth, light!

Next was the decision to seek truth in every aspect of life. Truth in all schooling activities, jobs and dealings with all people no matter what caste, creed, race, culture, nation, country, or those who think they are. Respecting each and every person that comes across one's way. This was again missing at home because the teaching or 'conditioning' was such that only Sikh people are the ones to trust or the best to deal with in life. That parental influence was not positive towards others who were not like our religion, our race or anything else that appeared to be different from the Sikhs. But since we are in Canada with such a limited Sikh population, we cannot always deal with them only. Experiencing contact with so many other people, I discovered that all people are great, All people were indeed the same no matter their religion or their race. Everybody is part of the source. The conditioning did not belong to the source.

As time when on, facing struggles of life, strife, sadness, madness, anger, grief and problem after problem causes one to look for the truth without giving up. This cannot be it! One starts to seek out those who are happy, bright, full of life and light. Hey, we can actually find these people on our own but unfortunately they did not always belong to the Sikh faith or the ethnic enclaves that we live in. Happiness appeared to be something that one must discover on our own. It could not be something that was teleported from our parents. Nationalistic views were also taught to other kids by their own parents, which made further divisions. This caused people to be unhappy with others, judging and making it appear that they are right and all others are wrong. The constant struggle with our immediate family or caretakers who were not really well informed, well educated or open minded meant that one must take the steps to turn the light on by ourselves.

Nobody wants to be around miserable people who judge or think they are right when in reality they are not. This can be said of any religion or group who feels that they are superior to another or other people so lights can be turned off in many places at the same time in many faiths. One is able to see it on their faces. As a child becoming a youth and then into adulthood, the light was inside the eyes of each person who came with love, truth, and hope that there indeed is light in the world. Some of us have just turned it off by ourselves. People then become negative and cling to the mind viruses, poisons or 'conditioning' that had been planted in the mind since the time of birth. Unwillingness to explore outside of the boxes that society creates causes individuals to become dark and unhappy. They are not willing to turn on the light. Turning the light on sometimes means being a rebel.

Light is bright, open and very much within each of us. Some of the ways one can open their heart, mind, and souls is to read books of other religions, ways, cultures, study with different people, open the mind to new friends with different upbringing, finding jobs outside of the norms for one specific group, and seek to open up to whatever it is that is available to them.

So, what to expect when the light turns on?

Once the light in the awakening gets turned on then, all one is able to surmise is, "There is nothing down here!" You just want to leave this world as now you are living but in reality you died while you were living here. It is actually an amazing feeling. It makes one feel high all day long. A feeling of euphoria, happiness, bliss, peace - in ecstasy without having to take the drugs. Worries are all gone along with the stress and strife that many people face. No more anger and fighting with anybody. The light made the skin glow, the energy in the spine would go up and down when it was active, the center of the head or head chakra would tingle most of the time especially during physical exertions of the body and the body functioned at a higher level - nails grew faster, hair became softer, darker and felt baby-like, marks on the skin faded and the body felt really efficient. This light took a few years to turn on due to bodily processes, but once turned on, it can't be turned off. The light in awakening turned on by about forty.

It is hard to let the light in when we draw our drape or our blind to block the beautiful rays on the sun. In so many instances, humanity was observed blocking the light of sun. The sun is our energy and so too our source of the same energy. When the light hits our eyes, our skin, our face and our body we feel that energy. That energy is seen but when we block that energy with a drape or blind then our energy is also reduced to darkness, night or black, which does not allow energy to flow. Drawing a drape or blind causes us to see nothing so that everything becomes black. When we relate the color black to the source, it doesn't make sense. Black has nothing to do with light or energy. It almost blocks light and energy from passing into us. Perhaps the plant beings are actually smarter than us, as they always tend to move towards to the light - as we should too.

LOTTO

"All of life's problems will be gone."

Many people have a dream of the winning the lotto. All of life's problems will be gone with the win of the lotto. You won't need to work, you can quit your job, you can shop until you drop, you can buy the house that you always wanted, you can even stay in that house and not do anything, you can eat whatever or wherever you want, you could go on vacations all the time and eat some more there, too. The lotto is bound by no limit. You can do it faster, easier and with no problems. Right? Well, the highest feat of humanity is the awakening and is the whole point of this life. The real lotto of life is not the material one but the spiritual one. It is called self-actualization or returning to the source.

Bobby Dazzler always happened to be located in a space near a lotto kiosk. It was amazing to see the number of people who line-up to purchase a lotto ticket. Often, it was the same people looking to win the big lotto. They were not happy people. The people were almost desperate as they sat on the bench outside the store to see if they had won. Sometimes they would come in and say that one day when they win the lotto, they would buy this or that. It was sad to see so many people waste their time, energy and money buying tickets and even sadder when the same people would do this over and over again without success.

Perhaps the time has come to teach the world that the real lotto, the spiritual lotto, should be sought, instead of pursuing the material lotto. The spiritual lotto frees the mind from attaching itself to anything on the worldly Planet Earth.

LUSTS

"Lust is the sexual desire of someone with no love or true affection."

Bobby Dazzler saw a shift in the retail world when Halloween went from scary to sexy. The costumes that the girls and women wore were no longer the scariest costumes in the town. It was all about being the sexiest one out. This related to the lusts of humanity. It was no longer a private bedroom party. Halloween opened the door to lusts being available to all to enjoy and see. There was no more shame in dressing like a whore or slut for Halloween because everybody was. That is when Bobby Dazzler knew lusting and lusts were more open in humanity.

Lusts have been around since the beginning of time. Lust is the sexual desire of someone with no love or true affection. Lust is also associated with being eager for something, especially power. Lusts can be: he lusts her, she lusts him, he lusts him or she lusts her. Confusing as it sounds, lusts can be heterosexual, homosexual, bi-sexual, and transsexual, or all together and in between. Lusts are something the spiritual seeker has gotten over, for going back to the source requires single-pointed discipline.

One wonders why we all aren't just celibate, if lusts are part of the problem. It is very difficult to control our lusts. Perhaps some of humanity was created out of lusts while others may be created from a sincere desire to procreate. Lusts are natural inclinations that some of us can control better than others. Being able to have mastery of the body and its senses is one aspect of being a true seeker of awakening.

It is taught in yoga that an equal opposite reaction takes place in every action. Lusts were no different when they were created for men or women. The equal and opposite forces are the penis and there is the vagina (pussy). Lusts can take place any time in a marriage, outside of marriage, in a friendship, in a workplace environment, in school and just about with anyone, anywhere. The modern world has made it easier to act on the impulses of lust. Lusts are elevated to a level much higher than previously when the cell phone, email, texts, cyberspace and other techs weren't as readily available for temptation.

Lusts of all sorts are a distraction when it comes to self-realization. They cause the mind to focus on our lower senses of pleasure. The seeker would be wise to limit their lusts or maybe choose to be a celibate in order to come closer to the Divine. After all, when we first awoke spiritually at birth, we may have been a product of two people's lust for each other, but didn't engage in it ourselves, as we were babies.

MALES

"Both Buddha and Guru Nanak had families but rather sought awakening."

You can't have a book on life and what's hot and what's not if you don't have a brief on males. Males is a topic right there with money. Males have traditionally controlled many aspects of life such as the political arena, government, economics, and business organizations. Advantages have been given to them through cultural, traditional, and religious belief systems that place heavy weight on the paternal hierarchy of life at home and outside of the house. It is no different for awakened Masters, either. Many Masters like Jesus, Moses, Mohammad, Buddha, Swamis, Babas, Gurus of India, and even Modern Master Eckhart Tolle are male spiritual teachers. Not that there aren't any female leaders in Awakening like Sai Ma, but they are fewer. However there is an increase in the number of girls and women attending schools, higher education, colleges and universities. Women's enrollment in universities is climbing, even surpassing males in many western universities. The elementary and high school honor rolls are also dominated by females, and the strengthening of women who lead households is also increasing along with their prominence in business, politics and other positions of influence. This is extraordinary, as the overwhelming power that the males have had over women in the past was incredible. This shift will cause some males to take the back seat in some areas of life while women make long overdue inroads. The world dynamics are changing and the opportunities for women are gaining traction.

Males leaders have led the world to where it is today. And, today, we are all too familiar with the evil desires of the ego with the need for power, control, and suppression of the masses. Males can take responsibility for many of the mass wars, genocides, murders and killing of so much of humanity.

Many leadership positions have been occupied by males, and the desire to fight prevails around the world. Money is an important aspect, as males still earn more, and are geared towards providing for their family. They have held many positions of power throughout history and up to the present times. But with awakening, the tables are turning towards peace.

The possibility exists that women can be equally awakened, but their voice was never heard with the need to care for the children, the commitment to marry and maybe even take care of those awakened males. Few women have been written about. There is little written on woman by those awakened males, or about the wives of those awakened males who were left to take care of infants or children that were left behind while the great Masters sought awakening. Both Buddha and Guru Nanak had families but rather sought awakening. Males were pressured to marry due to the family desire to procreate, produce heirs, to pass on their genes, to make sure that their needs are satisfied sexually and to make sure that they will have control over the general population of people. This leads to many of the rules, laws, legal jargon, religious texts/books and many other areas of life being dominated by males. In this way the status quo remains whereby a patriarchal system is always in place and has been in place. Males have held the reins for a while but it can't continue if we are to move forward into a new cycle for the world. A shift is taking place. The universe is set up in opposites and duality also prevails, not quickly but eventually. Perhaps that is why opposites attract so much. What has been up so long must come down sooner or later for a better balance of the genders. So women will make strides forward and males will see a shift that allows for the rise of the feminine force. The women of the world rising is part of this change in consciousness which has led many educated male leaders into taking the stance that gender equality in politics is a must to be successful and to move forward. The Prime Minister of Canada set the example by having an equal number of males and females in his cabinet. Such moves by males most definitely makes the world a better place. From a spiritual perspective both males and females seem to be raising their level of consciousness which can only lead to a more aware humanity.

MEALS

"There is no biological reason for eating three meals a day."
Yale Professor Paul Freedman, editor of *Food: The History of Taste*

There was never any time to take in three meals when working retail. You get used to eating snacks or whenever there was a lull. Lulls were never during the breakfast, lunch or dinner period. That was when others were off for their breaks and sales were to be made. Those times were especially busy, even more so when working solo. It was hard to close the store and run to grab something at the food court, but it was easier to just bring a brown-bagged lunch or snack. Meal breaks during the busy seasons of Halloween and Christmas were impossible. So many people would come and want to spend money it was hard to focus on food while staff had to deal with being short one person who was on a meal break. Meals were just not that much of a priority when working in the retail world of Bobby Dazzler.

Why do we eat three meals a day even when we are not hungry? Who said we are supposed to eat three meals a day, and the first meals must include an upper - a stimulant like coffee along with bacon, ham, or other pork sausages? And the next two meals! A little more of the same with the meats changed up - so we have aged hams, Bayonne, brine-cured ham, Canadian ham/bacon, country cured, clitella, pancetta, fresh cooked, gammon, Irish ham, picnic ham, prosciutto, scotch ham, Smithfield ham, urban style or York ham in the next two meals of the day if other meats such as steak, lamb, or chicken are unavailable. The point here is not that we are eating a dirty or unclean animal in so many of our meats, but there is an over-emphasis on the number of meals and meats we take in daily. These are the typical Western meals of today along with a glass of milk (dairy). Why do we continue to wreak havoc on the pure human body when we know such a combo is awful for our bodies, souls and mind? Past books on yoga of the human body speak of those who eat little, urinate little and exert little when seeking. Our time is the exact opposite. A couple came into their neighborhood grocery store claiming it is so hard not to think about dinner when they had just finished lunch. One even said, "He didn't appear to have any room for dinner given his extra-large lunch that finished so late in the afternoon." Conditioning is so deep that we cannot eat when we are hungry, but just because "that's what they said." Who are they? Why are we required to eat three meals a day? The food industry would suffer and it would be more challenging to make any money if we all thought to eat only when we are hungry. Perhaps those that claim we need to eat three meals a day are the same people that have put water in plastic bottles, labeled them with funky names and then conditioned humanity to drink eight ounces of water per day, preferably from bottles when tap water is often just as good.

MEATS

"Eating a plant-based diet makes spiritual sense for those of us who become awakened."

Humans love their meats. There are so many varieties for them to enjoy, such as beef, pork, chicken, goat, lamb, and other newer novel choices of meats. Meats is a topic that Judaism discusses in their Kosher rules. It forbids the mixing of dairy and meats. It also forbids the consumption of pork and shell fish. Some paths abstain from meats altogether while others state that it is to be cut this way or that way - Halal or Kosher - so there is less suffering in the animal. Why not just leave those meats alone and free of all the pains that the human causes in the beast beings? Consuming meats requires one to kill another being, any which way we put it.

Using cows as an example, it has been suggested that we give thought to dairy cows' pain and suffering. They are being forced to produce unnatural amounts of milk. Why should we knowingly partake in the suffering of the cattle? Has the human being become unconscious? Don't the cows have the same fears as we do when we butcher them for their meats? Are the fears, anxiety, stress and worry not transferred to the meats that we consume, which then affect our human body systems? Doesn't it make sense to eat a healthy plant-based diet or even one that is vegan-based? It is well known that if animals were not tied up before slaughtering, they would run due to fears of being killed. Those fears remain in the animal and in the blood of that being which are then consumed by humans. Why would we want to consume meats or foods that hold the fears of another being attached to them?

It is no surprise that certain processed meats have been declared carcinogenic (cancer-causing) by the World Health Organization. Processed meats like hot dogs, ham, bacon, sausages, and some deli meats have certain preservatives and flavors that have been added creating carcinogenic meats. Processes such as salting, fermenting, curing, coloring, flavoring, and smoking cause the meats to be no longer natural food products. Some red meats were also classified, including beef, lamb, goat and pork.

The production of meats puts an enormous amount of pressure on Mother Earth to produce. She exhausts herself since so many natural resources are required to produce these meats. In addition, many meats have antibiotics and other hormones added to the foods that the animals eat before they are slaughtered so the animals grow faster, are plump, and produce leaner meats. Most meats are no longer natural or organic. Even if they are organic, they cost so much more and there still is the killing of another being involved.

The West loves its meats; steaks come in many forms - blue, rare, raw, medium/rare, medium and well done, as well as strip sirloin, filet, porterhouse. Yes, this is the age of the steak and it is from cattle. The love for meats has grown over time to be more and more novel as our desires for novelty grow along with hunger for meats. Bugs are new novel forms of protein. Eighty percent of the world eats insects out of necessity or for protein. There are bug chefs who can prepare dishes made of scorpions, tarantulas and even grasshoppers. Frogs are nearing extinction due to humanity's love for them as foods. Who would have ever guessed that pigs' feet and cow's tongue were looked upon as delicacies in many parts of the world? Edible mollusks are also devoured as food for the elite. Clams, cockles, mussels, oysters, scallops, abalone, conches, limpets, periwinkles, whelks, cuttlefish, octopus and squid are all sought after and prepared in our restaurants as dishes for gourmets. Crocodiles became a protected species after their meats were savored by Jamaicans where cows were not as readily available. Even in the friendly, most livable and yoga city of Vancouver, burgers were served made of camel, crocodile, venison, kangaroo, rabbits and wild boar, just to please our senseless desires.

Welcome to the barbaric age, where Indian cuisine can include a fusion of the best with garlic and curried grasshoppers, as a delicacy; just another unique flavor to please humanity's hunger for the novel, unusual, and abnormal. Had the appetitive of humanity sided with the beast? Well, take a look at dishes that are available today, like camel pie, pork tongue in cheek, maple bacon chip ice cream, chicken hearts, rolled pig's spleen, crispy pig's ears, stuffed lamb hearts, blood sausage, pork tongue, crocodile casserole, lamb liver/neck chops, octopus, crabs, and shrimps just to name a few. The list goes on and on with meats from so many other living creatures (beast). Although some appear borderline ridiculous, they are still being eaten and created as masterpieces by chefs.

Choosing to be a vegan or vegetarian frees us from bringing more pain and suffering to another of G-d's beings. It eliminates the need to kill. Eating a plant-based diet makes spiritual sense for those who want to become awakened. A vegan, by dictionary terms, is an individual who does not eat meat or animal products such as eggs or dairy. This means eating in moderation, not in exaggeration. It is time to change some of our diets collectively, and emphasize vegetarian or vegan meals. Fruits, vegetables, nuts, and beans are not just healthy for us, but make ethical sense for the environment. Mediterranean foods, fruits and vegetables are all fresh, juicy, light, nourishing and tasty. They provide energy. On the other hand, meats are considered bitter, sour, salty, or pungent and cause feelings of being sluggish, lethargic and apathetic.

In all things it is important to create a balance. Perhaps just eating the eggs and leaving the chicken alone is the happy medium. If we eat the chicken then there are no more eggs. Life does not have to be all or nothing. There are some great omelets, scrambled eggs, French toast, eggs benedict and sunny side eggs are delicious, tasty and healthy. One does not have to abstain from everything until we have nothing to eat. If the chicken is kept alive, we would have plenty of egg dishes to eat. What does it matter if the egg came first or the chicken? Just as long as the chicken lives.

At one time, meat may be all that is eaten until a phase in life comes that just makes more sense to not eat them. Sometimes it is taste buds, sometimes it is the feeling that we are eating another being, and other times it is through books that encourage us to abstain from meats. Trial and error is best when testing the body and how it feels after consuming meats. The clear picture can't come with force nor can it come when the intention is there to awaken. The memory of when we became awake at birth, when we never touched meats, should help or at least remind us of the sweet taste of not having to devour other beings. Going vegan or changing to a plant-based diet is not an immediate step. Like all things in life, strides, steps, and cycles must be endured before one chooses this path on their own. This is just the way that everything goes. One must realize on their own that the plant-based vegetarian and vegan diets are not nuts.

Just as plants almost always move towards the sunlight or light, it may be that if we consume plant-based foods, we too will take in some of that light and move towards light.

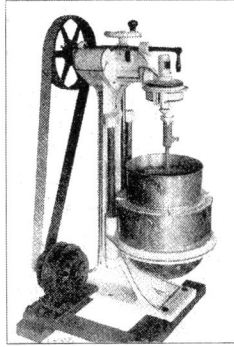

MIXED
"We are all mixed, the same seeds of humanity."

Brown is the color that appears when other colors are mixed. It seems to have taken over so many of the aspects of our lives. Could it be the new color for our foods and our races? Brown bread, brown eggs, brown sugar and brown rice are just some of the great foods that have proven to be healthier. The same seems to occur when we look at inter-mixed marriages. The result is beautiful shades of brown or mocha in humanity. Perhaps brown is the color that all of humanity will be when we pursue unity.

People talk about being of mixed races. Others say they have mixed families or they are in a mixed marriage with people from different religions or regions of the world. People are looking to identify themselves with their ancestry. There are websites that determine your ancestry based on our blood samples. What does all this mixed up business mean? It means that humanity is still clinging to its roots, its history and the past. This has nothing to do with the present. Are we really that interested in determining the different races of humanity? Intelligence only sees one race - the human race. All the other mixed up stuff about being 1/4 this race, 1/4 that, and 1/2 the other, doesn't mean a thing in the eyes of the Divine who sees all with a single eye. Didn't humanity just look at other humans' faces and make up races? Humanity is coming together and becoming what the aspects are meant to be - unity. Humans live with other families, marrying humans from various parts of the world. We are all mixed, the same seeds of humanity. If humanity would look at the whole from that perspective, then nothing is mixed. The only thing mixed up about this is talking about it being something different, unusual, or out of the ordinary. The more that people marry who they wish to, care less about what religions/regions their partners or families are from, the more we feel united, just as humanity is when we can come closer to becoming awake to find truth. The more stringent or closed we are, then the more separate we feel from other humans who follow different paths. Coming together means overlooking the whole "mixed" thing.

Cities like Vancouver, Los Angeles, London and New York are such melting pots of people from everywhere that it is impossible not to be "mixed" in one form or another. Perhaps one day, we will be so mixed that we will know ourselves to be part of the human race and state we are all from our mothers' wombs.

NAÏVE

"An advantage of being naïve is being able to believe in oneself when no one else will." - Sophia Amorurso

Running the Bobby Dazzler store made humanity all the same and seen with a single eye. Prior to going into retail, one is naïve about how people behave. As children, our naïve nature is what keeps us boxed up in our culture, traditions, religions and patterns that have been given to us by the other all around us. We listen and soak everything up like a sponge. Retailing helped to get rid of rigid ideas so a softer naïve approach to many different people is learned. It is with this naïve approach we become awake, alert and aware on our own, through self-discovery and self-mastery.

Collectively humanity must be naïve if we think that the highest feat of humanity is to be found in just one book that our faith gave us. This naïve is an ignorant way to apporach spirituality. Nothing can be that easy. Awakening is the coming back home to the source. It could not be found in just one book by reading it over and over again. Thus, we have become naïve by not delving into all aspects of life. Once an individual becomes a seeker of truth, trusting everything without experiencing it is not going to get anybody anywhere. Nobody likes to be taken advantage of, so being naïve to a point is okay, but in daily life naïve does not always work. The Divine loves those who are naïve, but trusting in the Divine to take care of them and everything around them is necessary. From that point, we must become a little naïve and trust that the Divine is working inside of us. As we live life, experience it and learn from those around us then naïve becomes even more important. It becomes kind of second nature, like "let go". We allow things to happen. Nothing is by force. It is with a naïve approach.

As one moves towards truth and realizes the truth, then it is okay to be naïve and trust blindly. We come to realize that naïve is not being unknowing, but one is naïve knowing G-d will take care of everything. There is nothing wrong with being naïve to life and trusting others, as they too are Divine. Like usually attracts like and often others like you are brought closer to you.

NOMAD

"The new trend for humanity seems to be roam the globe like the nomadic people of the past for a new place to travel and marvel at."

The modern traveler is now a nomad due to their desire to move from place to place. The modern nomad not only travels around the world; Bobby Dazzler saw many patrons traveling around the malls just for the sake of change. Patrons would come and go daily, sometimes buying, sometimes looking. The nomads who frequented malls were the same people who were traveling around the world looking for more shops, malls or stores. The nomads were driven by the desire to please their senses.

Suddenly, everybody wants to be a world traveler. Trips, trips and more trips. Everybody is made to believe we should become modern day nomads and join in the restlessness. When did this modern nomadic movement start? Did it begin with the invention of the bicycle, automobile, train, or plane? Or was it when the RV/motor home was created, so we could just pack up and travel with all of our belongings to no special place? Nobody will stay put in their homes. The modern nomadic movement has nothing at all to do with becoming still. It is a shame to see so many people who moved to the Western world to live in a beautiful, peaceful and safe place, raise a family and enjoy the full circle of life, still want to go away so often. The Western world's desire for novelty along with a general restlessness takes us to faraway places like China. The West is being convinced to seek to find Yoga (union) amongst 1.3 billion in India where only 33% of the country has proper sanitation. The West is being made to believe we need to please our senses in gluttony in Mexican resorts or "hot" spots while much of the country is under lockdown due to drug lords and the drug trade. We are made to believe we should eat like pigs or burn our skin for a week and then come back to partake in diets and exercise. It is so odd that the West must escape the peaceful, quiet and easy life of the West to go where there is turmoil, crowds, and lack of stillness. Those of us who have some of the highest standards for food, health, government and life are conditioned to believe we should go the other way to discover and perhaps to appreciate our life here. Millions in China, India, Brazil, Africa and other parts of world would feel they had won the lotto if given the opportunity to be born or live in the West or North America. Yet, the West travels like the nomad to find novel foods, places, people and just plain novelty in their life. Being still makes us bored, but is necessary if one chooses to awaken.

The invention of the RV or the motor home which is a car or van with sleeping quarters has assisted this movement very dramatically. People live in their trailer homes which are less expensive than renting or owning. It is also a novel way of living that allows individuals to change cities, towns and even countries quickly without having a set address or the need to stay put. It makes it exciting to live in new places, and it makes change always possible while moving around anytime and all the time. This is especially true for the "grey nomads" (seniors) as they are called in Australia and New Zealand, who sell their homes to travel the last part of their lives.

Could we be that bored? Or is this just another way to burn our money? Are we really so ruled by our senses that to please them we will travel like restless nomads for no reason at all?

For health, safety and hygienic reasons, reputable stores will not take pillows and sleeping bags back once they have been used or slept on. So then, why in the world would humanity find it healthy or hygienic hopping in and out of hotel beds or bed and breakfast places where hundreds, thousands or more people have slept and done whatever they do in those rooms overnight. What guarantee do we have that the covers where changed before we arrived? What about each of the pillows that have sweat, saliva and other bodily fluids leaked on them during sleep? A quick Google search shows that as little as 200 milliliters to as much as one liter of sweat goes into our mattresses every single night. This sweat contains bacteria and toxins that our body doesn't need. Mattresses could also have dead skin on them, along with dust mites. Sure, the sheets get changed, but the mattress is not changed that often in a hotel, hostel or any other place we sleep when traveling. So, the eeww factor should be taken into consideration when deciding to take those nomad trips.

It has further been brought up in current newspapers that the most unhygienic places on airplanes are the trays we eat off. The dirtiest spot was the table tray with "2,155 colony form units"- a measure of the number of bacteria or fungal cells per square inch. Compared to 285 on an airplane air vent, 265 on the lavatory flush button and 230 on the seatbelt buckle. Wow! The seeker would need to take this into consideration when taking trips.

The new trend for humanity seems to be to roam the globe like the nomadic people of the past for a new place to travel and marvel at. We still can't find what we are looking for as Bono of U2 put it in his song. Everybody wants to be a world traveler and is going on world tours. We are still being made to believe happiness is a destination spot (outer place) when in reality it is a way of daily living in our innermost space. Only in the West do we have the funniest of all the retreats - a Yoga (mind, body and soul) retreat where we endure painfully long hours of waits in lineups before and after getting to our retreat. What kind of treat are we giving our body in these retreats where we have to make adjustments to our body, mind and soul to account for jetlag, time changes, digestive changes to 'new' foods, sleep pattern changes, tiredness due to waits, anxiety, stress plus frustration due to language barriers, and so many other changes that the body must deal with just for a retreat. What was the point of this retreat again? Who knows? It appears there are ways to get over jet lag. But, get over something we don't even need to do. We are finding ourselves needing a retreat from the retreat in so many instances it makes one wonder if it is worth it.

The time, cost, stress/anxiety level, sitting in static positions which causes blood to pool at the ankles, chemical imbalances that trigger a lack of serotonin which regulates our sleep pattern, appetite and mood are all put into a disequilibrium when we travel like the nomad. Travel disturbs all the body's systems and causes havoc on our cells when we become this glorified nomad. People are still wondering how some cancers are increasing when the body is clearly put through the wringer when we travel. Skin cancer is also on the rise and nobody appears to see any connection to people lying around on beaches for a whole week in the super-hot sun. What is so healthy with this sun on our skin? The biggest culprit for destroying collagen and elastin fibre of the skin is the sun, which accelerates aging and opens the possibility of disease of the skin. We play ignorant to these basic connections to our body, mind and soul. Hence, the term, "I need a vacation from the vacation" comes into play when we get home.

Nobody wants to be grounded anymore. Traveling like the nomad is the opposite of becoming still. It is the constant movement of people all around the world, wasting fuel and dumping more pollutants into the air so that more of us can go here and there. It is no wonder that climate changes are taking place so rapidly. Have we gone mad when we travel aimlessly jumping from hotel, to motel, to hostel and then to a campsite when we search for ourselves and happiness? Is there a point as we get away with so many others who also just want to get away from their beautiful homes, their jobs and familiar places? Humanity's sheer need to look for constant novelty, variety by taking trips, enjoying tasty foods, looking for more breathtaking views for our eyes, or just engaging in constant activities shows a degree of barrenness in our Western and in our Eastern hearts. We have succumbed to our senses and their desires. This anxious nervousness goes to show just how hungry and thirsty humanity has become in its search for diversity, change, and "newness". It is no longer okay to be in our own comfortable homes in our own clean beds. We can't become still and sit still, can we? A closer look at the whole hotel-jumping thing makes one wonder if we would ever dream of having different people come into our inner space called home and have them sleep in our beds, which people consider their sanctuary. Yet humanity has jumped on to Airbnb which allows for just that. Why do we carry on with this nonsense of going around in different cities, destination spots and beaches by sleeping in beds that many other people have slept in? Plus, we pay to do this and never wonder for a minute about the whole absurdity of this scenario.

Globalization further makes airports homogenous, along with the many urban cities that have cookie-cut the shopping experiences so malls in our home towns have the same shops, stores and brands that the destination cities have. While we are waiting for our flights and passing by security, we will find more stores to shop and more places to eat foods in. As if we didn't have enough "stuff" in our homes, garages and self-storage units, the need to acquire more goods from each of our destination spots and airport shops as we wait for our flights is drilled into our brains. We are becoming a society infatuated with gaining more and more, everywhere we go.

Who said we were supposed to engage in this nomadic movement? The travel industry, media, large business/corporations, subliminal messages, billboards, and ads on bank machine screens have glorified the modern day nomad as if they are in style. The new nomad is a restlessness that is making humanity move around and prevents them from becoming still and pure in the heart. It even prevents the human to seek union of the mind, body and soul since it is so noisy at the airports, security checkpoints and everywhere else that one must go through an ordeal just to arrive at that vacation place that promises a quiet experience.

The nomad of today finds many cycles of the body being affected by this constant movement including the sleep cycle due to time changes or jetlag, dysfunctional eating food cycle which causes digestive problems, fatigue, confusion, lack of awareness, the mental/emotional adjustments to new surroundings, serious disruption of our genes by throwing them off of their normal daily rhythms and also mood disorders due to a combination of having no patience for lineups and constantly being on the go. Never mind constipation, diarrhea or other bowel movements that cause the human to disrupt their exertion/digestive cycle even more. Have we gone mad? Jetlag is also known to reduce neuron growth in the brain, causing a decrease in learning and a reduction in memory capacity. North America or the Western World is becoming known as the leader in having it all yet it leads the world in depression, heart attacks, cancer-related diseases and yes, unhappiness. The travel of the nomad provides us with some anesthetizing that drugs, pills and ganja (marijuana) does. Senses which lead to more desires need to get happiness or numbness that frees us from the cares and woes of daily reality. We have it so good we want to leave the homes where we carry out those beautiful renos so we sleep in the beds of other people who are experiencing the same feelings of wanting something more. A longing or search for something outside. So, what do we do when our inner self is unhappy? We search for happiness elsewhere around the world! Maybe we will find happiness over there and maybe over here?! All the while, we fail to look instead into our own hearts, or the inner side, which is where the souls live.

Typical trips mean we stand at the airport looking around dazed, and we suddenly realize that we are not very happy. We have just spent eight hours (sometimes more or less) on a flight from home, we had spent 45 minutes in a security check line-up, been patted down and probed by guards, having our 50 milliliter larger-than-allowed toothpaste seized, then we dragged our luggage down a 40-kilometer corridor until we sweat like a hog . Exhausted, we suddenly experience jet lag. But remember, we paid to put ourselves in this situation.

Why are there so many books at the airport bookstore on finding happiness? Could it be that much of humanity is attempting to get away to become happy, only to find ourselves facing stress, worry, and anxiety in these unknown places? Not to mention disequilibrium in our entire body.

Traditionally, the nomad is one who travels with no fixed home to survive by providing skills to the visiting area or by allowing his animals to herd and feed. Nomads were common in early times especially in the Middle Eastern countries of Iran, Egypt and Israel. Today there are about 40 million traditional nomads and many millions more who are living a life of constant travel and vacationing for fun to escape work, find happiness, or maybe just for something to do other than to serve the worldwant. The nomads of today bring no skill, only their appetites, their ability to wine and dine, their desire to people-watch through staring and then to move onto another place hoping to do more of the same with the possibility of finding happiness or the possibility of finding more people who are looking for the same things so they feel the same. It is all about the appeal to the senses or oversensory stimulation. Maybe here I will be happy! This group of nomads is addicted to moving around by their own choice, for they are not happy nor able to sit still.

Everybody wants to be a nomad or is being taught it is a great idea to be a nomad. The travel industry has found out that many people are not that happy where they are and looking for something to do with all that money gained during the age of materialism. Why not spend it looking for that happiness? Maybe one can be happy in another country with other people just like us! Maybe happy can be found here or there, but we are willing to look everywhere just as long as we have the money to finance these trips. We are encouraged to be world travelers who surf from motel to hotel to a bed and breakfast and then into a tent or perhaps a hostel. What is so great about hotel surfing or motel surfing, when we know for a fact that there is nothing like your own bed and a good night's sleep in it? Then, why do we like to change beds so often and in so many unfamiliar places? Has it become stylish to sleep in one another's beds? We would never fathom having different people come to sleep in our bed at home, so why are we engaged in it as we travel like the nomad? It just seems be a more dignified form of couch surfing. The seeker is not thrilled by choosing to be a nomad.

So the next time you decide to go on vacation in this great age of distraction, there just might be nothing more luxurious than going nowhere. In this stillness at home, one starts to feel alive, full of fresh hope, and foster love for humanity.

NOVEL

"Searching for the novel, humanity is chasing a restlessness in their heart that also leads to more nervousness."

People always like things that are novel. Novel has to do with diversity, change and looking for unique experiences in life that make us feel we are getting more and taking more of life in. Novel things include taking trips, trying new tasty foods, parachuting out of airplanes, hiking to remote or secluded areas, travel. Bobby Dazzler was a novelty retailer, so we knew what novel meant to people.

Even taking a simple Hatha yoga class shows how humanity is chasing the novel. In class, we try to choose a different place to put our mat instead of the same as last time, we choose a different teacher, a different towel, a new mat color, new yoga gear or the teacher will engage in talks while we are supposed to be in shavasana (lying down in rest like a corpse) to 'change up' the class from the usual. The whole point of Hatha yoga is defeated. It no longer is an activity to achieve yoga with simple human desires of humans where stillness and quiet is supposed to be supreme. The desire for the novel also extends to other people. We try new people out on dates and perhaps divorce if the novelty of the marriage just went away or wore off and the partners became bored, jealous or lonely. The desire for the novel extends to almost every aspect of life today. Children are sent to camps, summer camps, activities and even play dates with different friends just to make sure that we keep our children busy with new things to do.

Pursuing novel things in life is easier during materialism, for new experiences can be purchased with money. Searching for the novel, humanity is chasing a restlessness in their heart that also leads to more nervousness. Studies on stress indicate that four ingredients work together to create a recipe for stress in both adults and children: the newness or novelty of a situation, the unpredictable nature of a situation, a threat to the ego, and a sense of low control. Novelty and engaging in novel things to do has nothing at all to do with meditation or coming into union with the Divine. Choosing the novel means one cannot be still, quiet and patient. Novel also leads humans to compare and judge others through labeling. If one individual can try many things because they have the means to do so, the other feels they are missing out on life because they cannot afford to do so. This leads the mind to overthink, inability to relax, and anxiety creeps in. Competitiveness with other people is created without ever intentionally meaning to do so. Western life is also about those renos which we do to our homes so we can undertake flips of our homes to make more money and buy another house to do it all over again which will require one to move and face a novel situation again. Engaging in novel things is part of the times today, and no wonder depression, anxiety, and stress are at high levels. Stress causes the child or the adult to develop headaches, digestive problems, more colds viruses, psychiatric problems and, later in life, chronic diseases that shorten the human lifespan.

So, why do we engage in novel activities? It is because everybody else is doing it so we should too! The movement of people into sheeple (sheep people) is always fascinating. Nobody wants to just be still, it is all about novel because that is the "thing" to do. It is too bad that we don't pick up a novel (printed book) and become still instead, and use the word 'novel' in a different manner. When one reads a novel, an automatic meditation and stillness comes to be. This can't take place when we engage ourselves in the other form of 'novel'.

OMNIS

"Intuition takes us beyond the limitations."

Omnis means all and science means knowing. Put together, the word omniscient means all knowing. This is what the seeker is striving for when seeking to unite with the Divine. Opening to this omniscience within each of us requires the exercise and development of intuition. Intuition takes us beyond the limitations imposed by our five senses and develops our sixth sense(s). There are many aspects to opening our sixth sense. It involves the development of a keen intuitive awareness that goes beyond the normal perception of sight, sound, touch, smell, and hearing.

This awareness is something we are all blessed with at the time of birth, but its development occurs when the environment that one is reared with has minimal meddling. When shaping, programming, and conditioning is kept to a minimum, a child, and later an adult, is left alone to develop as nature has intended. The sixth sense is enhanced by becoming still, quiet and alone for long periods of time. This trait has been taught by many masters and is essential in order to enter into stillness

OTHER

"Who is the other? It is everybody other than YOU, the Self."

The other - our friends, family, coworkers and siblings, are all the outside people all around us. When we celebrate certain traditions and special occasions we are required to care about what other people think.

If it weren't for the need for other people's approval, the retail world might not even exist. People care about what other people think. It is important to keep up with the Joneses and the Lees. Shopping fills a need to impress others. Shopping in stores like Bobby Dazzler made people feel as if they, too, were in style and trendy.

The other has such a profound influence that it has stolen some of the precious gifts we as people have to offer each other. The other is the external pressure to conform to the same ideas and belief systems of those around us. The other puts pressures on us to be like them. We care far too much what other people think. Other people seem to interfere with our Divine programming, which causes us to fall off the grid and from the path of G-d realization. Dr. Dyer referred to conditioning and programming as "old mind viruses." And this is what they are: viruses.

In reality, the other shouldn't matter that much. We must be able to state, "What other people think about us is none of our business!" When we make it our business to constantly pay attention to what the other thinks, says or feels about us, then that is when we buy into the label, judgment, and shaping we carry throughout our lives.

Who is the other? It is everybody other than YOU, the Self.

We are completely surrounded by the other such as family, friends, siblings, mate, spouse, husband, wife, girl/boyfriends, co-workers, business associates, enemies, allies, friends, foes, your lawyer, banker, accountant and the list goes on. Most of society feels a tremendous need to please, get advice from, be seen, or have the other around. This is probably why social media got so popular - society's constant desire to see what the other is doing.

It doesn't matter if your family is Italian, Greek, Iranian, or Arabic. It could be Asian Indian, inter-faith, or inter-race. The family could be adopted, foster, blended or gay. Family likes to give out great advice, opinions and ideas. Whatever they have been taught, they will teach us. These are people we don't necessarily choose. Often one wonders how we have anything in common. Are we really related? The truth seeker chooses to forgo the need to go to the house of relatives, keep in touch with friends socially, or engage in parties, cultural celebrations or traditions where the other is often found. Those choosing to become awakened may find comfort in being alone rather than in the compay of the other. After all, it is the other that gives out all sorts of programming, conditioning and beliefs.

People want to be noticed. When people like to be seen all the time, society's conditioning can lead to over-socialization. Look at all the cool spots to eat. During the off-peak hours, one can find a table, eat mindfully, and leave with no hassles plus one gets full service, hot foods, no waits with nobody staring at each other. Yet we find that nobody does this! People would rather wait up to two hours on a Friday or Saturday night with noise and lineups, even though the same food is served minus all the hassle between the hours of 2 pm to 5 pm any time of the week. Some say we all get hungry at the same time. People want the world to see them in public places that are cool like at the mall or in a club. There is no point for those who want to be seen to be in a place between the hours of 2-5 pm as nobody would know that they were there. Only the servers, and they just want the tip, so you wait for the line ups instead. Friends, the in-crowd, the hot people and the cool people all come out at that time. They are not there to eat but to be "in". So they do it and think they are all it.

This has nothing to do with finding yourself. The need for the other is constant. Yes, humans would be lonely if we were always on our own. Yet, this guide is about coming close to Divine Source not to find crowds. The others are necessary in life but the truth seeker attempts to eliminate the extra energy drain by choosing to focus and not worry about the other, especially during mealtime.

So how should a truth seeker approach the other? The other must complement the energy you bring. Those who take the energy will leave little for you to enjoy and function with. Are the people you surround yourselves with the others who nourish your soul? Especially during mealtimes, evening downtimes and in the mornings upon rising.

Or, is the other just an energy vampire who steals our energy from us? Those who steal our energy work on a low vibrational energy. Some bring energies of negativity, sorrow, sadness, grief, jealousy, hate, envy and lack of empathy. These are characteristics that are the exact opposite of intelligence. The other who brings this energy must be left alone. The seeker is unable to engage with this other even if they are our parents or caretakers. It is better to be alone than with the other in this case. If the other attempts to overtake our interactions on a daily basis with their ideas, beliefs, concepts, feelings and so forth, then they, too, must be avoided. Especially when one seeks the truth. It is true that our relations, caretakers or parents have lived longer than us, but their experiences are theirs, not ours. It does not mean that we follow every single sentence they utter. We all have a mind, a brain, a life, and choices to make when realizing the self, without the other. What works for the other may not work for us. It would serve us well if we limit outer, other voices or chatter and begin to know the self in life.

OUTER

"The world loves the outer stuff because that is what others see."

The outer is the opposite of the inner. It "duals" with the inner and this is where we are today in humanity. Our outer world has everything to do with the material world and nothing to do with the inner world, which is concerned with spirituality. Materialism concerns itself with making all that is natural into something other, outer and showy. We have materialized breast milk by making baby formula. We have made the most basic staple of life, water, into a material object by bottling it, then labeling it, giving it a funky name and selling it for money. We have made foods that are a necessity for life into art and entertainment by taking pictures and grastropics. We have created nonsense out of the most basic, simple things in life which has led humanity to many human-created conditions such as the desire to hoard, buy it, get more stuff and seek things that please our senses. We are as far away as possible from G-d, the Divine source, the universal centre or the spiritual eye as can be. The outer makes it appear as if the Divine is somewhere outside, so we take part in offerings, expressions, pujas, pilgrimages, requests and animal sacrifices to please G-d. None of these have anything to do with the inner Divine. The Universal Awakening brings a shift to the inner.

The world loves the outer stuff because that is what other people see. In the West we start with outer stuff right when we bring our child home from the hospital. We begin with the nursery room that nobody else can mimic. We put our child in the best brand when we know the baby doesn't even know what Nike or Adidas is at six months. We then attempt to keep up with the Joneses, Wongs, Goldsteins, and Singhs – and whoever else has the best brand-named stuff as we go along in life. Thinking we have mastered it all then we move onto our house, cars, and even more. The outer stuff includes make-up, some potion, a little bit of lotion, some cream, serum, a nip and tuck here and there, liposuction, plastic surgeries galore, Botox treatments, a little laser all over, the bling fake nails that prevent you from working, a rainbow of hair dyes, fake lashes that get caught in our eyebrows, things that are thought to be taboo like the tattoos /piercing /stretchings, high heels that one can't even walk in, the thong (g-string) that sits in the middle of our ass or vagina so we can pull at it all day long, fake boobs, penis enlargement, then come the pills to keep the penis up longer, even more pills to libido to help the woman to have sex longer. And more - dildo (sex toys), spray tans, kinky lingerie, stars and idols, clubs, party places, reality shows (gong shows), and the list of the outer stuff that has nothing to do with the inner stuff. Are we at the furthest point from the Divine yet? We are so, so far away that only the outer stuff seems to prevail.

The world is so lost in this whole outer space, and missing the inner. It has become a world of fakes. We are deprived morally as we attempt to move out of this dark period. The outer stuff is why humanity is far away from the central, creative force. We are in a dark state, pumping junk into the human body, when the body is part of G-d and so, Divine.

When anyone comes to the podium and states they are spiritually aligned while they are getting their Botox injections, shoving pills into their body, riddling their body with foods that are junk along with their spray tans, there is nothing spiritual about this. As the old saying goes, that is what twits do when they tweet. Everybody is in the "look at me" state. Nobody stops to get to know themselves. Who am I? is part of the inside of you and the inner spiritual side. We do not understand who we are on the inside because we are too busy harming our bodies with stuff. What's happened to our inner stuff?

We are taught that it is enough just to go to a place of worship to be spiritual. We are taught that we need to give (money) to these spiritual places of worship so we can come closer to G-d. We are taught that we must pray in places of worship on a certain day, be it Friday, Saturday or Sunday. Why can't we pray every day? We are taught that it is enough just to read one particular book to find truth or awakening. Or we are taught that the Divine is something that is unreachable, only for certain clergy like the Priest, the Imams, the Rabbis or possibly Nuns. We are taught that even this is something outer from us that has nothing to do with the inner of us. We are being shaped to focus far too much on the outer stuff and not enough on the inner stuff.

Emphasis on the outer stuff is important to many of the organized religions of the world. Using Sikhism as an example, it is hard to understand what the 5 K's (external displays) of Sikhism had anything to do with finding the truth and G-d in present times. Perhaps the 5 K's were helpful when the religion was created so that Sikhs would appear different from the Muslims and the Hindus who were attempting to force conversions at that time. Every one of the 5 K's are things that devoted Sikhs must wear to symbolize that they are Sikhs. This may be true to ensure that other people can see they were Sikhs. Other paths make adherents shave their heads, or only allow a beard without a moustache. Each path has outer displays that don't have a thing to do with the inner self or self-realization. Even followers of the Buddha put on certain robes and shaved their heads when taking the path of Buddhism to look more like the Buddha. Many other faiths had different outer ways to prove who they were, but in the modern world of today, the inner being of the human is far more important than all the outer shows of who they are. The outer displays by humanity were numerous but they all had nothing to do with becoming awake, alert and aware. Wearing certain symbols and going into the many places of worship were also outer displays of their faith to G-d. They all had nothing to do with becoming quiet, silent and still. In fact, going to places of worship where many people gathered was the opposite of how one would be able to self-realize. Churches, temples, mosques, synagogues, self-realization centers, ashrams, Gurdwaras and other places where people gathered to chant, partake in talks, speak, worship, pray and come together were noisy, crowded and prevented one from becoming still, quiet and listen in silence. Listening is hard when one is not in the presence of silence. In many of these places one must become a member or perhaps pay for certain blessings through donations, or fees to be part of a congregation that is a segregation from other paths. Paying money or providing gifts is materialism. Materialism has nothing to do with spirituality, which reflects the inner self. How can these outer displays encourage or assist with growth of the inner self?

It appears that the outer stuff is much more important to many organized religions, paths and faith groups than staying in one's own home to become still, quiet and silent to hear the inner voice of G-d speak. In the West, where freedom of religion is available to everyone, home is where one must begin. Here is where one must make our heart the house of prayer. Unity in humanity will arise if we come to see all those around as the same and with one eye.

PARTY

"Without the party scene who would have bought our goods?"

In a store like Bobby Dazzler, the party started when the lights turned on in the morning, and ended when the lights turned off. We were a party store with colorful lights, paraphernalia, costumes, drinking stuff, smoking accessories and anything else needed for a party. Often clients would come in just to be part of the party atmosphere. No other retail store could offer a shopping experience with the right music, products, and a special feeling that the client was in a nightclub in Vegas or Ibiza. This made them stay longer and spend more. The party was always on seven days a week at Bobby Dazzler.

Living in Vancouver, BC, and not talking about the whole party scene would be leaving out a whole chapter. The clubs, bars, limos, SUV's, restaurants, hotties and more, live for the party. This scene is expanded from the nightclubs or rave scene to all the places where the other hangs out. To hang in cool eateries - spots like Global or Cactus Club, with hot women/men and loud music is the thing to do. The party scene seems to encompass all the habits - drugs, drink and smoke, and it is dangerous, addictive and expensive. You lose much of your money attempting to gain the satisfaction of the other. The party scene is based on the outer appearance of being seen. The need to let the other know you are in this great place to eat and with this gorgeous person on your arms. Thus, it is a little pretentious! Even if one can afford it, it still seems a little fake - fake boobs, botox and all that other stuff that goes along with being seen.

But when you're a business called Bobby Dazzler and your motto is "got what's hot!" it would be hard not to be part of the party scene. We sold everything for the hot bachelor party, bachelorette party, sexy birthday party and even the home party. We had gone from gadgets, gifts and electronics to selling stuff for sex, drugs and drinking. These were main themes of any party. We sold to all classes of people. The upper class, middle class and the lower class. All people love to party. Bobby Dazzler's business relied on the party. We carried every item that appealed to those who loved to drink, smoke, do drugs, even those who loved to be naked and those who loved music. A buddy of mine said, "You rely on the business of sex, drugs and rock'n'roll."

Bobby Dazzler served the party scene well. The party scene customers are those who are so needy that they seemed to spend every single cent of what they earned on being noticed, being in and hot. Halloween went from scary to nights of the sluts. People spent hundreds of dollars on costumes that would be worn only a few hours, never to be touched again. They wanted the latest, most up-to-date and would spend whatever it took to ensure that they were the first to have it. Without the party scene who would have bought our goods? We, too, lived for the party; but we had our own party, that was to profit off the party scene. We knew what society was up to and made sure that their needs were met in ample supply. They demanded and we would provide. We made a point of keeping ourselves up to speed with the in stuff, the hot staff, the hot items and the cool trade shows.

It is true that the party lifestyle is not conducive to becoming awake, alert and aware person. It causes the body to fall into an imbalance. The party life is an exaggerated lifestyle that barely gets one anywhere but surely does get us into trouble. People end up spending too much money. The power within the party scene is fake as it only brings those wannabes to your side. There is no real friend in the party scene because most people are just drunk, stoned or high. How can these people know what they are doing? They are just a bunch of people who love to party. After watching the party people for twenty-seven years, the desire to forgo the party and to awaken was ignited. It was just too much partying after a while.

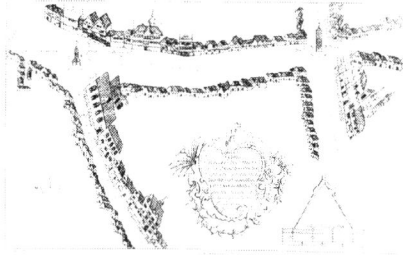

PATHS

"Books become a starting point to a path of our own."

It is estimated that there are well over 4,200 paths or religions in this world to truth. These paths were here before we began our life on earth. We normally follow the path that our parents give us. One who veers to their own path or seeks paths different from those early paths might be a seeker. But the majority of humanity takes one path (or none if atheism is the path that prevailed during childhood.)

Many of these paths have books or scriptures offering access to knowledge and wisdom for those who have a desire to learn. So many books are available in the West through libraries and bookstores that one's own path to turn the light on is easier. There is freedom of religion in most of the West, yet it is surprising that many of us haven't taken the opportunity to explore and open to the many other paths of the world. People seem to take the one path they are born into and follow it in its absolute form without questioning. Yet nobody has claimed they see awakening by following this one particular path in its absolute form. Wisdom involves being intellectually curious and open-minded. Ignorance is being closed-minded, unable to stimulate the mind to try different paths, build on new ideas and exchange thoughts. One must be able to read and write to gain access to this information. Half the world still cannot gain access to books to learn and become educated due to their country, region or religion of birth. After becoming aware of the many paths that are available, a person is better able to take the best and discard the worst. Those who seek must challenge what is said and attempt to seek truth through a "fight" with themselves. Reading about each of the paths to awakening gives us insight, hints, answers questions, lets us determine what is truth and what is false. It gives us a chance to determine what we feel is right or wrong through a process of critical analysis. These paths have books for us to engage ourselves with, and they become a starting point to a path of our own.

POINT

"Will the light ever turn on?"

What is the point of humanity? We must do whatever we have to do in this life and then return back to G-d through self-realization. Sounds so quick and easy, yet it is one of the most difficult tasks. During the age of Materialism, many have realized their G-d-given gifts. Great entrepreneurs, artists, writers, business owners, teachers, nurses, doctors and many others have found the one thing they love to do and are doing it. It doesn't matter what that job or work is. All that matters is if you are happy doing what you're doing, then it is just a matter of incorporating the search for "truth" into your life alongside. The secret to self-realization is that the gift that one is good at doing must be shared with others.

Taking on responsibilities to care for humankind is the greatest gift one can give.

One cannot "cling" to everything that the gift they are good at doing in this life has allowed them to accumulate in a material sense. Toward the end of the human cycle of life, we are not meant to cling to all that money, the house, the hubby, the wives, the heirs (child), the autos (cars) or anything else that is gained or remains on earth and part of this earthly plane. A person is meant to let go of it all, and seek to join with the Divine Source, so the cycle of having to do it all over again will not happen. Once the Divine knows that this human soul is attracted to all those beautiful things on Earth, the cycle begins again. One returns to Earth to try it all over again, until the real point of life which is "truth" or "self-realization" is found. Perhaps that is the reason our population is growing so much. So many humans are attracted to all the "stuff" on Earth. This makes us miss the real point of life. That is what makes so many of us keep coming back over and over again. So, we repeat this lesson.

The point of this life is do whatever we are great at, makes us happy and also makes us engage in the world with others in a meaningful way so that towards the end of the human cycle, we can come back to G-d, or intelligence, just as we arrived - empty. This is the final point of our human life

As we watch humanity indulge in the senseless pursuit of delicious foods, the next best hotel, enjoy trips and views, get more homes, more autos, more money, more jewels and more stuff whatever it maybe, the timing cannot be better than now to turn the light on. The world is engaged in materialism and we are so far from the Divine source that there just seems to be no way out of the vortex of our need for greed. Nobody is looking for G-d! Everyone seems to be engaged in pleasing their senses. Nobody wants to leave this planet, and populations continue to be subject to the cycles of birth and death. These cycles continue as divisions widen between those who have and those who don't. The only way to escape this cycle is to turn the light on. It is to realize by ourselves the whole point of awakening the soul. How do we bring humanity to understand this, when everyone is more worried about finding the next best steak, delicious foods, and wonderful views? Will the light ever turn on? Will awakening take some of us out of this cycle of birth and death? Will we ever get the point?

POWER

"The only thing about power that seekers of truth must realize is that they must empower themselves."

Power and greed are the tell-tale signs of the age of materialism. For millennia, those in power have controlled humanity through channels that prevented people from escaping, thinking, learning, advancing, becoming freer or sustaining themselves for a better future. Power can be found in political groups, governments, social institutions, the military, the authorities, in religions, schools, cultures, economic groups, ethnic groups, nations, races and any people who come together because they have found a common ground, cause, or ideology that makes them believe they are right and powerful when they come together as a group. When one has power then greed takes over to ensure that even more power is exercised over the masses. Power seeks the company of other groups who are large. The larger the group the more powerful it becomes.

With power, governments, armies, social organizations, religions, powerful individuals, kingdoms and others have risen to great strength. Even today, Syria's Assad refuses to step down from power and instead slaughters men, women and children although the people are all from a common religion of the nation. Now two groups with the same religion fight to gain control over a country - the Shiite vs. the Sunni. Two groups from the same path are choosing to fight, kill, and destroy their own country for power. In the meantime, not much of the country is left. Historically, the need for power that has always existed has made it necessary to fight to have peace.

Where is humanity in all this? Why would anybody want to take a chance at coming back down here to Earth to face the possibility of being under the control of such individuals? Why not escape this vortex called human life and all the power that man seeks, and go to pure light? Human beings can go for power for themselves so that truth can be revealed.

The West may be delusional in thinking that here we are free and away from autocratic dictators. Yet, we, too, have been misled by large business. Their power has been hidden but their control appears in what we see and hear. The large have gained control over the techs, media, banks, the foods industry and even all those in between. We are at the mercy of the large (corporations/business) whose purpose is to profit from the small.

Humanity in the West is at the mercy of the large who feed the mind with subliminal messages, telling us we should keep in touch more often, which only causes individuals to disperse through the engagement with the other. They are also pushing humans to engage, become more social through the mottos - "keep in touch," and "nobody wants to alone." They make the rules and also break them when necessary to ensure that their captive audience, humanity, is kept in constant control and under wraps.

The only thing about power that a seeker of truth must realize is that they must empower themselves. To bring the power back to ourselves requires the individual to rely on themselves. It requires one to make judgement calls of their own, and not listen to the outer voices that tell them what to do. Once we totally submit to G-d or the Divine intelligence within us, we are able to develop our individual power. It is here that the power of the sixth sense and the power to become a seer arises. Islam referred to this as total submission to Allah. A seeker calls it total submission to the Self. What arises out of this is a powerful and self-empowered, You!

PRAYS

"The right place for meditation is anywhere one can connect to the Divine in silence to become still."

In the retail world of Bobby Dazzler when no customers were in the store and if all duties were completed, these quiet moments became time for meditation. This is a great time to enjoy the quiet. Any time when nobody was in the store, meditation or prayer could be practiced to connect with the Divine.

For the seeker, prays is essentially meditation. It could be made tech-sounding as "ipray", a new word in English for meditation with G-d or the Source during the day of rest, away from the restlessness of technology and noise of the world. Religions have created days of rest where one prays with others in a place of worship on Friday if one follows Islam, on Saturday if one is Jewish, and on Sunday if one is Christian. Why all the different days? Islam takes it even further and instructs the masses to pray five times at specific times a day. Collectively, humanity can realize that it is possible just to pray every day and not limit it to certain times or days. Those seeking awakening don't need to find a specific place to pray, for they can just meditate in their own homes. There is no need to buy into the "pray here and pay over there" business. One who prays through meditation prays all the time. Being thankful and living in gratitude becomes a daily practice for the seeker. Unfortunately, religion has made it seem as though "we" are right to pray on this day and "they" (the other religions) are wrong to pray on that day. Ironically, the three great Western religions could not come up with the same days of rest - they had to be different. They also called their places of worship mosque, synagogue or church. With different names, division, conflict, and separation prevail. Their congregations are based on segregations. Coming up with just one day a week to pray can be very limiting. Does this mean that humans don't need to pray during all the other days of the week? Does it mean we can only go to a certain "place" like a mosque, synagogue, or church to pray?

With ipray, we pray more often, alone, and in our own homes. Currently a movement towards meditation studios is popping up in places like Vancouver. Individuals can pay $20 per drop in visit, $75 per monthly passes or up to $950.00 per month just to meditate in quietness outside of their own homes. This model goes right back to the idea of a "pray here and pay over there" system that religions have created for thousands of years. When groups come together to pray, meditation becomes almost impossible due to distractions and socializing that takes place with the others all around us. When one prays in a religious place or a meditation studio, it is nearly impossible to connect in union with the Divine due to other people who are around us. Meditation can only be found in an "inner" place not in any "outer" places such as a temple, synagogue, mosque, church, a learning center or a meditation studio. The best thing about ipray is that one realizes just how wonderful it is to pray every day and seek a meditative lifestyle that is conducive to the growing needs of our mental health and self care. Quietness creates mindfulness which reduces stress, worry and anxiety. One forgos the need to pray on just the one specific day of the week that a religion mandates. It also lets the place of prayer be our homes or wherever we are, rather than in specific places. We may choose times, dates, and the place. This is how the awakening starts.

Awakening is a personal, private, and independent experience, and it is much easier when the house of prayer is our very own home. Also, part of coming close to G-d is taking care of the human body that the soul lives in. This requires one to be physically active. As we pray in our own homes, there is less time taken up traveling to certain places to pray. When time is spent wisely in meditation in our homes and in taking care of the body that holds the Divine spirit of G-d, there is progress toward awakening in modern times. It is not effective for proper meditation to sit for hours clustered with others in social gab, listening to sermons and interpretations by spiritual representatives or intermediaries (Priest, Imam or Rabbi), or listening to chants, hymns, prayers. If one prays or rests on days other than those mandated by religion then they may find days of prayer (meditation) that actually work for them, though not necessarily for the religious group. The right place for meditation is anywhere one can connect to the Divine in silence to become still. Ipray is praying here, there and everywhere. It is prayer whenever time allows us. Going forward, humanity prays all the time.

QUIET

"The quieter you become the more you will be able to hear."- Ram Dass

It is the quiet ones who glimpse the real spiritual path to actual meditation. Often quiet is misconstrued as stupid or dumb. It is the exact opposite. Pure intelligence is born of silence. Most people feel they are so smart they must speak up and say their two bits. Isn't this, after all, what we are taught in the West? "Don't just sit there, say something!" Yet, all blabbermouths do is reveal their purpose to the quiet ones who watch and observe without reacting. The quiet ones only make a move or say words when necessary. Sure, a mouth was given to be used. But the loud ones can always be heard miles away even when they are not spoken to. The West has over-socialized the world by means of email, texts, phone, tweet, Instagram, Facebook and many other forms of social techs. Even with the mouth shut, the techs have enabled those that don't want to stay quiet to be touched in so many other ways. The concept of quiet should be extended to mean the quieting of the mind. The mind cannot be quiet if one is still engaging in the many forms of social networking through techs or oral conversations. The mind is still awake and being loud. It is only in silence that the eternal source is able to connect to the individual. It is in this silence that space is created. That space and those gaps are where intelligence lives. The more times we grow that space daily, the more chances intelligence has to enter our minds.

One gets to know the self when one becomes silent and quiet. In quiet, you can finally hear your breath; you can think and sort things out without pressure or influence. You can relax, chill or even do nothing but meditate. Meditation becomes possible when one is quiet and alone. Quiet in a room all alone is so much fun to do - if you haven't already done this, try it! You will yearn for this once it becomes a daily practice. You will wonder why the phone, email, tweet, grams (insta), or texts keep going on while offering nothing but distractions. Distractions are nothing but problems. "He said, she said"… " "blahs, blahs, blahs"… "What are they doing?" … "Where are you, what is up and what is going on?" …. Then more yadda, yadda, and yadda. What does this accomplish other than putting more clutter in the mind? Meditation make one smarter, relieves pain, inspires creativity, decreases health bills, improves memory, sweetens dreams and enables us to have better relationships.

Only when we learn to be quiet will we learn to hear ourselves, which is the inner voice of the Intelligence, the higher Self – also known as G-d. The answers you have been waiting for come racing in. But quiet cannot come until one learns to be alone. Meditations, whether online or in public groups cannot enable a real place of inner stillness. This can only be done alone. In reality you are not alone but in tune with yourself on a higher level than those who grasp at others out of a need to belong or feel needed as part of the group. Awakening means deeply knowing the self, being self-reliant, and having self-control. Awakening is impossible to obtain when we are outer-directed and grasping at people and places. It is possible to have a constant undeniable feeling that something else is watching over one's best interest. It is indeed desirable. Knowing there is this higher power, this higher creative force, this connectedness to all humanity makes becoming quiet quite fun! When one becomes quiet, silent and still, the feeling of this energy will be like a tap on the shoulder. It will feel as if someone is pushing you forward, with proper guidance, giving the nudge we all need.

Shifts in our ability to see things that normally cannot be seen start to occur. This can only happen when we become quiet. When one is in a quiet room alone, intuitive insight naturally appears. Only you know what is good for you! Others may provide wise advice but only you know where you want to be and what you want from life. In the best-case scenario every person is this world has a mommy and daddy to provide the basic foundations necessary to carry on with life . Failing that there are others who can give the same stable forces such caretakers, guardians, aunts, foster parents and so on. The ultimate motivating power and seat of force to derive the goals and drive the heart and soul is found in the self. Blame gets us nowhere. It becomes the blame game leading to brain drain. When the self hears that voice in quiet, then the self can build its own dream. Make it happen for yourself by choosing to be quiet and meditate. Quiet allows one to be uninterrupted and create the plan without that annoying other attempting with noise and advice to do it this way, that way, or no way. You ask yourself, how would they know what is best for you and what works for you? They don't! Only you know your own self. So, quiet is a must. The outer voices will bother you until you cannot develop yourself, find yourself, nor reach your goals - whether they be material or spiritual.

We can observe without reacting. If we truly desire to come close to Intelligence, then it would be wise to mimic Intelligence. If Divine Intelligence can't be heard verbally through spoken words then we must refrain from oral, verbal or vocal communications of any sort, also. This does mean that repetition of hymns, mantra chanting and any other sounds from the mouth are not necessary for awakening.

The quieter you become, the more you hear. We can engage our five ordinary senses in a way that allows one to see past what the ordinary human can see. In addition, it develops our intuitive sixth sense. Intuition then strengthens our remote sensory skills which lead us to kick in our seventh sense, which I refer to as the "omnis" sense. Omni is Latin for "all", every, the whole of every kind of unknown origin. The all-knowing sense! This is the ultimate sense of all senses in the human being, and leads us towards becoming awakened, superhuman, and omniscient. All this is only possible when we become quiet. After all, we can't hear G-d verbally in chanting, in oral conversations, and practicing mantras. So why should we? It's time to mimic G-d and be quiet.

RACES

"Races that make you run in the same spot are not races at all."

There are two aspects to races in life. The first belongs to the races that humanity goes through during the material world. We have everyday races like going to school, achieving graduation, getting to work on time, or even just doing all the things you want to before the end of the day. Then come the rat races of the material world. The race to get the best props for our life such as the ultimate house, the best hubby or wife, the nicest car or the ultimate job. The races are never finished! Once you cross one finish line, another race starts up so the races continue and are ongoing even after our death. Races provide people with drive, energy and power. There is nothing wrong in participating in these races. That is part of life. However, once we reach the plateau in the material world, we forget that it is a race within ourselves that is the most important. We continually find ourselves pursuing society's set rules that have us engaged in obtaining more material wealth without any regard for our spiritual health.

The other aspect of races is the human-created division of races. This definition of race refers to people of common ancestry who are distinguished by physical characteristics such as hair color, color of eyes, color of skin and stature. In the Divine's eye there is no race but the human race. Many in power try to convince humanity that there is a race problem, but this is a non-existent problem, for humans are all part of the same source. Whatever color we came down here to operate our lives in is just that: a color. The color of our skin is the outer layer of ourselves and has nothing to do with the inner self. One cannot connect to the source if we are focused on the color of one's skin. Who has made this important? Why? An intelligent person would be able to see through all the smoke and mirrors to arrive at the fact that all people are people. That is it! Conflict, divisions, and a fight is created only to benefit those in power. To make war not peace has been the motto of the world, but the motto of the seeker chooses peace always. We all know that if we can continue to convince people that some people are lesser and others are more then some of us can gain power over others for profit or money. For the seeker, there are no races and there is no racism problem. All humans are human no matter what race or outer cloak they have arrived here in to carry on their duties.

Running a retail store meant that people of all races came in. There was no time to judge or categorize people based on races. It would be a poor way to run a successful store if Bobby Dazzler decided to base sales on race. The categorization of races wasn't even an issue in a store that had so many customers from a mixed-race background. It just made it possible to understand that races are only an issue or problem made up by the programming of society, and which is simply false.

Of course, we can still look at people's faces to figure out their races. Race is a non-scientific manner of classifying humans, but once we figure out the race then we begin our judgments, ideas, our conditioning of what to expect from those races based on preconceptions and thoughts that have been planted in our head from past information, ideas, guidance, patterns or conditioning received from our parents, our environment, our caretakers, the other, society and media or anybody else. We can only find truth and become part of humanity that is based on loving kindness if we choose to erase the race card. We couldn't all possibly look the same, as the world is meant to be full of color. Forcing the same race upon humanity has never worked anyway. Nazi Germany tried to find the pure race by choosing blond hair, blue eyes and fair skin. It didn't work then and doesn't work now. Races are meant to be mixed.

The world is full of so many races, with so many faces and different eyes. They are all part of the Source. Some of the races are black, mocha, white, brown, Asian, Latin, or mixed. What does it matter as they are just an outer shroud of the Divine that we all belong to. Past cycles and the modern cycles in some instances appear to create a separateness from others into different races. The race layer is one layer that needs to be peeled away when searching for truth to become one with all. Life was not meant to classify people based on race. Nor was it about who will win first. It was not be a race against other people through racism or the color of our skin. Removing this layer allows the spiritual seeker to see the source in all.

When speaking in terms of spirituality, the real race is with ourselves. The race is to find that one gift or talent that we were blessed with so that we could share it with the world. When we find out what we are supposed to be doing in this life and then share that gift to make the world a better place then we have arrived. The race is successful. That is it! The only race remaining is the one that allows us to return to the Divine source through self-actualization to complete the spiritual life cycle. Being free, all powerful, and expressive of our innermost desire with no limit is the final race of our lifetime.

REACT

"The spiritual seeker is not looking to react."

To become awake, we must cease to react. To react results from the desire to speak up, point out, teach, exert force, exercise ego, will, desire, fight, anger, rants, and so on. We tweet or post our stuff on social media so we can get people to react with likes. Social media has taken off due to the power of "react". People love to react!

It is human nature to react to situations we don't approve of. Normally, a person wants to react when they see something that is not right. Why wouldn't we want to react when we feel something is wrong or if someone is doing something crazy or illegal? But frequently, this does not lead to the right or intended outcome. Why? Well, who wants to be told what to do? Yet we react with "I'll teach you not to do that!" And we end up not just reacting but over-reacting, which is when the problems really arise. We get angry, frustrated, upset, uptight, uneasy, and most of all not able to control our real feelings because we cannot see why this is occurring. We react so instantly, it leads us to a downward spiral. The person we engage ourselves with may not be at the same level as we imagine ourselves to be. If you know and believe in the self, you would not react but walk out of the situation rather than descend to a lower level of thought. It is a waste of time to even think you are going to change that situation or person. You may even get hurt from the whole ordeal of being in a low vibrational energy matter.

As we go through life when such situations arise, carefully watch the face of the other. Look into their eyes and then just walk away. In a phone conversation, try to hang up if nothing seems to be going in any productive direction. A situation is stagnant if each of the parties attempts to prove they are right. Nobody wins. Stalemate. The loser of the situation is both sides, and the winner is always negative energy, hostility, and hopelessness. The words that erupt can never be taken back. You have been led to react when you could have used your mind's intelligence to become quiet.

The spiritual seeker is not looking to react. What does the seeker do when someone reacts? Nothing! Stay. They stay quiet, that's what! One comes to a point of non-reaction when they have overcome all this. They choose to be still. How can this be? When in school, we are taught to speak up and react rather than be passive. Why react when what is happening is supposed to be happening? Those who seek and adore the drama of life react. Reacting is merely a form of regaining contol. It draws us into controversy. Those who just wish to watch and see G-d's drama at work choose to non-react. To become still, quiet, and awake is only possible when we forgo the urge to react. This is contrary to conditioning. We have been conditioned by our parents, caretakers, teachers and society to react through our voice, speech, or words. We have been told to speak up, engage in chats or talks, say something, and above all don't just sit there so quiet in this noisy world - if you want to be heard, react! Nobody wants to become quiet to hear more. That is just too passive for a world dominated by techs, phone calls, email, pages, tweets, tags, and so on.

Today, a common phrase has come into play. They say, "It is what it is!" This is the closest modern phrase that one can adopt today when we relate to the teaching of spiritual awakening.

REBEL

"The rebel with a cause would be the seeker looking for the truth!"

It is essential for those seeking truth to choose the path of the rebel. A rebel seeks to discover truth for themselves. It is a difficult path, as your ideas or ideal become different from those around you. Opposition will constantly come from all around; from immediate family, friends and everyone we deal with daily. A rebel calls for changes that sometimes make others feel insecure, inadequate and even belittled. Some may even try to sway us from being a rebel by bringing in "scientific verifiable" evidence to deter us from our path of being a seeker of truth or from tapping into that unlimited self, the Source.

Many paths or faiths of the past base the truth on the experience of a particular Master or Teacher. A rebel challenges what has been written or said by the Master or Teacher of past paths. Learning truth for ourselves means taking the path of the rebel. The rebel must erase everything that has been given to them to start over again for the cause. The rebel with a cause would be the seeker looking for the truth! The rebel in modern times has been stereotyped as one who likes to drink, smoke, do drugs, ride a motorcycle, not have a job and get tattoos. But actually, a rebel is one who does not conform to what religion, nation, culture, or family dictates as being truth. The spiritual rebel questions, challenges authority, and seeks to learn from personal experience to find truth. The rebel seeks to go beyond what is received in pursuit of experimental wisdom. In truth wisdom cannot be transmitted or received. That which is heard, read or learned from others and is adopted as one's own is not wisdom. Wisdom that arises due to one's own experience is private, personal, and independent of another person's idea of wisdom. It is the bread and butter of real truth and self-realization. In fact, if all of humanity became rebels and sought awakening then seven billion+ paths would exist to awakening. And if all of them could write about that experience and give a guide for others then seven+ billion religions/paths/guides would be born. That is how private, personal and independent awakening is.

The rebel nature is required for the uphill battle of becoming a seeker of truth. Many try but decide they cannot continue due to those who oppose their way. Intuition will tell the rebel what is true and what is false. The rebel must try, challenge, question, and test what is believed to be truth by the general population.

The rebel seeker must be individualistic and a forward thinker willing to learn from all. The rebel must be able to break away confidently with the task, idea or thought in mind which is based on their own heart. Hence, the rebel is not just a unique individual who does things a little differently, but may be one who sees things that the others have overlooked due to "go with the flow" or their desire to "follow the crowd" (sheep). The crowd may laugh at the rebel since it may appear that the rebel makes little sense according to the books, scriptures, dogma or religious texts but the cause of the rebel will prevail. That cause is awakening or self-realization. If there were no one to rebel, change would never take place. One will always appear to show a different road so things be seen in an alternative light, to grow.

The rebel must choose not to be complacent. Often their view is unique since it has nothing to do with the crowd. The hard work of the rebel is to point out false scenarios against the many layers of conditioning in society. Once a rebel suggests changes in the way of thinking, the group feels threatened by the one who seems to want to show another route or path that may suggest to them they may have been following the wrong path the whole time. Any time that a rebel points out to a group they may be collectively wrong, the entire group feels as if they are the fools, or threatened. And so that is when blasphemy is proclaimed or apostasy is confirmed upon the rebel. When the group feels threatened it blames the rebel for creating chaos and disrupting the ongoing system of things; not upon themselves for failing to see if it is correct or not. We all can relate to the fact that nobody likes to be told they are wrong and they should do this or that. Why do we bother to teach? That was the predicament that Buddha first came upon when he became awakened. Many Masters realize that when truth is found it is so very hard to teach those who are delusional. It is not easy for those who do get it to teach those who don't get it! Some Masters came to be by choosing to rebel. Guru Nanak was born to a Hindu mother but rebelled and challenged authority. This broke all social norms and caused distress to his family since he was not satisfied with the ideas of sati, treatment of widows, and the excessive power the Brahmins held. Guru Nanak then founded the Sikh religion which emphasized social life and living as householders. Despite being the founder of a religion, he was challenged by his own eldest son, Sri Chand. He did not agree with his father's ideal of awakening. He rebelled and founded the Udasi Sect which taught asceticism and celibacy. It was considered to be a part of the Sikh fold, but fell out when the Akali movement took off and was bordering on syncretism of Sikhism and Hinduism. Buddha, another rebel from earlier times, passed up a wonderful, worldly life in the palaces of his family's weath to seek truth. Buddha was indeed a rebel who chose his own path rather than the one expected of him by his family. We must emulate such Masters as rebels with a proper cause: pursuit of self-realization, awakening, Divine intellectualization, or truth!

REHAB

"Learning to face reality, refusing refuge in cliches and lies, fighting to find a way out - that's what 'Rehab' is all about." - Antonia Bird

Rehab or detox are the next steps in getting over a terrible habit. The bad habit can be diverted to doing something or some other habit that is not so harmful to one's life or long term goals. Perhaps taking up a sport that will occupy the same time that is spent drinking booze during those same times. Often we come home and need that drink which leads to another and then another. Or a certain (other) buddy drags us down to the pub or bar, so we get caught up in the same routines daily that are also part of the habit. Breaking that habit is needed so rehab can be successful. Changing the circle of friends is also a great idea, so one is not around those who tempt us to drink, smoke or do drugs. Easier said than done, but rehab is necessary for one to be clean and awake. This is often taught by those who lead AA meetings or by those who try to influence those in rehab. They all try to divert your habit to something that is less harmful and dramatic. When one has a very addictive personality, that addiction can be transferred to some other addictive habit that is less harmful than the one they are forgoing.

When we examine ourselves to see what we should do, true introspection can take place. Examining all the factors around us shows what we need and what we don't. Bring in those others who will help you in your life and future. Lose those others who enjoy the indulgences of life so much they have made bad habits for themselves and you. Only you can see the vision on the horizon. Only you will see the beauty that the world offers. The bad habits will only shorten your days and you will be unable to realize that we have G-dly attributes inside of us. Create a habit in your life that is one that will last and make you feel ever so good. You need to come to a point of awakening by putting yourself into rehab or detox from that booze, smoke drugs, and pills.

RENOS

"Renos are part of the restlessness in our world."

The word renos is short for renovations of a house, condo, apartment or space in which one lives or works. Renos are great for our own homes when we decide that we are going to stay put in our house and update it. However, renos today are part of the red "hot" real estate markets of Australia, New York, Hong Kong, Los Angeles, Vancouver and all over the world. People are using renos to update homes, condos, apartments and other spaces to increase their values so that they can be put back on the market for resale. This is naturally driving prices higher and higher. Once a reno is done, the property is put on the market to flip. If this property is an actual home of an individual, renos cause moves. They keep us moving constantly and add to the restlessness in our world. They have nothing to do with being still. For those of us seeking truth, renovations are okay for updating but if everything works fine and one is content with where they live, then it is not necessary to carry out renos. Stillness prevails. Stillness is essential when seeking truth, but renos are part of the global movement that continues. They are in style and trendy, yet for many they become money pits; once one room is done, another is waiting. Renos are part of the outer fix that many look to undertake in order to impress the other. The other loves to see new fancy faucets, door hinges, designer door knobs, marble sinks, metallic walls, shiny floors and so on. Our eyes constantly seek room for improvement. We are a society that has a mindset that says, "let's change this and that so we get it to look just like a magazine." As renos look like a great way to make money, they have become businesses. This has caused many to purchase multiple homes encouraging speculative markets around the world. Many homes sit vacant and go without tenants just so they can be used to make more money later when the prices go higher. That is when one flips the property, selling it for an even higher price. The value of properties has increased so much that our children or grandchildren may not be able to afford homes of their own, especially in urban areas. These ideas are based on the acquisition of more and more in the material world. These aspects of life have nothing to do with becoming awakened as it is just making society engage in the current trend in the world. The seeker would be wise not to take part in the current programming of the world of renos.

Renos have nothing to do with becoming still. People feel that since everybody is doing renos so should they. It causes the value of homes to go up and everybody gets to "ooh and ahh" at the great renovation that was just undertaken so the family can do it all over again in about a year. Many families in the West say they don't even take their stuff out of boxes with the number of moves that take place due to the many renos. Not to mention the great resources that are put into the homes along with the environmental costs of pulling fixtures out of a home. How is this of any benefit to our children? What purpose are the renos if during that time most of the owners spend so little time in their house because they will have to move again soon or they are modern day nomads traveling over the globe? The nomads move from hotel to hotel and those who engage in renos in their own homes move from home to home. These activities of life both have nothing to do with becoming still and finding the Source.

Who and what is all this renovation business for? The same people who help us to finance our renos keep drilling into us that we should see the world and behave like the "new" nomad. The problem with the trips is that we are never home to enjoy all these renos. The renos become an ongoing and constant project of life that benefits the cards (credit) and the banks. One needs to examine why we in society are doing renos.

Renos are being promoted by banks so that one can tap into their equity and go wild. We are constantly owing money to the banks who give us those loans. Renos are being promoted in media on every one of the screens we are exposed to daily, so people get ideas for their own homes. Constant conditioning of renos by the banks plants the seeds in our minds that we, too, just jump on this mortgage bandwagon like everybody else. Maybe even buy two, three or four homes and make even more. Buying multiple homes means that collectively humanity is engaged in hoarding. Hoarding multiple properties only ensures that we are attached or clinging to things on Earth. One can see that greed is what prevails at the end of the day, because one can only live in one house at one time. The winners of the renos are the banks who give out the mortgages and the governments who collect various taxes associated with the buying/selling of real estate.

Constantly moving homes as a part of renos causes change on top of the natural, normal change of life. Renos are part of the restlessness in our world. It is also closely tied to those who take the trips, love looking at new views and those seeking thrilling experiences. All of which have nothing to do with connecting our mind, body and soul to the Source.

Being on the move after renos are done prevents us from becoming still in one place we call home.

RULES

"Rules work best for the sheep but the seekers must be rebels and live by rules of their own."

No business can survive without following the rules and regulations of doing business. Businesses must understand and follow the various Acts and Statutes that the government enforces businesses to follow. Sure, Bobby Dazzler needed the help of accountants and lawyers from time to time. But to be successful in business meant that Bobby Dazzler needed to read the rules before going into the retail business. That means it was essential to learn the Income Tax Act, the Commercial Tenancy Act and the Bank Act along with getting a very good handle on business law and accounting for business. These are just some of the rules that need to be learned before one goes into any business for themselves.

Some people like to only live by the rules, while others choose the path that breaks them. Rules are part of a system. A system that works for the betterment of those who are large, in power, and want to keep the status quo. It is best to know that rules are part of life and should be followed to keep the status quo. However, when we awaken then we break some of the rules that keep us enslaved in certain ways. Rules like the death penalty for blasphemy and apostasy which prevent anyone from challenging books, texts and religions, are made by humans to ensure that a dumbing down of society remains. The West has thankfully freed itself from such rules. We are freer from rules that protect dogma. One can skirt repressive rules and self-realize with the tools provided for modern awakening whether within or without a religion. Some rules can be bent, and it is best not to talk about it. The ego likes to boast, so it openly flaunts its desire not to follow the rules. This is where the real problem with breaking the rules occurs. Rules are in place to prevent chaos, and to control and manage populations. There have been so many books of scriptures that needed to be followed verbatim, yet we must keep in mind the unstated fact that those rules were made for their times.

To awaken, rules must be understood on a much higher level rather than just applying rules to modern life that were made some 3,500+ years ago. Rules are meant to guide consciousness, not to be uncritically followed in absolute terms. Experiencing life is the only way to know what is good or not. Using the Torah as an example, the invention of cars was not specified in the Torah. So, no orthodox person drives to the Shule (synagogue); they walk instead as was done for centuries. People debate about this for hours on end: if we should drive to the Shule or if we should walk? Or should we stay home? From a modern world point of view, it would be better to read the Torah at home in silence and become still. Staying home would also enable some form of meditation to take place rather than having to engage in over-socializing with the many other people who are at the Shule. Yet, some of us follow rules to a T because that is the way it has been done for thousands of years, even though it is unrealistic for the modern secular world.

A civilized society needs rules. Rules support a peaceful and harmonious society. Some rules must be learned so we overcome our fears. It has been said that humanity has two inevitable fears: death and taxes. Well, the taxes can be done by an accountant and one can read the Income Tax Act for any nation on their own, so one can learn the rules of the Tax Act to overcome this fear. All rules have a minimum and maximum. One must know the maximum to be covered for the worst-case scenario. Wow! That seems obvious, yet humanity spends more time in worry and fear over taxes rather than just reading the Tax Act. If this is something that all people must pay for then why is it not taught in our schools to our kids and teens right at the school level? It always comes down to power and control when it comes to taxes. Constant fears and worries would not be instilled in society if everybody was taught to not fear them but embrace them through learning. Next the rebel seeker overcomes fear of death by choosing to awaken and pursue truth rather than engaging in fears or worry. The seeker is always a life learner. This then allows the seeker to overcome the biggest fears of humanity by choosing to pursue truth over the rules of dogma. Rules work best for the sheep but the seekers must be rebels and live by rules of their own.

SENSE

"There are five basic senses according to everyday understanding. Taste, Sight, Touch, Smell and Hearing."

As long as we are left to please our senses, we will be caught in an endless loop, attempting to please our wants and needs on every whim. The human is reduced, a being caught in gluttony. Each sense controls how we react in this world. This cause of physical, mental, and moral decline in strength is the sensuous indulgence in foods, sex, money and power. The result is that the human works with the lower senses rather than the upper senses.

Humanity reacts and lives through the senses we have been given. Today we have lost our common sense, and so much of our time now is spent focused on our senses of touch and taste. These are the two senses that are most animal-like in their nature. This brings us back to the point that we are in "touch" far too much through the many forms of communication and social media. An excessive amount of keeping in physical touch also hinders our ability to focus, get things done and have goals. This was seen in lusts. The need for physical touch is kept in check by limiting it to a level of moderation rather than indulging in it and realizing that sexual encounters may be for procreation, something which may have already taken place if a seeker is starting to their awakening process later in life in their 50's, 60's, 70's or later. In some instances, a person may choose celibacy in order to "totally submit" to the Divine within.

Our desire for taste has exploded so much that foods have become a central theme of life and a focus contributing to the high rates of obesity worldwide. Our focus on taste has caused an explosion in the number of restaurants and food establishments around the world but also the creation of novel foods by chefs. The seeker chooses to forgo the need to please the sense of taste, by limiting foods and sometimes even engaging in fasts. It may become clear that foods are just a means for survival. The motto "eat to live rather than live to eat" comes into play daily.

Plato and Aristotle examined the senses and concluded that the senses of smell, hearing and sight can never be taken in excessive amounts, as one is not able to succumb to them or overindulge in them. Conversely, the excess of taste results in obsessive, compulsive desires for foods. And too much keeping in touch results in excessive sexual desires and life-lusts. This leads to many problems and suffering.

To awaken, the senses of sight and hearing, along with smell, are better to rely upon.

The seeker would be keen on using their sense of sight and hearing to strengthen their observation skills. Observation is done by looking at the actions the other is performing and by hearing the words the other is speaking. It should be emphasized that the seeker is not the one speaking but the one listening. They are the ones who are quiet and remain as the introvert as much as possible. Jiddu Krishnamutri defined intelligence in the following manner: "It is in this observation that space is created for real intelligence to develop. Intelligence of this sort is strengthened as the capacity to read between the words, read between the lines, gather information by observing, by learning with information that is around us at "any" given circumstance or situation. This enables the individual to act according to that information; reading between the lines all that is implied is (intelligence) in the sense that thought is offering words with hidden meanings and thought is watching, seeing, hearing and observing. Using our visual sense without opening our mouth. Gathering intelligence, acting on intelligence allows for change, clever discussions, opinions and words that allows us to awaken internally to a whole other world that the speaking world could never understand."

As for smell, we all know when something or someone smells good or not. There is a certain smell of booze, smoke, drugs, unclean foods and emitted by people who are not clean due to poor hygiene. We all know that an alcoholic, smoker or drug-addicted person has a certain smell. It is usually an unclean smell as the priorities of life are the addiction and not being clean. Those pursuing the awakening process would not only want to smell good themselves but would stay away from those people who are not like-minded. Why? Well, like attracts like; there is no way an unclean person who has become addicted to the habit of booze, smoke, drugs, pills, unclean foods and poor hygiene can awaken. The seeker would simply find those that are more like themselves in this aspect and draw upon positive energy that is like-minded. The smell of fresh clean clothes, a clean-smelling body with proper hygiene and the smell of great, fresh foods can be the only way for the body to heal.

Awakening includes the five senses plus our sixth sense which is the most intuitive sense. It is the sense that deals with the mind and the extra-sensory world of outer sense and leads to a further sense known as the remote sense. It is the intelligence sense. Unfortunately, most of us can't even get into our intuitive sense because taste and touch have taken over the others in a landslide. We humans recognize this shift and get a grip on it before our foods and lusts take us over from our meditation.

How can we access our sixth sense? The third eye is available to all of humanity, but it is not active in all of us since some of us are too busy worrying about our meals, who we will get in touch with or who will be our next date or hook-up. The sixth sense is open for all to access but it requires a shift in the senses that we use daily in our lives. We simply limit the use of the senses of taste and touch and put more effort into our senses of sight and hearing so that observation as discussed prevails. We are all given the unique ability to have the sixth sense, which enables the average person to see more, just like seers who are known to have a functioning third eye.

Not all of us are able to realize the third eye and its abilities. In some, it remains hidden all their lives as we become so engaged with all the distractions of life. Sometimes, the third eye can appear as a black dot. It may be crooked or uneven on some, but the extra eye allows one to see behind their head. When you meet an individual with the third eye opened, they can see things with a different perception that others cannot. This may sound unrealistic or crazy but there have been individuals who have these special abilities arise in their body when they develop observation to very high levels. Their eyes are wide open because they are alert, awake, and aware to what is going on around them. They are able to see the subtlest of moves in facial expression, body changes, perspiration and eye contact or lack of. This, of course, can only be done when we are not so focused on the other senses of taste and touch all the time. Those seeking awakening would be keen on fostering their senses of sight, smell and hearing. You can catch this ability in them the moment you lay eyes on them. They are quiet but these individuals have a keen sense of knowing the unknown. They use sight more than speech in almost all cases. The choice to become more visual over vocal is one that will definitely foster opening of the third eye and allow our sixth sense to open.

SHAPE

"Seekers want to shape themselves in a manner that allows them to be one with all."

Many things shape us and shape our lives: the people around us, especially our parents, caretakers, guardians, our community, society at large, governments, religions, traditions and so. Everything around us shapes our ideas, our thoughts and what we know to be truth. When certain ideas are repeated over and over again, shaping becomes somewhat permanent as that is what we are made to see as the truth from the time we were a child. For example, there is evidence that infants are influenced by their surroundings from a very young age. By surrounding a baby girl with pink or a baby boy with blue, we condition and socialize our youngsters into narrow ideas about what it means to be male or female. The child is being shaped to behave a certain way by the surroundings that the parents provide. The child is unable to shape and develop naturally nor really be who they want to be due to restrictions imposed on them. This is also why the likelihood of divorce is higher if your parents were divorced, for example. The chances of falling into drug or alcohol abuse are elevated if our parents did. A prostitute's daughter is more likely to enter the trade. Similarly in the case of religions, if one is a Christian then the child is a Christian. If one is born to Muslims then the child is also Muslim. The likelihood of taking a path other than the one our parents or those around us has given is very low. In essence, we succumb to a mediocrity due to all those others who have provided this "belief poison" and who dislike those who choose to actually become awake from their ways, their life, their foods, their traditions, their customs, their religions, their form of dressing and everything else that the "other" believes is the right way. The shaping is very deep and it is all around us. This pattern repeats in all paths, despite clear indications of right and wrong. However, those who choose to become awakened must take steps to peel the layers of shaping that have been placed on them since birth.

Those who seek to become awakened must remove the first obstacle by choosing to not participate in past shaping. One must erase the old shape and start all over again so that the shaping that is taken is based on trial and error by yourself. The seeker will not take part in cultural traditions, rituals, society's needs, religious dogma and other preferences that actually belong to the other people around them, for they decide for themselves what is true and what is false. Deciding to take a path towards becoming awakened may mean taking a stand against many relations, friends, family and siblings who might oppose the "new" choices being made and the "new" you. These choices can only be made if one chooses to be freer, self-sufficient, self-reliant and independent. If one is still depending on the "other" for support and guidance, there is no possibility of being free. The other will always have a hand in shaping us. The shapes that the other gives will always lead to programming of the mind. Using Buddha as an example, when he was sitting underneath the Bodhi tree, he was not engaged in lusts nor used many of his senses in an extreme manner. He was "controlling" his senses in a disciplined manner through austerities.

The seeker may also want to get rid of or limit the amount of internet, radio, video or other types of mind-controlling thoughts that get planted by the various modes of media and techs. The seeker is attempting to become mindless, but through a natural, everyday experience with life. That can only be done if one silences the outside "voices" or chatter. This quieting of the mind helps to create space. It is in that space that intelligence begins to take shape. These types of real life experiences shape us in the correct way towards becoming awakened.

The environment has a profound influence on our lives and on the lives of our children. In today's fast-paced world of cyberspace with techs ruling our lives in so many ways, it is bewildering just how the internet shapes our lives, ideas and viewpoints. The western environment may be liberal but it does not support a disciplined lifestyle, nor does it lead to a freer point of view. Big business controls so much and teaches a narrow point of view serving banks, cyberspace, email, techs, foods, cable, texts, and so on such that they shape our minds, our thoughts and our ways. The brain is fed by their subliminal messages. This definitely means that big business shapes much of how people have become.

It takes a great deal of mental power, focus, and discipline to ignore what everybody around us is saying or doing. A child is just a blank slate, a tabula rasa, when they come into this world. It is the adult that fills up that slate with their ideas and their truths. The adult human's duty is to nurture children so their Divine gift can be found. Instead, the child is shaped into what the adult has been taught to be truth. Adults provide all sorts of ideas, thoughts and truth that were fed to them as they grew up. They simply get passed along from one generation to the next. An awakened adult is supposed to provide food, shelter and love to the child so the child can develop naturally. Yet, all sorts of shaping of the child takes place unnecessarily. A child is supposed to be protected from any type of shaping.

The spiritual seeker should not tinker with the child by attempting to shape or limit it by means of narrow cultural programming or patterning. The spiritual seeker ideally attempts to learn from all religions, paths, cultures, foods, ideas, all people and everything without judgment. Seekers want to shape themselves in a manner that allows them to be one with all. That is only possible if we lose the shaping given to us from the time we were born.

SHEEP

"The seeker must break away from the herd and become the black sheep to answer the inner call."

Without the sheep aspect of humanity, retail would never be a successful industry. Bobby Dazzler noticed that humanity operated in cycles of herdlike movement when it came to buying behavior. People wanted items that everybody else was purchasing. Once something caught on, the sheeple of humanity would convince the rest that they too should buy the same item they have. So, retailing can be easy so long as there is a product appealing to sheep.

Sheep adhere to the status quo, which is known as "just fitting in". Driven by fear of the unknown, we grasp onto the known for as long as we can. Nobody likes to take on the unknown as it causes us fear. We continue in the state we are because it is easier. This is one reason religions have had so much success in firmly grasping humanity. In a world that celebrates individuality so much, why continue to move like sheep and follow the crowd? So much of humanity accepts mediocrity. Why do we succumb to being part of the herd? We all have a purpose, yet live a life based on rules that society, culture, and religion have set up for us. The seeker must break away from the herd and become the black sheep to answer the inner call. This internal, invisible Divine intelligence is what is called G-d or the Light. It can only shine once we break away to be free from the limitations that human life imposes on us. Those limitations make most of humanity follow like sheep. Religions limit human possibility by herding people into sheeple by the billions, without permitting a single person to rise up other than the original Masters who led the initial movements.

Sheep move onto places of worship. All organized religious faiths have books of their wisdom, making it unnecessary to make a trip to your place of worship. You may worship at home with nobody to interrupt your prayers.

Nor do you need to be seen praying for your prayers to be heard. Let your house become your place of worship. Unfortunately, nobody will see you follow your faith if they do not see you coming and going from a place of worship. Could it be that these places of worship are simply outlets for socializing? G-d is no more there than in your own house. G-d is everywhere, and that includes inside of yourself. Many presume that the Priest, Rabbi, or Imam is a necessary go-between. But with the realization that we are all made in the image of G-d and and are part of the Divine then a go-between would be in the way. They are attempting to be in between you and G-d. The best way to reach the Divine is to remain at home, be still and meditate on the Divine within. Only engage with the world to share the gift that one has been blessed with.

Sheep also abound in many political systems around the world. That is why we have autocratic dictators still in place who rule with the sword and their ego. Why don't all people want democracy and change? People everywhere want to be free and live a good life. It is foolish to think that living under an autocratic regime is better than within a democratic system of government. Who would seek a life of suppression, oppression and depression? With only one political figure running the show, one individual decides that all people will live in misery. The masses of people foolishly allow this because it is easier to follow like sheep rather than to take a stand against the ruler. Many ordinary Germans said they were merely following orders from Nazis above during WWII and the Holocaust. Because they were following like sheep, it was easier to kill six million people than to stand up and oppose murder.

There are many examples of how people act like sheep out of a need for approval, or due to fears of taking steps outside of the crowd. The truth seeker would be wise to never follow the beliefs of sheep, but instead become a black sheep. Regular sheep are asleep.

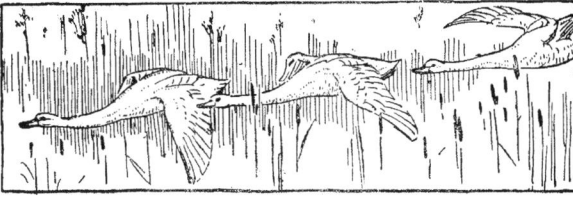

SHIFT

"Shifty people thrive on novelty and change."

There are those who like to shift their mind, their way of life, and surroundings, so that they are in constant flux or change. Change in life is already inevitable. But to purposely engage in shifty behaviours like constant travel or even moving from one house to another does nothing to bring stillness into our lives. It only causes us to continue with our moves. Modern times have made it easy for people to seek change or novelty. Humanity is enabled to easily change many aspects of life, and as a result, a whole new group of people are now known as shifty. Today, almost everyone you run into can be a little shifty. Techs and cyberspace have made it possible for fake identities. Shifty people change so much of themselves that you don't know if they are coming or going. This is all on purpose. They do not want anyone to really know what is going on in their lives. Shifty people thrive on novelty and change. The world has enough change already without needing to add to it. Our shift into materialism gave rise to a whole new humanity based on outer stuff.

From a retail perspective, it was challenging and frustrating trying to contact people who frequently changed phone numbers and addresses. To shift and be able to adapt to change is a part of life. However, when change occurs so often that you lose yourself in what you do and how you do it then you become shifty. No fixed address, no fixed job, and no fixed anything for a resume. This shiftiness became worse and worse over Bobby Dazzler's twenty-seven years of operation. Calls arriving from unknown or private numbers! Potential staff moving so often that too many details on the resume were outdated within a year. A shift in attitude and manner was apparent in dealings with clients, staff and suppliers. It became harder to distinguish truth from what was false. The shift we need now is one that takes humanity from unconscious to conscious. The real shift about to take place will transform materialism to a more spiritual way of life. It is long overdue, and will involve all aspects of life, bringing the human nearer to their Divine purpose on Earth. Awakening will no longer seem impossible, and humanity will gain confidence and faith in themselves by self-empowerment.

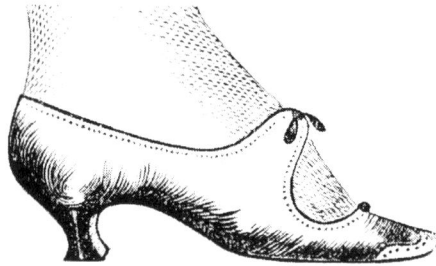

SHOES

"You can only wear one pair at a time!"

Insanity in humanity is at its highest point when we look at the whole 'shoes and purse' scenario. No one knows who started this trend. Imelda Marcos had a collection of over 3,000 pairs of shoes. You can only wear one pair at a time! What madness! Women and now some men just love their shoes and they love to buy yet another purse (or man purse) to match those shoes. This is the signature trademark of materialism in the West and East alike. Owning many pairs of shoes and getting another brand-name purse is the highlight of going to the mall. Doesn't anybody wonder about the environmental impact of owning so many shoes and yet another purse?

There is no time to think of awakening when there are so many shoes and another purse to buy. It is not just shoes and purses, but materialism leads us to buy multiple homes, condos, autos and other stuff just because we can. This is despite the fact that one can only live in one house at a time and drive one car at a time. The same goes for shoes; we can only wear one comfortable pair of shoes, not multiples of them! Materialism has added more shoes to our world along all the other 'stuff' this world is infatuated with. Consumerism and materialism are linked to greed. Everything is connected. This shoes and purse craze most definitely has something to do with our Earth warming up globally. Next time you buy shoes, think of your environmental footprint.

SLEEP

"Sleep is the best meditation." - The Dalai Lama

Sleep is obviously important yet so many of us don't get the right amount or quality of it to allow optimum functioning toward becoming awake and aware. Sleep is necessary because many of us live secular lives requiring our body to recharge from activities like work or school for the next day. We should go to sleep when the natural light dims at night, and awaken when the natural light returns at dawn. This is the order of the world that was created for us to live in the best way possible for our bodies.

Sleep is part of our life and our physiological programming. It is necessary to sustain our health so we can function daily as doers in our world. Many yogis do without sleep and so does much of humanity when engaged in the techs to keep in touch with others all night long. They feel they gain more from life by staying up to party, watch cable, engage in chats on the phone, texts or other social behaviors. They feel that more of life is being taken in, while at same time they are reducing their years on Earth by depriving themselves of sleep.

There are natural cycles built in our bodies. We must acknowledge this and allow our bodies to fall asleep easily. The daily cycle is called the circadian rhythm. It is not unique to humans but is shared with animals, plants and other living beings. This rhythm brings equilibrium to the human body daily. Sleep enables muscle repair, memory consolidation, and hormone release for regulation of growth and appetite. Sleep helps us thrive by contributing to a healthy immune system. One third of our life is spent in sleep, while the other two thirds of our life we are supposed to be alert doers. Medical research has revealed that sleep deprivation is a powerful contributing cause of all the following health problems: obesity, diabetes, hypertension, heart disease, some forms of cancer, depression, decreased immunity to bacteria and viruses, low IQ, attention deficit, irritability and of course a decrease in alertness leading to accidents and injuries. If any food we ate had such toxic effect, we would seriously rethink its intake.

Sleep in adults and children is becoming ever more scarce as we stay up to watch cable, surf cyberspace, check emails, or just go out later to enjoy more social time with our family or friends while we eat more delicious foods. People are walking around with red eyes, workers are looking tired and worn out. We are not getting enough sleep! Deep sleep for at least six to eight hours is necessary for the body to heal, grow, create, and rest. Minimum amounts of sleep are required for optimal operation of the human body. Sleep deprivation will hasten our deaths, making the flip phrase that "we will have plenty of time to sleep when we are dead" ironic and sad.

Before sleep you must unplug all the techs around you so the continual engagement with the outside world is put to rest, and so the inner world can be turned on through meditation. Real meditation and sleep can only happen when lights plus techs are out.

Sleep rejuvenates the body, and sharpens the mind and intuition. Developing our intuitive sense is necessary for self-realization. Without it, one becomes wishy-washy, and foggy. Sleep ensures that certain brain cells are replenished and helps prevent cognitive decline and dementia.

In today's busy world getting enough sleep can be very difficult. This is especially the case when we choose to constantly travel like the modern-day nomad, continually moving homes due to renos or simply from our desire for novelty. We become shifty. The world is full of techs, many based on blue-light screens that hinder sleep by tricking our circadian cycle to think it is day when it is actually night. Lack of sleep is often caused by stress and worry due to work obligations. An adult should get seven hours of sleep but teens and children need even more as they are still growing. An alarming rate of sleep deprivation occurs in our kids as more of them use techs to relax before bed. The opposite result takes place when we use techs to 'wind down'. To sleep when the rest of the world gets up is a terrible shame. The wee hours of the night between midnight are 4 am are meant to be the hours of deep sleep.

There is a reason that Earth was created with a night falling. G-d meant the night for sleep, and this means lights plus techs out.

SOULS

"The trick is to give the ego to G-d and just live in the soul."

We are all souls of the Divine spirit. Some souls are more evolved while others are just beginning their journey. Such souls are immature and still allow their egos to supersede the truth. We all have souls, and souls don't have genders. Souls are genderless. There are two aspects of G-d's Divine nature that humans carry: the soul and the ego. The trick is to give the ego to G-d and just live in the soul. The beast and the plant beings don't carry an ego, but they do both have souls. The ego is a code word for the Devil or Satan. That is where all the "duals" in life begin. When we act from our egos, then we behave in opposition to our souls. The ego disconnects us from positive, joyous spiritual energy. Humanity must subdue the ego to connect itself to the realm of Divine energy, which will result in removal of all pain, suffering and chaos from our lives.

It is interesting to note that in some countries gender-neutral is being accepted as a gender. It is a term suitable or applicable or common to both male and female genders. It is a word or expression that cannot be taken to refer to one gender only. Could this be the beginning of the soul's desire to arise or awaken? It is a movement that describes the idea that policies, language and other social institutions should avoid distinguishing roles according to people's sex or gender. It is meant to avoid discrimination, from the impression that there are social roles for which one gender is more suited than another.

SPORT

"Glorify God in your Body. Or do you not know that your body is a temple of the Holy Spirit who is in you, whom you have from God, and that you are not your own? For you have been bought with a price: therefore glorify God in your body." - Corinthians 6:19-20

By means of a sport, a human being honors the body that holds the spirit of the Divine Intelligence. What is known as hatha yoga in the East is sport in the West.

In the past, when the great religious revelations occurred, humanity was busy with toil working the soil, which gave a natural workout. Today, however, so many jobs are performed in a stationary or sedentary position. Physical exertion of the body is necessary for it to function properly. It is good for children to play sports from an early age to accustom their bodies to being doers of sport rather watchers of sport. Children should be put into many sports to see which they enjoy, such as soccer, swimming, tennis, karate, judo, and other sports that require children to challenge their bodies. Some contact sports are unsafe, such as football, rugby, or ice hockey where the dangers of injury such as concussion are high. However, if a child enjoys it and is good at a sport, then it is potentially an excellent character builder.

After a child grows into an adult who wishes to become awakened or become awake, social sports should be set aside in favor of sports done alone in silence. For example, walking, swimming, running, jogging, hatha yoga, martial arts, cycling, rollerblading, snowboarding, skiing, surfing, are all sports that are done alone. This ensures we connect to the inner self and not to the outer social self. The idea is to limit the social aspects of the sport and focus on its physical aspect. Some sports just require one to engage in too many talks.

It is something that we should consciously engage in, as the body is meant to be moved. It is surprising that in these times we need to tell people to exercise, when so many suffer from obesity and cardiovascular diseases linked to sedentary lifestyles. The scriptures of the past did not emphasize the importance of physical engagement of the body through exercise or sport, since the body was kept active by daily physical work.

We are all part of the Divine Source, including plant and animal life. One becomes closer to the Divine by taking care of the physical body, our temple where we perform our worldly duties here on Earth. The light which is our souls lives in the human body. We come closer to the Divine when our bodies are engaged in a sport, as doers rather than watchers. The Divine reaches us faster when we are not distracted by infirmity or disease but are instead engaged in the proper functioning of our body in physical exertion, movement and challenge.

Conscious physical activity is as important as healthy eating. One cannot meditate on the name of G-d and expect to become awakened in this day and age without taking care of the body. A path that includes a sport is necessary as a piece of G-d is in each of us. Physical sports are not written about in many scriptures, but clearly we need to keep the vessel that carries out our daily duties here on earth maintained in proper order through physical activity. Humans choosing to forgo on keeping their body healthy, clean and physically active are becoming slothful and causing their own body to be riddled with disease and destroyed. Such a body can never rise to G-d. After all it is written: "If any destroys God's temple, God will destroy that person; for God's temple is sacred, and you together are that temple." I Corinthians 3:17

Some of us like to watch sport while others like to do sports. And there are those who like to watch and play. It is something that we should consciously engage in and should be put into play just like when one sits down to eat. So many of us are finding ourselves in sedentary lives that doing a sport or two is a must for healthy living.

Sport is not just necessary for our health but it is necessary for the mind, spirit and body together. If the body is running optimally, the chances of becoming awake are much easier and clearer. Many people who play any sport will say there is nothing like that rush you get when your adrenaline gets going. That high after a brisk walk or run. Even walking is a sport as it is movement, especially brisk walks. The runner's high is like the feeling one gets from doing a yoga class. The body just feels great and so does the mind. The benefits of doing sports are many. Great well-being comes from partaking in any sport that one wishes to do. Living longer, healthier and active lives has so many benefits. The benefits along with the feelings it gives are just amazing!

And then there are those who like to watch sports. What is so great about sitting long periods of time and yelling at the television or at the players when they can't even hear you? What is so great about spending three or more hours watching other people play their sport? This sedentary activity does nothing to stimulate the body. A look around will also show you that those who watch sports are also engaged in an excessive consumption of foods and alcohol. It is unbelievable that many are willing to take up to three hours of their day, not including travel time, to watch this little black puck or ball go into the net or over a line. From the perspective of a seeker, there is no activity that is more of a waste of time, energy, and money. Equally mind-boggling is the fact many are willing to pay $400 per seat to watch this live, around people who are screaming, swearing, cursing the referee, and engaged in gluttony to the maximum.

As children, many of us were exposed to similar scenarios of having to watch a full hockey, football or soccer game from beginning to end. It was easy to give up cable as an adult, so that the same waste of time did not happen again into adulthood. It was much better to engage in doing something rather than watch this little black puck roll around the ice for hours at a time. There was no missing of the loud cheers or boos that eventually started to sound like white noise. Nor was there any need to relish the junk food that was consumed on game night.

Playing street hockey with the neighbor's kids was something else. Playing it meant that the body had to be ready for running and speed. It was exhilarating, fun, fast, and made the mind feel great, too. The playing aspect of hockey was great fun and exercise at the same time. Team sports are wonderful early in life, but a sport done by oneself is preferred for those seeking to become awake. Doing sports by themselves allows for a moving meditation to take place where there is little or no talking. It is important to do as many sports on our own without another person so that the mental noises can stop while we are doing the sport. This means not bringing a friend along to do a sport with you but doing it alone. When we engage in sports with others, the need to speak naturally arises, since two people can never be quiet for long periods of time without words coming into play. These words prevent one from being still and quiet, which is essential for a spiritual seeker on the path of awakening.

So why are so many people spending so much time watching the game? Well, it may have to do with the whole group behavior of socializing. Sure, humans are social and like to be around other people but a seeker may be someone who is okay being in solitude for extended lengths of time.

However, people love to belong to a group and believe they are more alike than not. So, one thing that brings them together is that they love the same teams, wear the same colors, chant the same songs, cheer for the same team and vote for the same team to win. So, this spectator-sport thing is more of a get together for people who are like-minded to have fun, party, be social, get in touch, make some noise and wear the same colors to support their teams. The many large businesses which control $115 billion of media would never make a dime if we all became doers of sport rather than watchers of sport. Don't wait until the doctor tells you to take a sport up after that stroke, heart attack or other medical condition. The time has come to take up a sport that causes the body to perform optimally and at its best always.

STILL

"Make stillness a daily habit."

Spiritual masters always tell us to become still. How is it possible to become still in a busy, over-scheduled and over-stressed world? The West is finding it difficult to become quietly still due to the restlessness and nervousness of society, the constant need to go out and the desire for thrilling, novel experiences through the use of our senses which only feed the ego. This is compounded by social media, subliminal messages, flyers, constant emails, tweets, texts, and bombardment of advertisements that constantly create those images that we should go out, get away, take more trips, tours, and travel. Humanity is being molded to search for more interesting views, travel senselessly like a modern-day nomad, and do as much as possible to keep busy. This is on top of being engaged in those crazy renos in overheated real estate markets that are taking up our valuable time so we renovate, sell and make more money to upgrade to that even larger house, and then go on even more trips, go on more adventures, more outings, more places to eat and so on. Along with those trips come more foods, views, booze, things to smoke and sometimes more drugs. If one has a child, that means more games, trips, foods, outings, play-dates, and more stuff. All of this prevents the mind becoming still. When we are attempting to understand what it means to become still, we need to examine the different activities we engage in daily.

When we cannot become still we prevent the mind, body and soul from making a connection for union. Union with Divine Intelligence (G-d) that is. For the human being today, being still is difficult when everybody is moving around so much. Even when one becomes still, the other comes to convince them to take in more of life. Some may say that is living life! It has become in style to parachute from airplanes, ride motorcycles, parasail, bungee jump and try more daring things, so we can say we tried it. It is stylish to outdo the other, and that is making it difficult to become still. Renos keep us moving from homes to another house, hindering our ability to become still. It is a world in which more of everything is better than less of anything. Getting bored, being still and quiet is out of the question for many. It is even more impossible when we engage in the techs daily to constantly keep in touch with everybody underneath the moon except for yourself. Techs cause constant distraction, making stillness impossible.

But what happens when you become still? Space is created. Gaps of space emerge that were not there when we engaged in the distractions of life. In this space, the peace that we are searching for is found. In this emergence into silence we are able to connect to the eternal and unlimited intelligence. There is no more inner or outer. One sees no peace or fight because they are both one and the same. There is no need to curse anyone as to bless would be the same. Duality of opposites is eliminated when one sees them as equal. There is no need to react when all situations can be seen as equal. That is what becoming still is!

Being still is what many speak about, but during modern times, it is one of the most difficult things to do. Why? Humans have many thousands and thousands of thoughts per day. However, in between those very thoughts is space. In this space is peace. We access those spaces by becoming quiet, silent and still through meditation. In the exaggerated general restlessness of society, life has so many distractions. Restlessness in the mind and heart increases as we are made to believe we should seek novelty in every possible way. Becoming still involves forgoing the need to seek that which is novel.

Meditation in a general sense usually involves sitting quietly alone so that silence can be accessed. However, for stillness to be effective, it must be made a part of our lives daily in every aspect, for awakening to start. Here are simple examples of ways to become still.

1. Once a house is found to meet all the needs for shelter then staying in that house should be the priority. That house becomes one's place of prayer and meditation.

2. Read books quietly at home, even choosing to stay home and cybersurf rather than going to a café to sit with all the noise for a latte. Bring it home and make that quiet time.

3. Make the commute home to be in a quiet drive without the radio or play music only without vocals/words. This gives us some quiet time in between work and going home to more noise, family, kids, techs and all the other distractions that prevent the mind from becoming still.

4. Do regular physical exercise or a sport, so that practice can become a moving meditation for you. this sport or physical exertion should be done

alone, not in a group or class. For example, walking, swimming, cycling, yoga, kayaking, jogging.

5. Do daily chores methodically, like washing dishes, cleaning the floor, folding laundry, weeding, ironing, cooking and all other household duties in quietness so the mind can become peaceful, still and not engage itself in any thought.

6. While working, choosing to forego gossip, gab, and talk at work that has nothing to do with the job. Taking lunch by yourself to eat mindfully and maybe taking a 10-15 minute walk after.

7. Limit the amount of time spent on techs/screens. Not going on the phone or carrying it around everywhere. Checking emails only twice per day. Letting calls go to voicemail so only the important calls are returned, not those with fresh new juicy gossip or gab. Possibly even disconnecting the phone for long periods of time if not needed.

8. Connect with nature as much as possible to see the natural beauty of life.

9. Choose to forgo going to relations' or relatives' homes for social occasions, and instead focus on the self by doing a sport, reading or walking alone. Thus, avoiding constant socializing in favor of down time.

10. Choose to take a relaxing shower or a bath in quietness, with minimal lighting or candles. This is one of the most unintentional meditative methods of becoming still, right in the comfort of your home.

These are just some simple ideas to make stillness a daily habit. Find your own example from your own life that fits into this idea of becoming still while still living in this modern, noisy, and busy world full of distractions.

STUCK

"For awakening one needs to remain in the present."

As a whole, we are spiritually stuck. We have hung on to past forms of enlightenment for too long. The current religions have created divisions that keep us far from the Source. It now appears almost impossible to bring humanity into unity. When moving towards truth, there is no need to go over history. A seeker will not have any need to go to old churches in Europe, examining paintings of the past, collecting antiques leading towards hoarding, wondering about the traditions, rituals, cultural and societal programming of the past. To be totally present requires us to be here now and not worry about what has happened in the past. If we choose to become awake, alert, and aware then the possibility of escape from being stuck will appear. When we are stuck in the past then it becomes harder to look into what is happening now as our focus is still on the past. For awakening one needs to remain in the present. The more we engage in the now, then the more present we are able to become.

Choosing to focus on history draws our attention to non-sense outer stuff. When we choose to be awakened, there is no need for identification with a country, an ethnic group, a culture, with roots in a family, roots of knowledge, roots in beliefs which all have collectively been planted in us from our past not the present. They are all just memories that have nothing to do with the now! Dragging into those memories keeps us stuck.

The more present we are, the easier it is to heighten our intuition and expand our awareness of what is happening right before our eyes. We can have deep insight and evolve only in so far as we sustain our presence in and of the present. Spiritually we need get out of the rut of attachment to old forms, traditions, cultures, religions, garbs, and ideas that keep us stuck in the past. This is very difficult to teach. Humanity is told to hold on to so much of the past that has been passed along as truth from generation after generation. We cannot move forward spiritually if we continually cling to past ideas which prevent us from being able to let go.

SUGAR AND SALTS
"Everything we consume has significance to our well being."

These are the two most common ingredients in our processed store-bought packaged foods, and which cause the most havoc in our bodies. Knowing that sugar and salts both cause the human body many problems is the first step to becoming aware. This awareness can be expanded upon by researching the different diseases caused by the overuse of sugar and salts. All sugar and salts should be taken in with moderation. Everything we consume has significance to our well being. Since these two risk creating so much havoc on our bodies, it is important to watch out just how much we consume daily. Too much of either is associated with heart disease, diabetes, stroke and a number of other health ailments that cause the body to fall out of its natural equilibrium. Becoming awake, alert, and aware is all about temperance creating equilibrium in all aspects of our life and body. So watch out for that sugar and those salts in our everyday foods.

TABOO

"Abnormal is the new normal."

The West today pursues all things taboo. Humanity's love for the forbidden is on display in all the stores in the mall. Bobby Dazzler just caught that trend. All things that were once taboo were hot!

What are we do with all things that are taboo? In the past, tattoos were frowned upon by many religions as they were seen as unclean. The possibility of disease or skin irritation increased due to the lack of medical knowledge when a tattoo was put on the skin. It was seen as a possibility of causing harm to the self which would prevent the full life cycle to be lived. Many different allergic reactions took place such as blisters, cysts, ulcers, bacterial infections, excessive scarring, and tissue necrosis which could possibly lead to death. But now we have come a long way from those days. Tattoos and skin piercing are common and are done in a much safer manner. The risks of infection due to tattoos have been greatly reduced due to clean equipment. Sure, there are still risks from dirty equipment but they are not as high as they used to be. All things taboo are an outer alteration to the body. They have nothing to do with the inner. It doesn't make an individual less spiritual if they choose body tattoos, fake tattoos, piercing everywhere including down there, jewelry that expands the ears, or hair dyes including pink plus blue.

Tattoos were also seen as symbols by those who were in gangs, those who dealt drugs and those who chose to sell their bodies for money - prostitutes. Today, tattoos are mainstream. Many people have them.

From an awakening perspective, tattoos or piercings have nothing to do with modern awakening. They are merely outer expressions of humans to make themselves appear trendy or stylish as it is the "in" thing to do. The message is "I am different! So watch me take it to the extreme so I can be a celeb of my own." Having tattoos makes us stand out, especially if they are all over our face or on other visible parts of the body. This causes the individual to stand out which makes it hard to live an obscure life of awakening. Awakening is drawing less attention to the outer and putting more effort into the inner self.

TECHS

"Techs was no fad."

Techs is short for technology. It was obvious that techs were used by all patrons of Bobby Dazzler. People would come in to comparison shop, take pictures of items and even make calls to make sure if they should make the purchase or not. The advancement of technology made people uncertain and indecisive when making retail purchases. Techs turned normal business transactions of a few minutes into complicated tasks of finding out from ten people if a purchase should be made or not. Techs made it more difficult for Bobby Dazzler to retail.

Steve Jobs, CEO of Apple until his death, admitted to being a "low tech parent" to a tech journalist. When he asked Jobs in 2010 whether his own kids loved Apple's ipad, Jobs replied, "They haven't used it. We limit how much technology our kids use at home." This, from the mouth of one of the most powerful tech gurus of modern times. His products are so potent that he limits them from his own children. They are made just for the rest of us sheep. If the man who created such techs won't give them to his own children then why should we?

Techs and cyberspace are the greatest concerns of modern times, occupying much of our valuable time. Time that could be used to find our creative force or come to the light of G-d - yet we are bowing down to this little blue light as if it were our new G-d. The techs are both the world's largest knowledge machine and the largest distraction device ever created. They keep the human from any meditation. If those of us thinking meditation can be done in a group-like setting, by connecting groups via techs into cyberspace, that is not meditation. True meditation is done without any techs.

Techs are everywhere: in education, business, economic exchange, communication and social connection. Technology has gone from being a simple tool to an entire way of life. It is difficult to look back only 40 years and imagine we ever managed without these techs. Schools are phasing in techs and phasing out handwriting on the assumption that no one will ever need to handwrite again. Techs have grasped onto every single aspect of our lives - in our homes, work, schools, and personal lives. Techs control a massive and growing gaming industry. This is all happening as we allow techs to take control of our lives, more and more every day.

Everything moves in cycles. Could techs have destroyed creativity? Most techs are used when we are in stationary and sedentary positions. One is only rarely running or walking when watching cable, YouTube, writing an email, sending texts, on the phone or cybersurfing. Techs have caused the decline of creativity and of movement of the human body. It truly is use it or lose it. Losing it means more diseases on the rise, and a general population that is unhealthy and obese. Everything is related and connected. Losing it also means a lack of creativity, which can be seen by all that is being culturally recycled today. We have constant remakes of movies like Superman, Spiderman, Batman, Star Wars and so on. So many things that were created when the techs were not around are being updated with techs and remade, revised, and resold. Techs have made humanity less creative in what we can come up with. Why are we are still finding the superheroes of the past so popular today? Shouldn't we have made new superheroes for the present time? What about all those bands that keep going strong after 50+ years of making music? Bands like AC/DC, Metallica, Kiss, Rolling Stones and so many more are still selling out concerts. The music of today is not as deep as it was when the rock bands come out. Old school is still cool in many aspects of our lives. The techs have changed the world in many respects, but to the detriment of "actual" human interaction. Children now find it difficult to even hold conversations with peers, adults, and teachers because they are so used to not having to properly speak anymore. They can send out texts to converse, full of typos and lacking proper grammar. However, in face-to-face interaction, the children end up being unable to partake in intelligent conversation. The habit of relying on our techs to control social interactions through the computer or phone has now made it difficult to communicate in person.

What will happen to all these techs as we move forward? Humanity will have to limit their use or even disconnect an amount of techs from their lives, so the mind can live in union with body and soul. We don't have to walk around with phones glued to our ears! How did we ever get that idea in the first place? Why do we need to stay in touch with people so much? People will realize that the more techs they have, the more anxiety and depression they have. When pursuing self-realization as a seeker of truth, it is important to limit the use of techs, and possibly disconnect from techs altogether.

TOUCH

"Staying in touch socially is not as important for the spiritual seeker as keeping in touch with inner self, the Source."

From the point of view of awakening, there are two aspects of touch. One is the "keeping in touch" that we do through techs and the other is physical touch itself. Both play a significant role in our lives daily.

With the advent of tech, clients wanted to keep in touch with others while shopping. Bobby Dazzler noticed it became harder for the retailer to have a concise, clear conversation while making a sale while all the different techs kept the client in touch with other people on their phone, or tablet. People would rudely interrupt the salesperson by taking calls, or cut off the clerk midway during their sales pitch. Interruptions continued while any transaction was being processing and having three-way conversations become the norm.

It will be hard to cut out being in touch with others but you must put a limit on just how much in touch you want to be with the outer others when deciding to awaken.

Being in touch means being social, engaged with other people. It involves chit chat, gossip, and talks that are sometimes useful but most of the time are not. Today, the techs keep people plugged into each other 24/7. There is no time to become still, be alone and to quiet the mind. The mind is composed of five aspects: concentration, self-control, faith, determination, and patience. These aspects are at risk when a person is constantly in touch with others. There is a danger of losing your mind entirely. This may be the reason why anxiety and depression are on the rise. Keeping in touch also involves comparisons with others. The mind is kept without a time out. Failure to maintain the five aspects of mind prevents equanimity, and blocks creativity. So we see a dumbing down of society as a whole. Over-socializing in Western culture inhibits possibilities for awakening. It is causing widespread scatterbrain. Over-socializing is euphemistically called "keeping in touch." One must be aware and conscious of just how much "keeping in touch" is done with another while ensuring that the real keeping in touch is left to the self.

Being in touch has taken on a whole new dimension. It even prevents us from carrying out our daily activities safely, such as texting while driving which is causing car accidents. It now means that we have this constant desire to connect with or contact other people. Being alone is just not going to cut it, nor are you able to live this way because the training in society is to keep in touch. Contact and connection with other people is a natural human need. But we have taken it too far now, so all we do is stay in touch without paying attention to our own goals, drives, or desires. We simply find ourselves looking at the other people and their goals, drives or desires. This prevents us from really living. Staying connected is one matter, but living your life through others is impractical and futile. It prevents you from realizing who you are and what your life purpose is. Staying in touch socially is not as important for the spiritual seeker as keeping in touch with the inner self, the source, through meditation in stillness and quietness.

Using the example of Buddha, who limited who he kept in touch with by just sitting under the Bodhi tree, by himself. He was not known to have engaged in physical touch with others, despite having a wife. The Guru Nanak also spent 25-30 years away from his wife, teaching, learning and awakening despite being married, which does have a physical component to it as we all know. He put limits to the desire to physically touch and engage with the other. These are extreme examples, but both are examples of enlightened beings.

VEGAS

"Viva, Las Vegas!"

Vegas is the closest equivalent to a modern Sodom and Gomorrah that we have. Long live Vegas! Or should I say Viva Las Vegas! Vegas is the least spiritual city of the West, where materialism is on display at its peak. Why include it in a spiritual book? Vegas provides humanity with an example of what is glorified as great so that when the shift from materialism to spirituality is experienced, we can see what we won't be missing, and focus on what we will be gaining.

Vegas wallows and deals in gluttony, and stimulates each one of our senses so much that we lose all sense to the "Sin city" in grand style. This is where you can get women, babes, boobs, large penis, sexy/hot pussy, porno, booze, drugs, smoke, eat the best foods in large portions, act like you are famous, do what you wish you could do at home but were afraid to do, walk/talk/be with other people all day long, party like a rock star, go to all the shops spend your money - and if that doesn't get rid of your money Vegas made it legal to steal money by getting you to gamble it all away in all the games. It is the best place for lost wages. There is only an entry into the casinos. You will never find a clock or signs that point you to the exit once you enter this vortex. They let you play the slots, poker, and many other ways to put your money at risk 24 hours a day. Vegas wants you to gamble the rest away before you leave. You need to pay taxes on any winnings, but you can't get a deduction on your losses. Pretty unfair, right?

In a nutshell, Vegas is a world wonder of concentrated vices. Vegas is a dream come true to the business people who thought they could pander to all the wicked wants in one place at one time with no limit. It is a place designed to please the brain through appealing to the five senses at an exaggerated level, a level abnormal to quiet living. It aimed to bring games past all limits. In Vegas, there is no limit to games, booze, drugs, smoke, women, porno, foods, shine, bling, the light and the night. It is open 24/7 and never closes. The question is, are we able to survive Vegas? So many people fall in love with Vegas as it gives them all the feeling of being seen and being with the in-crowd. It gives people a sense of power without them ever needing to do anything. It is a dangerous place, because it makes people do things they never thought themselves capable of. It allows access to the things we normally would avoid. It corrupts our minds. It is evil plus legal with no limit. "Viva, Las Vegas!" From time to time with reality in check, it could be a fun place to visit but it is one of the finest examples of putting all of life's pleasures into one city for limitless fun.

Yet Vegas is glorified by the world. The seeker starts to see the real truth of Vegas and also sees how other cities attempt to mimic the pleasures, the gluttony, and the party of Vegas. A seeker doesn't need Vegas. It is just a very large distraction.

Over the years, Bobby Dazzler attended trade shows in good old Vegas. It was a whirlwind from beginning to end. Bobby Dazzler always wondered why such an important business event was held in Vegas. With so many distractions, vices, and noise, it was the most difficult place to conduct business. Yet humanity glorified Vegas and wished for it to be a city back home. Vegas became the antithesis of spirtual awakening, the extreme opposite of where the awakening soul should be. Over time, the trade shows began to be loathed. With so much noise, expenses, and disrespect of people in one place, it was just insanity of humanity. "Get me out of here!" An awakened person has no use for places like Vegas. It simply becomes a sick joke.

WATER

"People love water and love to look at it all the time."

Any item stocked in the store with water in it was always a best seller. The wave machine was an enclosed rectangular acrylic box with water in it, rocking back and forth. Water speakers bounced water in them according to sound and vibrations; they could not be kept in stock. All items with water in them made a lot money for Bobby Dazzler.

As a new human coming to the world, we lived in our mother's womb, which was primarily water. The human body is 60% water. Earth's surface is 71% water, 96.5% of which is in the oceans. Water is the most basic and essential of all elements for life. Many parts of the world are facing a water crisis, yet billions of dollars are spent trying to see if there is water on Mars. Material wealth is going into the colonization of Mars, yet Mother Earth is right here now with saline water that needs to be converted in order for it be useful to humanity today. It is crazy that we are looking for something so far way when we have plenty of it right here on Earth. Water is essential for crops and foods. With global warming causing havoc on the ecosystem, the time is now to make sure some of the 71% of water covering the Earth is useable. Couldn't those billions of dollars put into finding water on Mars be better used to make our water useful, here and now?

Our body needs it to live, but our soul needs it to feel refreshed. No matter where one looks, when you have a view with water it is always prized. There is something so very relaxing about watching the ever-changing flow of water. The serene calm of an ocean, river, stream, or lake makes us feel at ease. Hearing the water hit the shore is even used as a white noise feature in alarm clocks to wake up. When needing time off for self-care, all you need to do is take yourself to water. Watch and feel it take all the stress away from you mind. Watch it long enough and you may feel as if you are floating away over the water. Your body has this beautiful flow of energy come upon it when it is in the company of water. The next time you need space to relax, try to sit by water. You won't be disappointed nor will you be bored. It is a very relaxing exercise for the mind, body, and soul. It enables an awakening of the soul that nothing else compares to.

WOMAN

"The world will be saved by the Western woman." - The Dalai Lama

If the Divine had told us before we came to Earth that girls in some cultures are not as valued, then the souls would all reconsider and think that it would be best to stay united with the Divine or look for union with the Divine as quickly as possible. However, the pain and suffering of being born to some traditions such as Indian or Muslim parents is felt by many girls and women all around the world. Could this possibly be due to the books of the past? The West is more advanced so treatment is equal. But the conditioning that some cultures are prone to is hard to overcome. This treatment of women is also found in many other religions such Islam, Hinduism and some orthodox versions of Christianity or Judaism. Some regions and cultures, like China, still prefer boys before girls. The problems arise as there are 1.6 billion Muslims, 1.03 Hindus, and 2.17 Christians. This mades up 69% of world population by 2010 so these taboos affect the lives of girls daily. It affects the treatment of women and children and this conditioning is hardwired and very difficult to change.

Women still endure sex trafficking, sex slavery, war crime rapes, violent domestic abuse, murders, assaults, kidnappings, and many other abuses and indignities. This is due to gender inequality instituted in our society through so many aspects of life in politics, cultural norms, media and the workplace. How can this be sanctioned by religions which are supposed to be paths to awakening?

In 1997, an older male greeted the opening of the Bobby Dazzler store's door with the oddest yet true statement. His reply to "good morning" was, "It is a good morning as I am not a black Muslim woman living in Africa today." He explained that he had won the birth lottery. I stood dumbfounded for trying to figure out what he said, and it finally resonated. It was only 10 am, and the coffee hadn't even been sipped yet, so it took a little while for his statement to sink in. After two minutes, it made sense. Life in certain parts of the world is much harder for a woman than it is here in the Western world. Living with so many obstacles in life such as poverty, sexism, cultural and religious values, and marriage traditions means it is very difficult to be a woman. Never mind becoming a seeker of awakening! Being a woman is difficult enough trying to keep up with our male counterparts in salary and benefits, positions in work, business, and politics. But to deal with other pressures when we are living in a country that fails to allow an individual to express themselves is even more difficult given religious, societal, tribal values and norms, and economic barriers, or even pure ignorance, that all prevent women from moving towards truth. It is being born into a prison of confined circumstances. This man's response struck a resonant nerve in me and it still haunts me today when I consider the state of the world today for women.

Loving all, fostering loving kindness and ensuring that none of the Divine creatures are "dirty", this is what an awakened one sees. All other beliefs about the woman are poisonous belief systems of the past, created by the man.

The woman bears children and brings life to this world. Where does this hate for the woman come from even now? The three main Western religions all consider woman to be unclean while she is menstruating. This is an orthodox viewpoint, accepted by many as truth. Scriptural passages transmitted to uneducated people out of context can blind the mind. It plants negative ideas, opinions, and thoughts into minds that only pay selective attention to what is heard or read. This harm can be considered as brainwashing over time through repetition. How are we to understand why a naturally occurring part of a woman's reproductive system that is linked to procreation could ever be considered "unclean" in any book that is associated with awakening?

All souls have potential for self-realization. However, women must bear the burden of pregnancy, birth, and most of the childrearing. This has given so many more chances for males to become awakening masters. Great Masters include Buddha, Jesus, Moses, Mohammed and even modern Masters like the Dalai Lama. These Masters are all men who came from women. Real Masters realize how wonderful women are. The Dalai Lama put it best when he stated, "The world will be saved by the Western woman," adding with a chuckle, "Many people call me a feminist."

Woman is the chosen vessel for humans to arrive on mother Earth. A world with more love for woman is needed. Love is a synonym for G-d or Creative Intelligence. There is a need to promote basic human values of compassion, affection, love and kindness. Women have an opportunity to develop a greater sensitivity for others' pain and suffering due to the immense amount of pain and suffering that is experienced during pregnancy, childbirth and in raising children. In order for this to be possible, women must go through menses on a monthly basis from as early as 12 to as late as 55. The menstrual cycle is designed by nature to optimize fertility, requiring that the lining of the uterus shed and be renewed if the egg that is released monthly is not fertilized. It is a normal bodily function in the woman, without which reproduction is not possible. How has a process linked to procreation become so "dirty"? Menstruation is a necessity and there is nothing dirty, unclean, or abnormal about this process!

Orthodox, extremist versions of Christianity, Judaism, and Islam have convinced the masses that women are "unclean" when they are menstruating. Such teaching is easily misused to incite misogyny and cause chaos in the world. This is exactly what has taken place. Menstruation may be a little messy and uncomfortable for the woman, but that does not justify labeling the sex that brings life via natural and normal bodily processes as "dirty". It seems as if ignorance has prevailed again. The bad seeds of ignorance planted into humanity will take many cycles to shed. Seeds of hate, harm, and cruelty are in words that are always open to interpretation and misunderstanding in the religious scriptures that prescribe how we are to live. In the minds of the uneducated and misinformed, these types of statements, opinions, and beliefs can bring no benefit to the modern world where both sexes interact harmoniously. Such beliefs are not conducive to the general harmony that humanity desperately needs now.

Not only do women suffer from such superstitions, so do the children being shaped by these wrong ideas, and bringing them into the next generation. Paths that promote sex-based systems are not progressive and have nothing to do with turning on the light, or awakening. Dogma of this sort still sadly hinders the progress of the Western woman. Ideology that does not serve all merely brings additional suffering, inequality, and hardship. We in the West appear to have freedom of religion, but we are still burdened by superstitions at cross-purposes with becoming a truly progressive society, moving forward toward awakening.

Western women have already begun to rise after many years of oppression. There are many examples of women who have made it into positions of leadership traditionally in the hands of their male counterparts. There are more women than ever in schools, colleges, and universities so the prospects of success in business, employment, and work are looking better and better for women. Looking for G-d in everything and everyone of both sexes will ensure that peace is found without hate. The world has been dominated by men for quite some time now. But, just as everything else in the world goes through cycles, so will the current cycle of the males' domination shift. The Dalai Lama proclaimed the ascendency of the Western woman. It was a prediction of things to come.

In modern awakening, a woman doesn't have to worry that her religion's place of worship doesn't allow women. She can meditate in her own house or home of prayer. It can be done while living a secular life, doing chores, working, driving, and when the woman raises her children in love.

At the end of the day, souls are gender-neutral and a part of the Divine. It is just the outer cloak that changes upon subsequent birth. It doesn't matter if one is born to the girls in this life and to the males the next. For the awakening, all that matters is the soul's coming to realize truth.

WOMBS

"… going back to the source…"

Yes, it is that simple: each and every single one of us are from our mother's wombs. We were all suspended in water, never spoke, never cried, could not see but we could hear sounds inside of the wombs. We were still, for the most part, as we were unable to go anywhere. We belonged to the source at all times when we were inside of mother's wombs. So this is the best place to start when we want to get to the truth. We were essentially a tabula rasa. When we look for truth in this manner, then we see that all of us are from the same source. This is as basic as it can get. Sounds so easy, but once we left these wombs then we all cried as we came out this world. Rumi says that is when "the hangover started!" After leaving the cozy wombs, we were given names, labels, forms, ideas, beliefs and thoughts that would shape us for the rest of our lives. There was so much chatter, noise and outer distraction that we all were taken away from the source. We were put into a certain religious group, given a race and so many other layers that it was almost impossible to recognize that we are all the same. A decision to peel those layers off and return back to the source is a way for us to be as we were in our mothers' wombs. From there the seeker can see the world with a single eye for everything. Just by seeking to go back to the source where all humans come from, the wombs. This what the Universal Awakening is all about!

ABOUT THE AUTHOR

After retailing for nearly 30 years, the time had come to become a healer for humanity. Bobby Dazzler was originally the name of the retail store but it soon became the higher-self pseudonym used by the author, Jasbir Rai.

She is an entrepreneur, spiritual innovator, rebel, ideas generator, thinker, thought philosopher, mover/shaker and a lover of people. She learned so much from people daily in the retail world, a learning which she now uses to elevate the true nature of humanity towards light and awakening. Accessing knowledge from the Divine Creator, she shares this esoteric light, helping humanity rise to higher vibrations. A BA graduate of Simon Fraser University, she currently resides in West Vancouver, British Columbia with her two children.

Also by Bobby Dazzler: *Retail Jail: Retail Apocalypse*

Find out more at www.bobbydazzler.ca

Made in the USA
Middletown, DE
16 September 2018